The Language of Hermeneutics

SUNY Series in Contemporary Continental Philosophy
Dennis J. Schmidt, Editor

The Language of Hermeneutics

Gadamer and Heidegger in Dialogue

Rod Coltman

State University of New York Press

Published by
State University of New York Press, Albany

Printed in the United States of America

For information, address State University of New York Press,
State University Plaza, Albany, NY 12246

Production by E. Moore
Marketing by Dana E. Yanulavich

Library of Congress Cataloging-in-Publication Data

Coltman, Rodney R., 1957–
The language of hermeneutics : Gadamer and Heidegger in dialogue / Rod Coltman.
p. cm. — (SUNY series in contemporary continental philosophy)
Includes bibliographical references and index.
ISBN 0-7914-3899-6 (alk. paper). — ISBN 0-7914-3900-3 (pb : alk. paper)
1. Gadamer, Hans Georg, 1900– —Contributions in hermeneutics.
2. Heidegger, Martin, 1889–1976—Contributions in hermeneutics.
3. Hermeneutics—History—20th century. I. Title II. Series.
B3248.G34C64 1998
121′.686′0922—dc21 97-42842
CIP

10 9 8 7 6 5 4 3 2 1

Contents

Preface

As intellectuals at the end of the twentieth century, we seem infatuated with manufacturing labels for ourselves. We refer to ourselves as "postmodern," "postmetaphysical," even "postphilosophical" thinkers, as though all of this "self-posting" allowed us to gain some kind of temporal or critical distance from the modern, the metaphysical, and the philosophical. We postmodernists, however, know very well that this is impossible. The postmetaphysical critique of objectivity renders such a distancing illusory at best. But our habit of self-baptism is no hypocrisy or a simple-minded logical blunder; nor is it merely ironic. Rather, we call ourselves *post*modernists precisely because we recognize the irony of our own situation in the postmodern world. If the suffix "-ism" connotes a doctrine of some sort, then our wry concoction of a postmodern "ism" would seem to indicate something like an ironic complicity, a knowing participation in an antidoctrinaire doctrine. We postmodernists, in other words, not only understand but delight in the fact that our own "ism" undermines itself.

A certain smugness, however, comes along with such intellectual audacity. Brilliant though they may have been, modern, premodern, and classical philosophers, we assure ourselves, were never quite so savvy. As post-Derridean intellectuals who pride ourselves on maintaining our historical consciousness without falling into the trap of naive historicism, as intellectuals who thrive on plurality and cultural diversity, we fancy ourselves as having surpassed the tradition of monolithic systematic philosophy. Though, of course, we feel compelled to avoid all notions of "surpassing," of "overcoming," of any hint of a "beyond" which might tend to impute a metaphysical superiority to our position. And yet, with our constant will to the polyphonic and the multiple we find our own ironic attitude—the awareness of our own irony—somehow unique, if not in the histories of literature and art, then certainly in the history of Western philosophy. Moreover, we congratulate ourselves on our intellectual deftness; we pride ourselves on our ability to read the texts of the philosophical tradition with a literary eye, with a "chiasmic" eye, with an eye to the subtle preconceptions and rhetorical prejudices lurking within these texts. Although we admire the towering achievements of our progenitors, it seems to us that these figures—despite their undeniable acumen—never did quite manage to see the trees for all their attention to the forest. We postmodernists, of course, freely acknowledge our debt to the tradition. However, our attitude (if not our rhetoric) signals a subtle disdain for what we tend to see as 2,500 years of metaphysical self-delusion. We may not be able to escape entirely from the trap of metaphysics, but at least we are aware of the trap, and this awareness itself we take to be the great advantage of our own late-twentieth-century vantage point. Of course, in many respects ours is a very real advantage. The political and intellectual merits of a careful feminist, or neopragmatist, or deconstructive critique of traditional texts are difficult to deny—nor do I think we should deny them. For what could be more appropriate to the liberal-democratic, pluralistic worldview that permeates our ever more homogenized global culture? (Need we remark on the irony of a "homogenized pluralism"?)

But perhaps we are not such clever readers after all; perhaps we have a thing or two yet to learn from these "naive" metaphysicians—other than how to ferret out and expose their metaphysical presuppositions. Perhaps we can learn to read just a little less programmatically, a little less destructively, a little more sensitively to the productive possibilities of these texts. Not that we postmodernists have been deliberately misreading the traditional philosophers—far from it. For what does a deconstructive approach do but constantly defer any decision about what a text might mean? And is this deferral not hermeneutically justified? Are we not guilty of something like "metaphysical violence" when we try to impose a single "correct" interpretation on a text? How, in other words, can we misread a text when we refuse to assign a meaning to it?

But perhaps, in keeping with our ironic postmodern self-awareness, we should ask whether or not *all* readings are misreadings—including deconstructive ones, insofar as they do, after all, force us to make semantic choices (even if we need not ultimately decide among them). If all readings are misreadings, however, does it not follow that all readings are guilty of textual violence? For is there nothing violent in the act of deconstruction, in the act of *Destruktion*? But, of course, isn't the entire history of Western thought itself a history of destructively—that is, violently—misreading texts? Didn't Aristotle misread Plato? Didn't Aquinas misread Aristotle? Didn't Hegel misread Kant? Didn't Heidegger misread everybody? Without such fruitful misreadings, the philosophical tradition might have come down to us as little more than a kind of pedantic scholasticism.

What, then, will come of our own textual violence? Are we forever caught between the Scylla of infinite hermeneutic deferral, on the one hand, and the Charybdis of pedantry and mere scholasticism on the other? Or is there a third way, a way of risking an interpretation while remaining sensitive to the inevitable destruction inherent in the very act of interpreting? I would suggest that a careful reading of the work of Hans-Georg Gadamer can reveal just such a third way. I would also suggest that Gadamer, a man as old as the twentieth century itself, a man whose rehabilitation of the hermeneutic tradition seems anything but radical to most readers, actually provides us with an astonishingly simple yet amazingly powerful way to approach philosophical texts—or any texts, for that matter. Gadamer exhorts us to go ahead and interpret. He exhorts us to go ahead and decide what a text means and argue for our interpretation, but—and here we find the postmodern key to his protreptic hermeneutics—he also exhorts us to always remain open to the eventual inadequacies of our own considered opinions. Philosophical hermeneutics, in other words, is all about putting our interpretations at risk; it's all about recognizing that along with textual violence comes a hermeneutic danger—the danger (perhaps, the inescapability) of misinterpretation. Gadamer teaches us to recognize that we are always limited by our own hermeneutic situation, that all our readings are to some extent circumscribed by our own facticity, our finiteness as human beings. That is, he sensitizes us to the fact that our finitude precludes the possibility of our ever achieving a perfectly "objective" or "true" reading. Thus he also sensitizes us to the interpretive damage that we inevitably inflict upon the texts that we deconstruct. But this much we also learn from the Derrideans. Gadamer, however, also teaches us to have the courage to strive for an understanding of the texts we read; he encourages us to risk an understanding, to risk an interpretation, while at the same time remaining alert to the expectation that each of our interpretations not only will be but should be subjected to further deconstructive violence. In other words, like Derrida, Gadamer too recognizes the danger of assigning meanings, but his approach to reading does not attempt to avoid or somehow circumvent that danger through constant deferral but boldly confronts it by engaging the text as an other, a dialogue partner with whom we can only have a genuine conversation if we are willing to admit the limitations of our own understanding.

But Gadamer offers us much more than just a general hermeneutic approach. He offer us the possibility of recuperating the very idea of philosophy in an era in which our society at large finds it to be irrelevant (and, therefore, a waste of time and money) and the academy finds itself ever more frequently engaging in various modes of philosophical evasion. As philosophers, it seems that these days we are forever trying to find new ways of avoiding philosophy. Sometimes we flee from it (as though its systematizing tendencies were contagious) into a kind of diaspora of the chaotic. Sometimes we take refuge safely within the most arcane analytical specialties and subspecialties, perhaps so as to embrace the systematic for its own sake and thereby pretend to ourselves that God has not died after all. Or (more and more frequently, it seems) we insist that the time for theorizing has come to an end, and we find value in philosophy only to the extent that we can apply it to the practical political and moral issues of the day. Perhaps by falling into this third academic trend—this will to "ethicize"—we are merely reacting to society's antipathy toward the perceived idleness of the first two. But all three of these attitudes strike me as symptoms of a widespread and expanding intellectual phobia—a kind of fear of philosophy.

The contrary idea, however, the idea that we ought to embrace philosophy rather than fear it, is no obvious and unproblematic truth. If the deconstructive tradition beginning with Nietzsche and running through Heidegger and Derrida has taught us anything (and I think it has taught us a great deal) it is that any conscious effort to produce a coherent, systematic metaphysics that can provide logical and complete answers to the most basic questions of being and knowing cannot help but undermine itself and subsequently fail. I would argue, however, that our demolishing of the metaphysical tradition is not the radical innovation that we sometimes take it to be. Heidegger himself, in fact, reminds us that the Presocratics and the poets have been propounding just such a critique from the very beginnings of Western thought—if only we have ears to hear. But Heidegger's monolithic vision of the history of metaphysics tends to deconstruct with one hand while hypostatizing with the other; it dismantles certain texts and retrieves what it finds useful while relegating the rest to a netherworld of the hopelessly metaphysical. He seems unaware that this own *de*structuring of the tradition inadvertently and simultaneously *con*structs an equally entrenched philosophical edifice—the so-called history of *Seinsvergessenheit*. And continental thought since Heidegger has tended either to adopt his architectonic wholesale or retreat further and further into what some would see as a death-spiral of self-undermining deconstructive strategies, which, for all their supremely sophisticated rhetorical pyrotechnics, sometimes amount to little more than a constant reifying of a will to *anti*reification.

But do such comments serve as an effective critique of deconstruction? Does it even make sense to try to undermine a mode of thought that forever beats us to the punch by constantly undermining itself? Should we even want to? I suspect not. Imagine how less rich our intellectual lives would be without the likes of Jacques Derrida and Luce Irigaray. In fact, I would argue that, rather than merely erecting philosophical roadblocks or luring us into intellectual aporias, postmodern thinking—and especially deconstruction—has not only excavated metaphysics and displayed for us its utter untenability but has also (ironically) opened up the possibility of not just retrieving a series of philosophical artifacts, à la Heidegger, but of recovering the very activity of philosophizing itself from the ruins of the philosophical tradition. Perhaps the supreme irony of our late-twentieth-century intellectual situation, however, is that the one figure whose work really allows for this possibility, the thinker with arguably the most radical, and, at the same time, the subtlest command of deconstructive modes is a man with one of the most conservative reputations in all of contemporary continental thought—not Jacques Derrida, but Hans-Georg Gadamer.

In Gadamer we find that rare postmodernist who remains undaunted (and unhaunted) by the specter of metaphysics, one of the few who is not afraid to engage the metaphysical tradition head-on—not so as to simply deconstruct it, to expose its rhetorical chiasms and logical presuppositions, but to carefully yet forcefully dismantle it and retrieve that which he finds hermeneutically and phenomenologically viable. His great mentor, Heidegger, of course, showed Gadamer the way; but Heidegger focused his most concerted efforts at *Destruktion* and *Wiederholung* on certain figures who (with the notable exception of Aristotle) fall outside of the tradition, while Gadamer carries the Heideggerian project directly into the heart of the history of metaphysics. We see Gadamer's radicality, in other words, not so much in his ability to deconstruct, but in the boldness of his retrieval. For who else would even dare to recuperate for postmodernity a whole series of quintessentially metaphysical concepts—including Platonic participation and Hegelian dialectic? Who else would dare to offer a phenomenological rehabilitation of consciousness in the face of the withering postmodern critique of subjectivity? Who else would dare to call his project *philosophical* hermeneutics at a time when the very idea of philosophy is under relentless attack? Of course, the question that arises immediately for us as postmodernists is how Gadamer can hope to negotiate such radical retrievals without falling prey to the very metaphysical naiveté that he confronts. At one level, whether or not Gadamer actually *succeeds* in recovering a new mode of philosophizing is almost irrelevant—for the idea of remaining open to the possibility of being wrong, the idea of constantly putting one's own ideas at risk, constitutes the very core of philosophical hermeneutics. I would argue, however, that Gadamer's postmodern philosophizing finds its effectiveness precisely in that he never approaches traditional texts with the expressed purpose of finding metaphysical and logical impasses but with the hermeneutical attitude that the tradition itself still has something important to say to us—if we only have ears to hear.

Acknowledgments

I want to thank Will McNeill and Stephen Houlgate for guiding me through certain crucial stages of this project. I also want to thank Charles Bambach for his friendship, his hermeneutical sensibilities, and his keen editorial eye—not to mention his good taste in beer. Special thanks to my mother and father for never expressing their frustration at my wandering ways, to Victor Worsfold for initiating me into the wonders of philosophy, and to Richard Palmer for contributing far more constructive criticism than I had any right to hope for. But, most of all, I want to thank my wife Candace for her patience, her intelligence, and her metaphors.

I would also like to extend my appreciation to J. C. B. Mohr (Paul Siebeck) for their permission to quote extensively from Gadamer's *Wahrheit und Methode* and to *Philosophy Today* for permission to republish the better part of my essay, "Gadamer, Hegel, and the Middle of Language," which originally appeared in volume 40 (1996), pages 51–59.

Abbreviations

I have relied on standard English translations when available, unless otherwise noted. In cases where no English text is listed below, all translations are my own. In cases where both German and English editions are listed under the same abbreviation, page numbers correspond to the edition listed first.

Texts by Gadamer:

GW3 *Neuere Philosophie I: Hegel Husserl Heidegger*, Gesammelte Werke volume 3, Tübingen: J. C. B. Mohr, 1990.

GW1 *Hermeneutik I: Wahrheit und Methode: Grundzüge einer philosophischen Hermeneutik*, Gesammelte Werke volume 1, Tübingen: J.C.B. Mohr, 1990. (All translations my own.)

IG *The Idea of the Good in Platonic-Aristotelian Philosophy*, trans. P. Christopher Smith, New Haven: Yale, 1986. Original German text: "Die Idee des Guten zwischen Plato und Aristoteles," GW7, 128–227.

PA *Philosophical Apprenticeships*, trans. Robert Sullivan, Cambridge: MIT Press, 1985. Original German text: *Philosophische Lehrjahre*, Frankfurt: Vittorio Klostermann, 1977.

PP "Plato and the Poets," *Dialogue and Dialectic: Eight Hermeneutical Studies on Plato*, trans. P. Christopher Smith, New Haven: Yale, 1980, 39–72. Original German text: "Plato und die Dichter (1934)," GW5, 187–211.

PHC "The Problem of Historical Consciousness," *Interpretive Social Science: A Reader*, eds. P. Rabinow and W. M. Sullivan, Berkeley: University of California Press, 1979.

TM *Truth and Method*, 2nd rev. ed., translation revised by J. Weinsheimer and D. G. Marshall, New York: Crossroad, 1989. Original German text: GW1.

Texts by Hegel:

EPW *Enzyklopädie der philosophischen Wissenschaften im Grundrisse*, Frankfurt am Main: Suhrkamp, 1970.

PdG *Die Philosophie des Geistes, Enzyklopädie der philosophischen Wissenschaften im Grundrisse*, Dritter Teil, Frankfurt am Main: Suhrkamp Verlag, 1970.

PhS *Phenomenology of Spirit*, trans. A. V. Miller, Oxford: Oxford University Press, 1977. Original German text: *Phänomenologie des Geistes*, Frankfurt: Suhrkamp Verlag, 1970. (I have consistently used Miller's translation with the one exception of rendering "*der Begriff*" with "Concept" rather than "Notion.")

SL *Hegel's Science of Logic*, trans. A. V. Miller, trans., Atlantic Highlands: Humanities, 1990. Original German Text: *Wissenschaft der Logik I*, Frankfurt: Suhrkamp Verlag, 1970.

VuA *Vorlesungen über die Ästhetik III*, Frankfurt: Suhrkamp Verlag, 1970.

Texts by Heidegger:

BT *Being and Time*, trans. Macquarrie and Robinson, New York: Harper & Row, 1962.

GA19 *Platon: Sophistes*, Gesamtausgabe volume 19, Frankfurt: Vittorio Klostermann, 1992. English translation: *Plato's*

Sophist, trans. Richard Rojcewicz and André Schuwer, Bloomington: Indiana University Press, 1997. (All translations my own.)

GA24 *Die Grundprobleme der Phänomenologie*, Gesamtausgabe vol. 24, Frankfurt: Vittorio Klostermann, 1975. English translation: *The Basic Problems of Phenomenology*, trans. Albert Hofstadter, Bloomington: Indiana University Press, 1982.

GA39 *Hölderlins Hymnen Germanien und Der Rhein*, Gesamtausgabe vol. 39, Frankfurt: Vittorio Klostermann, 1980.

GA52 *Hölderlins Hymne Andenken*, Gesamtausgabe vol. 52, Frankfurt: Vittorio Klostermann, 1982.

GA53 *Hölderlins Hymne »Der Ister,«* Gesamtausgabe vol. 53, Frankfurt: Vittorio Klostermann, 1984. English translation: *Hölderlin's Hymn "The Ister,"* trans. William McNeill and Julia Davis, Bloomington: Indiana University Press, 1996. (Translations my own unless the English is cited.)

GA65 *Beiträge zur Philosophie (vom Ereignis)*, Gesamtausgabe vol. 65, Frankfurt: Vittorio Klostermann, 1989.

KPM *Kant and the Problem of Metaphysics*, 4th ed., enlarged, trans. Richard Taft, Bloomington: Indiana University Press, 1990. Original German text: *Kant und das Problem der Metaphysik*, Vierte, Erweiterte Aflage, Frankfurt: Vittorio Klostermann, 1973.

NI *Nietzsche, Volume One: The Will to Power as Art*, trans. David Farrell Krell, San Francisco: Harper Collins, 1979. Original German text: *Nietzsche I*, Pfullingen: Verlag Günther Neske, 1961.

PhA "Phenomenological Interpretations with Respect to Aristotle: Indications of the Hermeneutical Situation," trans. Michael Baur, *Man and World* 25 (1992): 355–393. Original German text: "Phänomenologische Interpretationen zu Aristoteles (Anzeige der hermeneutischen Situation)," ed. Hans-Ulrich Lessing, *Dilthey Jahrbuch*, vol. 6 (1989): 236–269.

PLW "Platons Lehre von der Wahrheit," *Wegmarken*, Klostermann: Frankfurt am Main, 1967, 109–144. English translation: "Plato's Doctrine of Truth," *Philosophy in the Twentieth Century: An Anthology*, Vol. 3, eds. William

Barret and Henry Aiken, New York: Random House, 1962, 251–270.

SZ *Sein und Zeit*, Tübingen: Max Niemeyer Verlag, 1986.

Texts by Hölderlin:

DE "The Death of Empedocles," 3rd version, trans. Michael Hamburger, *Friedrich Hölderlin: Poems and Fragments*, Ann Arbor: Univ. of Michigan Press, 1967.

ELT *Friedrich Hölderlin: Essays and Letters on Theory*, trans. Thomas Pfau, Albany: SUNY Press, 1988.

OT "On Tragedy: 'Notes on the Oedipus' and 'Notes on the Antigone,'" trans. Jeremy Adler, *Comparative Criticism*, 5 (1983).

Introduction: The Hermeneutical Proximity of Philosophical Distance

Whether or not a particular student was present at the actual moment when, in the Winter Semester of 1923–1924, a young Marburg professor exhorted his students to adopt a more "phronetic" attitude, I cannot say.[1] But certainly none of Heidegger's many illustrious protégées has taken this advice more seriously than did Hans-Georg Gadamer. Unfortunately, heeding the call of one's mentor can have its slight drawbacks. In the United States, for instance, the temptation to read Gadamer as a mere Heideggerian epigone explains to a large extent his rather tepid reception among Continental philosophers—at least when compared to such figures as Heidegger himself, Jürgen Habermas, and Jacques Derrida, whose works have spawned veritable industries of translation and scholarship. Gadamer's work has, of course, gone a long way down the phenomenological path blazed by his mentor. This very disquisition could even be construed as further evidence of a seemingly umbilical relationship. My intent here, however, is to bring into focus what I see as the most intense points of proximity between the student and his teacher, but which at the same time show as clearly as I think is possible the critical points of departure that set these two thinkers on separate albeit parallel thought-paths. This book will attempt to illustrate the immense philosophical power that Gadamer's thinking has achieved precisely by *departing* from Heidegger's at certain crucial moments. Not only, for instance, does Gadamer wish to retrieve from the tradition a dialectical and dialogical mode of thinking directly via Plato and Hegel while Heidegger seems to have a rather ambivalent relationship with these two and rejects the dialectic outright as hopelessly metaphysical; not only does Gadamer refuse to follow Heidegger into the "abyss" of poetizing thinking, but Gadamer even maintains that within the history of philosophy there never has been a so-called "language of metaphysics" in need of *Destruktion*.[2] This is not to say, however, that Gadamer himself remains trapped within an outmoded and rather naive metaphysical framework. Quite to the contrary, he finds his own radicality precisely in and through a Heideggerian dismantling and retrieval of the metaphysical tradition itself.

One could argue, as I will, that Heidegger's project of overcoming the history of metaphysics constitutes an effort to displace the infinite teleology of knowledge to which metaphysics aspires with a radically finite "topological" approach to the question of being (pacé Reiner Schürmann and others).[3] At the same time, one could see Gadamer's philosophical hermeneutics as an attempt to reinterpret the history of metaphysics in a way that allows its own language to speak in nonteleological, nonmetaphysical terms, from out of what he calls "the middle of language." Even at a cursory glance, certain points of similarity and difference between these two general characterizations tend to exhibit themselves. But rather than engaging in a straightforward comparative study intended to highlight these points, I would like to complicate rather than simplify the issue. I would like to offer a possible way of reading Heidegger and Gadamer together without attempting to either homogenize them, divorce them entirely, or even to "reconcile" the two. Instead, I want to allow for a kind of dialogue between them—a "counter-turning" dialogue that goes beyond both Gadamer's published interpretations of Heidegger and Heidegger's reputed comments about his student's work.[4] I borrow Heidegger's neologism, "counter-turning" (*Gegenwendigung*), to indicate a dialectical interaction that is also a phenomenological *Auseinandersetzung*, a hermeneutical encounter that not only lets them speak to each other but also against each other and themselves by, as it were, dwelling in the neighborhood of language and being. More specifically, by examining these two thinkers' respective relationships, first to Plato and Aristotle and then to the poet, Hölderlin, and the philosopher, Hegel, I hope to allow the implicit topology of the Gadamerian "middle of language" and the latent hermeneutics of Heideggerian ontology to reveal themselves in their mutually finite philosophical/phenomenological proximity.

As an initial movement in this philosophical investigation, I would like to pinpoint what I take to be the most telling moment in the intellectual proximity of these two thinkers—namely, their respective explications and appropriations of Aristotle's concept of *phronēsis* as laid out in Book VI of the *Nicomachean Ethics.* I can think of no more appropriate place to begin my study primarily because Aristotle and, more specifically, the concept of *phronēsis* constitute hermeneutically significant points of departure for two of the most widely read texts in contemporary philosophy: *Being and Time* and *Truth and Method.*

For the most part, these two thinkers do not differ greatly in their basic readings of *phronēsis,* which is of course to be expected given that Gadamer became Heidegger's student precisely in the midst of Heidegger's first and his most serious investigations into Aristotle.[5] And they both hit upon and embrace essentially the same proto-phenomenological characteristics of this so-called "intellectual virtue." Again, this is no mere coincidence—Gadamer himself actually credits Heidegger's Aristotle seminars for putting him onto this path. What actually distinguishes their respective appropriations of this ancient Greek idea may seem slight at first—a mere question of emphasis. The young Heidegger wants to stress Aristotle's distinction between the deliberative faculties or habits of the soul (i.e., *phronēsis* and *technē*) and the scientific faculties (i.e., *sophia* and *epistēmē*) while Gadamer is more interested in exploring the difference between the two forms of deliberation themselves—*phronēsis* and *technē*. This, however, is no mere academic subtlety but goes right to the heart of one of the most important distinctions in twentieth-century Continental thought—the one between fundamental ontology and philosophical hermeneutics.

By stressing the deliberative/scientific distinction and consequently reading Aristotle against himself by coming down on the side of *phronēsis* rather than *sophia*, Heidegger, in his Aristotle lectures and writings of the early to mid-1920s, gathers together yet another key ingredient in the hermeneutical melange that is to become *Being and Time.* Unlike other important terms for the early Heidegger, such as "formal indication" and the "hermeneutics of facticity," however, Aristotelian *phronēsis* does not show up explicitly in the project of fundamental ontology. One can indeed discern its traces in certain concepts such as "circumspective concern" or the "call of conscience" (as we will see shortly). But I would argue that its real importance for *Being and Time* is that it becomes subsumed immediately within the context of the book as a general, albeit implicit, comportment of the text itself or, one could say, as a fundamental attitude of the Heideggerian enactment of phenomenology. In other words—much like the hermeneutics of facticity and perhaps even in some ways synonymously with it—it names that which formal indication indicates: a particular mode of being-in-the-world.

Gadamer, on the other hand, while taking off almost directly from his mentor's early work and teachings, takes this particular aspect of *phronēsis* (i.e., its distinction from scientific, calculative ways of revealing truth) as almost a given, and proceeds to adopt a slightly finer distinction as a primary model for his hermeneutical project. Although he does not dwell on it throughout, Gadamer places his discussion of *phronēsis* precisely at the center of *Truth and Method* and, I would argue, at the virtual center of philosophical hermeneutics as well. To put it in more specific terms, if a central problem of *Truth and Method* is the destruction and retrieval of consciousness not as an epistemological but as an ontological, hermeneutical, and factical phenomenon, then the crux of the endeavor would be to rethink the prototypical element of all traditional epistemology—the element of applying the universal to the particular. And, precisely because Gadamer sees "*the task of application* [die Aufgabe der Anwendung]" as "the central problem-dimension of hermeneutics,"[6] it becomes essential to distinguish between the two Aristotelian habits of the soul for which application is a defining characteristic—i.e., *phronēsis* and *technē*. The opening sections of my inquiry, therefore, will deal with this distinction of Aristotelian distinctions in order to show how Heidegger dismantles and retrieves *phronēsis* as a fundamental comportment implicit in the hermeneutics of facticity while Gadamer proceeds to take this facticity for granted and retrieves *phronēsis* from out of its Heideggerian subsumption to serve as an explicit paradigm for hermeneutics in general. The following section will deal with their somewhat conflicting attitudes toward another ancient Greek figure: Plato.

Here, Heidegger's well-known rejection of the received Plato (i.e., Plato as paradigmatic metaphysician) will come up against Gadamer's life-long attempt to interpret Plato against (and retrieve him from) the traditional metaphysical reading. Heidegger, of course, also criticizes the traditional analyses and is careful to distinguish Plato's own work from "Platonism," and, as we shall see, his reading of Plato in many ways follows the same hermeneutical path as his Aristotle interpretation. He insists, however, on reading Plato through Aristotelian eyes, and thereby focuses on the dominating permanence of *eidos* (the Platonic Idea) as holding sway over *alētheia* (truth as unconcealment or disclosure). Heidegger thus sees the Idea as profoundly metaphysical and directly responsible for the all-important corruption of truth from disclosure to correctness. His reading of the Platonic Idea, therefore, although running counter to the tradition of Platonism and even (in some respects) against Aristotle's critique, forces Heidegger away from rehabilitating Plato's thinking and appropriating it for his own project.

Gadamer, however, having been steeped in the dialogues for most of his philosophical career—even before he became Heidegger's student—and having been particularly attracted by the thinking of such innovative Plato scholars as Paul Natorp and Paul Friedländer, found himself much more well-disposed toward Aristotle's teacher. So much so, in fact, that by the time he had been "heideggerized" Gadamer had already become convinced of the philosophical value of the dialogues, and this led him to venture something like a Heideggerian deconstruction and retrieval of the dialectic. Platonic dialectic, in fact, would become a complement of sorts to Aristotelean *phronēsis* as a further model for philosophical hermeneutics. That is to say, whereas *phronēsis* would serve Gadamer as paradigmatic for rethinking human understanding itself as a factical and hence ontological phenomenon—the phenomenon of *application*—dialectic, via the phenomenon of *methexis*, would become the model for a hermeneutics of dialogical *participation*. Gadamer's study, in other words, attempts to overcome the standard interpretation of Plato as the original propagator of the split between the physical and the metaphysical by attending to the contexts within which theses so-called doctrines arise. By focusing on the dialogical structure itself, Gadamer develops a hermeneutics of the conversation—the movement of language, the event, wherein understanding occurs. By taking the dialogues not as Plato's didactic expressions of a rigidly metaphysical doctrine but as exhortations to engage in live philosophical conversations, Gadamer not only overcomes the Aristotelian problem of how the physical world participates in the metaphysical world, but he manages to relocate the entire question of understanding within the structure of human dialogical—hence dialectical—participation. One could say, given Heidegger's treatment of these questions, that by appropriating Plato in this way, Gadamer effectively reads Heidegger against himself in much the same way that Heidegger reads Aristotle against himself (though perhaps more indirectly).

This question of the dialectic, however, clearly extends beyond Gadamer's appropriation of Plato. Hegel's rethinking not only of the Socratic art but of logic in general and the implicit collapse therein of the distinction between being and thought provides Gadamer with yet another excellent model for his own ontologizing of the phenomenon of consciousness. Gadamer, in effect, attempts to do for Hegelian dialectic what Hegel did for traditional Aristotelian reasoning. Just as Hegel rethought the static logic of the syllogism, releasing it into the dialectical movement of the Concept, Gadamer wants to release Hegel's dialectic from the straitjacket of systematic grammar into the openness of actual living dialogue, into what he calls "the logic of question and answer."

On the face of it, given Heidegger's adamant rejection of Hegel and the dialectic as the metaphysical capstones of the philosophical tradition, one might naturally conclude that here we have reached the point of greatest disparity between Gadamer and his mentor. And this view would not be altogether incorrect. In the second half of this inquiry, however, I will try to narrow this gap somewhat by way of two hermeneutical approaches. First of all, I will try to show how Gadamer's appropriation of Hegel can be seen as boldly carrying the Heideggerian project of dismantling and retrieval directly back into the teeth of the metaphysical tradition itself rather than following Heidegger into the realm of *Dichten und Denken*. At the same time, however, I will attempt to show how Heidegger's own most radical philosophical movement into poetizing/thinking never quite gains a foothold outside of the very metaphysical and specifically dialectical ground that it seeks to deconstruct. Such a critique is, of course, nothing new; many commentators have made similar claims (Derrida, Habermas, and Rorty come quickly to mind). But I am not asserting by this that Heidegger's later thinking is somehow ineffectual or that it simply runs into a dead end; far from it. I simply wish to explore the possibility that in his various encounters with Hegel's friend and roommate, Friedrich Hölderlin, the movements within Heidegger's own language inevitably display some of the same quasi-dialectical characteristics that one finds in the theoretical writings of this poet who was so intimately associated with the re-inventor of philosophical dialectics. I am merely claiming that an argument can be made for a hermeneutic affinity between Gadamer and the later Heidegger even at one of their most obvious and radical points of departure. My project, therefore, will be generally twofold (if somewhat multiform within the larger structure), while at the same time maintaining a double guiding thread throughout. The two main historical loci of my endeavor will be fifth-century Athens and nineteenth-century Germany, with the questions of *phronēsis* and dialectic serving as hermeneutical focal points for an encounter between Heidegger and Gadamer and their respective ways of dismantling and retrieving language and being throughout the philosophical tradition.

Part 1

Phronetic Application and Dialectical Participation

ONE

Heidegger and Gadamer on Aristotle: The Facticity of Phronēsis *and the Phenomenon of Application*

Even though, as both Heidegger and Gadamer would tell us, every hermeneutical engagement is thoroughly conditioned and mediated by its historical circumstances and so, in a sense, is always already underway, any specific conversation (even a counter-turning dialogue) must have a beginning—or at least our discussion of it must begin somewhere. Though by no means the beginning of either of their respective academic lives, the ongoing dialogue between these two men gets its start in the summer of 1923 at the University of Freiburg when Gadamer sits in on one of Heidegger's Aristotle seminars. But it is not so much the biographical circumstances of their meeting that I find valuable for my project but the fact that this pedagogical encounter establishes a point of near identity in their respective philosophical journeys: Gadamer adopts Heidegger's reading of Book VI of the *Nicomachean Ethics* seemingly without hesitation or alteration and carries it almost entirely intact into the very heart of his own hermeneutic theory. And yet, when it comes to Plato, the two phenomenologists will definitely not see eye-to-eye. Perhaps because of his classical philological training, Gadamer seems to have a natural affinity for Plato. Heidegger, on the other hand, finds the dialogues less helpful than Aristotle's treatises and effectively places the blame for the correspondence theory of truth squarely in Plato's lap. In fifth-century Athens, therefore, we find the site within which the first major turn of our counter-turning dialogue can show itself—a site at once of intense nearness and striking remoteness. As a way of entering into this hermeneutical location, I would like to frame my initial discussion in terms of a response to Robert Bernasconi's insightful 1989 essay, entitled "Heidegger's Destruction of *Phronēsis*."[7]

Heidegger's Phronetic Retrieval of Aristotle

Responding to the recently rediscovered text of Heidegger's 1922 article, "*Phänomenologische Interpretationen zu Aristoteles: Anzeige der Hermeneutischen Situation*" (the so-called "Aristotle *Einleitung*"),[1] and relying on a fragmented typescript of Helene Weiss's notes from Heidegger's 1924–1925 lecture course on Plato's *Sophist,* Robert Bernasconi offers a coherent and valuable reading of how Heidegger retrieves Aristotelian *phronēsis* for the project of *Being and Time.* He locates this retrieval generally in sections 15-18 in which Heidegger discusses the worlding of the world and equipmentality and more specifically in the word "*Umsicht*" or "circumspection" as a direct translation of *phronēsis.*

Of course, as Bernasconi himself points out,[2] this reading is clearly at odds with a number of other interpreters, including Jacques Taminiaux, who sees *phronēsis* in *Entschlossenheit,* John Caputo, who opts for *Verstehen,* and the anecdotal evidence of Gadamer and Oskar Becker (by way of Otto Pöggeler), who independently report Heidegger, during a particularly difficult moment in the 1924 seminar, announcing bruskly, "*Das ist das Gewissen!*" And, indeed, in the now published *Platon: Sophistes* lectures[3] we find Heidegger himself declaring explicitly that "it is indeed clear from this context that here Aristotle has hit upon the *phenomenon of conscience. Phronēsis* is nothing other than conscience put in motion . . ." All of this would seem to militate directly against Bernasconi (not to mention Taminiaux and Caputo)—especially since the sections on conscience fall squarely in Division Two of *Being and Time.* As it turns out, however, Heidegger had indeed been translating *phronēsis* as something like "circumspective insight" or, as Bernasconi indicates, "solicitous looking around oneself" (*fürsorgliches Sichumsehen*)[4] even up to the 1924 "would-be journal article" called "The Concept of Time," which Theodore Kisiel identifies as "the very first draft of [*Being and Time*]."[5] In fact, in the early going of the *Platon: Sophistes* lectures Heidegger repeatedly identifies *phronēsis* as "*die Umsicht*" and even "*Einsicht.*"[6] But whether or not *Umsicht* or *Gewissen* or perhaps *Entschlo-*

ssenheit is the proper way to interpret the Heideggerian *phronēsis* of 1927, I am more interested in examining Bernasconi's insistence upon locating "Heidegger's debt to Aristotle in the . . . distinction between *technē* or craft and *phronēsis* or practical wisdom"[7] and how his overall reading might help us to flesh out a series of almost off-hand comments made by Kisiel in the course of his invaluable survey of the early Heidegger.

In his introduction to *The Genesis of Heidegger's 'Being and Time'*, Kisiel explains that "The project of BT [*Being and Time*] thus takes shape against the backdrop of an unrelenting exegesis of Aristotle's texts, especially *Nicomachean Ethics Z*, from which the manifestly *pre*theoretical models for the two Divisions of BT, the *technē* of *poiesis* for the First and the *phronēsis* of *praxis* for the Second, are derived."[8] And later in the text, referring to how in 1922 "*alētheia* already understood as a process of unconcealing disclosure enters into the Heideggerian thematic" through the understanding of *phronēsis*, he asserts that "This influence lasts into BT, for the *phronēsis* into [*sic*] human action constitutes the exemplary paradigm of its Second Division, just as the other nontheoretical 'dianoetic virtue,' *technē*, concerned with making and using, is the basic example of the First."[9] And, yet again, in a personal conversation in February of 1995, Kisiel explained how three distinct moments of the text constitute, as he put it, the "Aristotelian insight of *Being and Time*" by elaborating ontological transpositions of *technē*, *phronēsis*, and *nous*, respectively: in Division One, the concern for the "tool-world" corresponds to *technē*; in Division Two, the phenomena of coming to terms with life as a whole, being toward death, and the call of conscience all allude to aspects of *phronēsis*; and, throughout the book, the unity of temporality expressed in terms of *Lichtung* and all of the attendant "light" metaphors, Kisiel sees as expressions of *nous*. On the face of it, it would appear that both Bernasconi and Kisiel (and Taminiaux before them), despite any differences with regard to the Heideggerian word for *phronēsis*, wish to see *Being and Time* in terms of the two nontheoretical modes of Aristotelian "being true." The subtler distinction here, however, is that Kisiel does not seem to follow Bernasconi in stressing the difference between the two as the *real locus* of Heidegger's debt to Aristotle. Admittedly, Kisiel does not elaborate on this point, and Bernasconi did not have access to all the materials that Kisiel did, but I think if we read Bernasconi to some degree against himself, with the aid of Kisiel's vast archival insights, we can begin to get a picture of Heidegger's

Destruktion and *Wiederholung* of Aristotle that will allow us a glimpse into not only how *Gadamer's* reading of *phronēsis* gains its phenomenological thrust but how, in his very appropriation of his teacher's interpretation, Gadamer begins to depart from Heidegger's path of thinking. As we shall see, by specifically distinguishing *phronēsis* from *technē*, Gadamer manages to dismantle and then rehabilitate the notion of "application" [*Anwendung*] that lies at the heart of all prior conceptions of hermeneutics and traditional epistemology as well.

Bernasconi finds a moment of tension in Heidegger's presentation of *Nicomachean Ethics,* Book VI when Heidegger identifies *sophia* as the unexpected *aretē* (excellence) of *technē* (an identification, incidentally, which Gadamer will follow some forty years later). The issue here turns on the basic schema of the five modes of *alētheuein.* In the Aristotle *Einleitung*—in line with his famous interpretation of *alētheia* as unconcealment and against the traditional rendering of "to attain or to seize hold of truth"—Heidegger defines *alētheuein* as "to take the being which is intended, and which is intended as such, as uncovered in truthful safe-keeping."[10] Thus the verb form of the noun, *alētheia,* attains an appropriately active character as well as a sense of preserving (*verwahren*). Kisiel renders *alētheuein* for us with the neologistic "trueing." Aristotle separates the five primary habits or *hexeis* of trueing along an axis, the symmetry of which one does not expect to be breached: *sophia* and *epistēmē,* as belonging to *epistēmonikon* (the scientific faculty of the soul), each apprehend that which "always is" (*aei*), whereas *phronēsis* and *technē,* as belonging to *logistikon* (the "estimative" or deliberative faculty), apprehend that which can also be other than it is. *Sophia* (which Heidegger translates as "authentic, observing understanding") and *phronēsis* (at this point, still "solicitous circumspection" [*fürsorgende Umsicht*]) are described in the Aristotle *Einleitung* as "the authentic ways of the actualizing of *nous,* of pure beholding as such" ["*die eigentlichen Vollzugsweisen des reinen Vernehmens als solchen*"],[11] hence their designation as the *dia-noietic* virtues, the excellences or perfections attained by way of or in association with *nous.* This leaves the two lesser modes of being true, *epistēmē* and *technē* apparently on opposite sides of a clear axiological distinction, and yet, as Heidegger sees it in section 8 of *Platon: Sophistes,*[12] although *sophia* is clearly the virtue or perfection of *epistēmē,* it also turns out to be the perfection of *technē* precisely when one would expect *phronēsis* to fill that role. For how could a disposition that apprehends that which changes have for its perfection a virtue that contemplates the eternal? According to Bernasconi, Heidegger relies too heavily here on the first part of Book VI, Chapter 7, in which Aristotle explicitly characterizes *sophia* as the *aretē* of *technē*, but this passage, as Eduard Zeller had already pointed out some years before, seems to refer to a popular usage of the word *sophia* rather than the technical/philosophical way in which Aristotle wishes to employ it himself. I would contend, however, that this passage would not be atypical of Aristotle's very un-Platonic tendency to use popular consensus as evidence of philosophic truths (cf., for example, the first book of the *Metaphysics*). But Heidegger does invoke a passage from Chapter 5 (1140b 24) where Aristotle points out that "*phronēsis* is an *aretē* but not a *technē*" as evidence of a severing of the *technē-phronēsis* relationship in regard to *aretē*, although there is perhaps no pressing syllogistic necessity for drawing this conclusion. Nevertheless, as Bernasconi is quick to point out, Heidegger does not completely separate the two, either in *Being and Time* or in the *Sophist* lectures.

Bernasconi looks to an earlier passage in the *Ethics* in which Aristotle explains the significance of the *hou heneka*, the "for-the-sake-of," which ultimately governs both *poiēsis* or making and *praxis* or doing. This common governance derives from the notion that *eupraxia* ("doing well" or "good action") is the end of all desire (NE 1139a 35–b 4).[13] Presumably, if one desires to make something, one does so for a reason, for the sake of something; and if the ultimate goal of every desire is some good action, then making can be said to have the same end as any human action, albeit deferred. And since *technē* is concerned with *poiēsis* and *phronēsis* with *praxis*, this would amount to an understanding of *technē* as being, as Bernasconi puts it, "piloted by *phronēsis*."[14] (One might hasten to point out, however, that the specific *hou heneka*, the immediate end in each case, is quite different. The *eupraxia* of *phronēsis* is the perfection of the individual "self," whereas that of *technē* is the accomplishment of the work at hand.) Although unable to find a direct reference to the above-mentioned passage in the *Sophist* lectures, Bernasconi suggests that Heidegger's accounts of equipmentality and the worldhood of the world in *Being and Time* bear a striking parallel to Aristotle's discussion of the common *hou heneka* of *poiēsis* and *praxis*. Not only does Heidegger use the word "*Umsicht*" here—the very word he had used many times in the early 1920s to translate *phronēsis*—to describe that special kind of nontheoretical sight that comes into play when one manipulates a hammer or makes something, but he also invokes the notion of the "for-the-sake-of-which" (*das Worumwillen*), the same word with which he translates *hou heneka* in 1924–1925.

Although I am not entirely compelled by Bernasconi's argument here (which I have truncated somewhat for the sake of brevity), it does seem to complicate Kisiel's view of Part 1 of *Being and Time* as an ontological transposition of *technē* and Part 2 as similarly transposing *phronēsis*. But, of course, Kisiel makes no claim, as far as I can see, that this scheme is either a pristine or an exclusive one. So long as we bear in mind the one essential commonality of *technē* and *phronēsis* that Aristotle himself is quite clear about—that they both apprehend that which can be otherwise—then there is no reason to assume that Heidegger could not have found it quite appropriate to include aspects of both habits of the soul in *both* sections of *Being and Time* and still keep the overall scheme intact. For if nothing else, *Being and Time* is a phenomenological investigation, and what are phenomena but things or events that can be (or at least appear) other than they are at a given moment. In other words, both *technē* and *phronēsis* are concerned with temporal, factical phenomena. Indeed, although he never refers to Heidegger's identification of *phronēsis* with conscience, even Bernasconi acknowledges that his reading of sections 15 to 18 "needs to be continued into the Second Division . . . When Heidegger in contrast to the tradition emphasizes the primacy of the ecstasis of the future he is developing his account, already latent in the 1922 Introduction to Aristotle, of the temporality of *phronēsis*."[15]

But what intrigues me here is that Bernasconi's Heidegger sees the two deliberative dispositions as intimately related to one another, and I want to suggest that by stressing this intimacy, Bernasconi is tending to undermine his own thesis that this particular distinction is the location of Heidegger's debt to Aristotle. The difference between *technē* and *phronēsis* is unquestionably an important one for Heidegger, especially if one follows Kisiel's rough sketch. But I would suggest that the real location of Heidegger's debt to Aristotle comes more clearly into focus with the aid of *The Genesis of Heidegger's 'Being and Time'*, where Kisiel gives us an unprecedented bird's-eye view of the early lecture courses leading up to the 1927 publication.

The picture that Kisiel draws for us establishes Aristotle as a pivotal figure for Heidegger. The *Nicomachean Ethics* and the

Metaphysics presented Heidegger with a fork along the path of philosophy. The more heavily trodden and well-worn route bore the sign "*Epistēmonikon*" and led proudly down the royal road to metaphysics and the ascendency of science and technology. The other way, somewhat unobtrusive and seldom traveled, was labeled "*Logistikon*" and held the promise, as only Heidegger could have seen, of a radically different way of thinking about both being and human being. By and large, the metaphysical tradition, in its great respect for Aristotle, kept traveling dogmatically down the path of *epistēmē* and *sophia*, those habits of the soul whose lofty goal was to contemplate the eternal, the path which Aristotle himself identified as the high road to the best life a man can live—the life that the scholastics would later refer to as the *vita contemplativa*.[16] Heidegger, however, saw *phronēsis* (which for Aristotle happened to run a very close second to *sophia*) as embodying some very particular advantages for a phenomenological project that wished not only to rethink being and temporality, but thinking itself and human existence as well.

The most important of these advantages, I would argue, is what Heidegger sees as the inherent facticity of this practical mode of being true. "The *alētheia praktike*," writes Heidegger, "is nothing other than the uncovered, full moment-of-insight (*Augenblick*) into factical life in the How of its decisive readiness for dealing with its own self, and it is such within a factical relationship of concern with respect to the world which is thus encountered."[17] We can discern here a distinct foreshadowing of fundamental ontology in the references to "factical life"—which Kisiel identifies for us as a Heideggerian precursor to *Dasein*[18]—as well as the circumspective concern of factical life with itself and the world that becomes a hallmark of *Dasein*'s hermeneutical comportment in section 34 of *Being and Time*. But, of more immediate importance for the present discussion, we see implied in this passage a sharp distinction from *sophia* in the sheer practicality and facticity of *phronēsis*.

Although Heidegger does read Aristotelian *epistēmē* and *sophia* phenomenologically rather than epistemologically and therefore against the tradition, this does not entirely obviate all those aspects of the two scientific ways of being true that metaphysics found so valuable. For instance, in their orientation toward the eternal, there is obviously little room for a consideration of temporality or the concrete situatedness of human *Dasein*. In other words, unlike *phronēsis*, and to a lesser extent *technē*, *sophia* and *epistēmē* are by definition incapable of accounting for the facticity of the world and human being-in-the-world. And it is in this more fundamental distinction, I would argue, that the location of Heidegger's true debt to Aristotle is to be found. This is not to suggest, however, that the difference between *technē* and *phronēsis* is an insignificant one for Heidegger or for *Being and Time*—just that it does not strike me as the essential Aristotelian catalyst for fundamental ontology.

For Gadamer, on the other hand, whom Heidegger's Aristotle *Einleitung* had affected "like an electric shock,"[19] the whole problematic is inverted. To a certain extent, one could characterize philosophical hermeneutics as attempting to do with traditional epistemology what Heidegger did with ontology. Aristotelian *epistēmē*, therefore, would seem like a natural target for a destructive hermeneutic, and *Truth and Method* does indeed operate, generally speaking, as an elaboration of deliberative over against scientific modes of being true. However, we must not forget that Gadamer has had the peculiar advantage of being able to take his teacher's deconstruction of metaphysics as an already accomplished task. Thus he can almost blithely state that "the distinction that Aristotle took up between the ethical knowing of '*phronēsis*' and the theoretical knowing of '*epistēmē*' is simple [!], particularly if one considers that for the Greeks science is represented by the figure of mathematics, knowledge of constants, a knowing that calls for proof and which anyone can learn."[20] The so-called theoretical ways of knowing, in other words, are modeled on the objectivity of mathematics and thus would seem to fall outside of the realm of *ethos* or behavior, which, as we have already indicated, brings us within the realm of *praxis* and hence facticity. And it is precisely this practical aspect of deliberative knowledge that Gadamer finds valuable for the project of interpretation in the human sciences. Ironically, however, it is only with the recognition of a *similarity* between *technē* and *phronēsis* that we reach "the point at which the analysis of ethical knowing in Aristotle can be placed in relation with the hermeneutical problem of the modern *Geisteswissenschaften*."[21] That is to say that they are both forms of knowing something in advance, and they each seek to determine and guide some kind of action; therefore, they both must contain within themselves, as Gadamer says, "the application [*die Anwendung*] of knowledge to the concrete task in each case."[22]

And with this notion of *Anwendung* (literally "turning toward") we also find ourselves at our first noticeable *Gegen-wendung* or counter-turning: Insofar as the traditional theories of truth and most traditional ethical doctrines have been concerned with the application or correspondence of *a priori* principles to *a posteriori* "facts," Gadamer turns boldly toward an area of metaphysics (i.e., epistemology) that Heidegger intentionally circumvents by drawing on the preplatonic idea of *a-lētheia*, truth as dis-closure or unconcealing. But, as we shall see, Gadamer turns away from Heidegger only by turning toward him at the same time—that is, by engaging in a Heideggerian *Destruktion* and *Wiederholung* of the traditionally epistemological concept of application.

Gadamer's Appropriation of Heideggerian Phronēsis

In the middle third of *Truth and Method*, Gadamer discusses how historical consciousness and the epistemology of the human sciences both share with human being the fact of being determined by tradition. Tradition, in turn, reveals itself hermeneutically in these modes of understanding as prejudice. That is to say that prejudice, in the positive form of critical self-understanding, makes historical consciousness both possible and meaningful by locating the self in the concrete context of historical experience. Aristotle's concept of *phronēsis*, though lacking this explicitly historical dimension, offers Gadamer, as he says, "the only methodological model for self-understanding of the human sciences if they are to be liberated from the spurious narrowing imposed by the model of the natural sciences."[23] In other words, in looking to the example of *phronēsis*, the *Geisteswissenschaften* can find their proper sphere over against Dilthey's attempt to find room for them within the purview of scientific method. But, of course, this merely constitutes an adaptation—albeit an extremely important one—of Heidegger's original insight, which we have discussed above. As we have already pointed out, however, what Gadamer really finds interesting is the slightly more subtle difference to be discerned between *technē* and *phronēsis*.

An important aspect of the *technē/phronēsis* distinction is whether one can be taught moral knowledge in the same way that one can be taught a technical skill. Gadamer balks at this idea, and points to the priority of being-situated: "We learn a *technē* and can also forget it," Gadamer writes,

> But we do not learn ethical knowing [*sittliches Wissen*; i.e., *phronēsis*], nor can we forget it. We do not stand over against

> it, as if it were something that we can acquire or not, as we can choose to acquire an objective skill, a *technē*. Rather, we are always already in the situation of having to act . . . and hence, we must already possess and apply ethical knowing.[24]

Phronēsis, in other words, is not in the least objective in the sense of something that stands apart from a subject. Rather, we always already (echoing the Heideggerian "*immer schon*") find ourselves in possession of moral knowledge. But given that moral knowledge is supposed to be an intellectual virtue, and, as Aristotle himself states, "Intellectual virtue owes both its inception and its growth chiefly to instruction, and for this reason needs time and experience,"[25] how can Gadamer argue that "we do not *learn* moral knowledge"? For that matter, have we not already alluded to the fact that *phronēsis* can involve (at least implicitly) previously learned knowledge of general principles?[26]

The question at this point reveals itself as a matter of translation and interpretation. Witness the following passage from Book VI of the *Nicomachean Ethics*:

> Although the young develop ability in geometry and mathematics and become wise in such matters, they are not thought to develop prudence [*phronēsis*]. The reason for this is that prudence also involves knowledge of particular facts [presumably as well as universals], which become known from experience, and a young man is not experienced, because experience takes some time to acquire . . .
>
> Again, error in deliberation is with reference either to the general principle or to the particular fact . . .[27]

Should we understand from this that moral knowledge, as Gadamer claims, cannot be taught, but that general principles nevertheless have a bearing on it? One could perhaps conclude, without fear of contradicting either Gadamer or Aristotle, that general knowledge is a necessary but not a sufficient condition for *phronēsis*. (If this is the case, however, one might wish to modify Gadamer's claim that we "*always* already possess moral knowledge" with the qualification that *adults*, those who have already become experienced, possess such knowledge and can apply it.) This question has significant ramifications for hermeneutics. For central to *Truth and Method* is the idea that hermeneutics cannot be reduced to a method or a technique (either in the modern scientific sense or the sense of a craft to be learned)—hermeneutics is not something that is taught per se, but is a process in which we are always already engaged. For Gadamer's analogy to cohere, the application of *phronēsis* must be similarly immediate and processual—*unterwegs immer schon.*

Aristotle is less than clear on this point, but Gadamer's reading becomes plausible if we follow his distinction between "ethical consciousness" (*phronēsis*), and what he calls the "ethical sciences." In "The Problem of Historical Consciousness," he explains how

> it is essential to the phenomenon of ethics not only that the agent knows in general how to decide and what to prefer, but also, he must know and understand how he ought to act in the given occasion, a responsibility that he can never evade. Thus it is essential that ethical sciences—while they may contribute to the clarification of the problems of the ethical consciousness—never usurp the place properly belonging to concrete ethical consciousness.[28]

The ethical sciences, of which Gadamer sees the *Nicomachean Ethics* itself as a prime example, provide only general outlines or schemata that may help guide the moral person. But, he argues, even the teacher of ethics "always already stands within an ethical-political restriction from out of which he acquires his image of the matter [*die Sache*; i.e., the moral ideal to be achieved]."[29] The guiding principles that are taught by the ethical sciences cannot predict or determine the end result of a particular moral decision the same way that an artisan employs a plan or blueprint (the *eidos*) that determines (albeit contingently) the end product of the craft.[30] Instead, as Gadamer says, "They concretize themselves always only in the concrete situation of the person acting,"[31] and this means that *phronēsis* is a process wherein the application of a specific act of intellection cannot be divorced either from the particular circumstances that give rise to it or from the particular person who is engaged in it. But this raises yet a further implication.

If, as Gadamer argues, *phronēsis* is at once both an intellectual capacity and a mode of being, then the means-ends distinction becomes blurred and the traditional dichotomy between knowledge and experience begins to collapse. Gadamer correctly points to the fact that Aristotle's definitions of moral knowledge, especially with reference to means and ends, are sometimes uncertain. He explains in a footnote that generally for Aristotle, "*phronēsis* has to do with the means (*ta pros to telos*) and not with the *telos*."

He goes on to conclude, however, that "*phronēsis* is no mere ability to correctly choose the means, but is itself an ethical *hexis* [a fully developed habit or comportment] that also sees the *telos* toward which the person acting is oriented through his ethical being."[32] *Phronēsis,* in other words, is an experiential phenomenon in which the means of acting and the "product" of the act (i.e., ethical being) occur simultaneously within the situation itself. Hence, in contrast with *technē,* wherein the means (the *eidos* and the materials of production) and the ends (the finished work) are patently separate and distinguishable, the means and ends of *phronēsis* are both subsumed in experience (and perhaps become distinguishable only on subsequent reflection). Gadamer even goes so far as to suggest that *phronēsis* becomes thereby "the fundamental form of experience [*Erfahrung*], which, over against all other experience, represents an alienation, if not to say a denaturing [*eine Verfremdung, um nicht zu sagen Denatierung darstellt*]."[33] That is, *phronēsis* becomes what he calls "genuine" or "real" experience, insofar as its application both participates in and reflects upon the immediate human situation. By "real experience" Gadamer means "that in which humanity becomes conscious of its finitude. In it the ability to make (*das Machenkönnen*) and the self-consciousness of its planning reason find their limits."[34] *Phronēsis,* in other words, not only distinguishes itself from *technē* but also acts as a critique of all purely cognitive reasoning by partaking in what Gadamer refers to as the "experience of human finitude."[35] He thereby reiterates the radical facticity of Heideggerian *phronēsis* in opposition to the systematic and teleological modes of *epistēmonikon* (i.e., *epistēmē* and *sophia*) that Aristotle himself stresses and the tradition embraces.

This insight into the situational, factical, and therefore ontological aspect of what might otherwise be construed as an epistemological concept becomes decisive for Gadamer's interpretation of *phronēsis* in that, so far as it is both immediate and situationally dependent, application and cognition remain undifferentiated. That is to say that *knowing* (at least in the sense of practical knowledge, but ultimately, for Gadamer, all knowing) does not precede and is not something other than either *doing* or *being.* As Gadamer sees it, following Heidegger, these ontological and self-referential aspects of Aristotelian practical knowing clearly distinguish it from theoretical knowledge, which objectively contemplates only the invariable and universal.[36] For Aristotle, however, technical knowing is objective as well, at least insofar as its acquisition and its application are separate moments. But *phronēsis,* says Gadamer, "is clearly no objective knowing. The knower does not stand over against a situation that he simply observes; rather, he is immediately confronted with what he perceives. It is something he has to do."[37] This nonobjective quality of *phronēsis* (and the fact that it always grounds itself in a particular situation) allows for a direct analogy with Gadamer's view of hermeneutics: *Phronēsis* reveals itself to be a form of being-conscious (*Bewußt-sein*) rooted in its own concrete *ethical* circumstances, while hermeneutics consciously interprets texts within the overlapping horizons or concrete *historical* circumstances of both the text and the interpreter. Situationally determined application, therefore, becomes the common feature that allows for the analogy: *Phronēsis* applies itself as *ethically*-effective understanding and hermeneutics applies itself in the form of *historically*-effective understanding or being conscious (*wirkungsgeschichtliches Bewußtsein*). Gadamer thereby deconstructs the traditional role of application in ethical situations and retrieves it as a phenomenologically viable occurrence. In other words, rather than coming from the outside and involving a theory or rule such as Kant's categorical imperative, which is often seen as standing prior to and existing independently of any particular circumstance of action that one identifies as ethical, application becomes the name for a central aspect of the phenomenon of understanding as it occurs in every human situation. To say, however, that "*phronēsis* applies itself" amounts to little more than saying "*phronēsis* occurs"—it amounts, that is, to a merely formal indication of the hermeneutical occurrence. But by formally indicating application in this way as an inherent element in all human interaction and not just an occasional technical procedure, Gadamer hopes to illuminate the universality of his philosophical hermeneutics. We can thus see how Gadamer's approach to Aristotle is at once Heideggerian—in his leaning on Heidegger's already accomplished retrieval of *phronēsis*—and uniquely Gadamerian insofar as re-injects *phronēsis* right back into its traditional role as a dimension of ethics while at the same time redescribing ethics itself as a universal hermeneutical phenomenon rather than a specialized scientific or technical scheme. And he does this precisely by retrieving the central moment of ethics—application, *Anwendung*—and interpreting it directly against its usual employment throughout the history of philosophy.

If *phronēsis*, then, provides Gadamer with a Heideggerian/Aristotelian model for interpretation in the human sciences and in human life, one might well ask how this phronetic mode of being actually occurs. How, in other words, does the *Wirkung* in *wirkungsgeschichtliches Bewußtsein* carry itself out? One can begin to answer this question by looking to Gadamer's primary interlocutor from the ancient world, Plato, and the way in which philosophical hermeneutics revivifies the long passé notion of the dialectic. His hermeneutical dismantling and retrieval of Plato marks perhaps the most dramatic point in which Gadamer turns away from his great teacher, and yet this, too, would have been unthinkable without his also turning back toward the factical insight of Heidegger's Aristotle interpretations. Gadamer's Plato studies, in fact, while predating even his visits to Freiburg in 1923 to hear Husserl and Heidegger lecture,[38] came to their first real fruition under Heidegger at Marburg in 1928 with his *Habilitationsschrift*, entitled *Platos dialektische Ethik.*[39] Gadamer, however, specifically credits Heidegger's Freiburg readings of Aristotle with providing the phenomenological orientation for his own Plato studies.[40]

But what of Heidegger's own reading of Plato? His most famous Plato piece, after all, "Platons Lehre von der Wahrheit," though not published until 1947, was written in the early thirties, not long after publication of Gadamer's *Habilitationsschrift.* One might have expected Heidegger to deconstruct and retrieve at least some aspect of Plato here in much the same way that he did with Aristotle, and to a certain extent this is so. What separates his readings of the two Greek figures, however, is that he opts out of the *Wiederholung* of Plato at a hermeneutically earlier point than he does with Aristotle. That is, whereas he reads both Plato and Aristotle brilliantly against the metaphysical tradition, he goes so far as to read Aristotle against Aristotle himself, thereby salvaging, among other things, the notion of *phronēsis* as a productive aspect of his own phenomenological project. He attempts no such reading of Plato against Plato, however, and if he can be said to appropriate anything specific, it would be a kind of historical delimitation rather than a positive hermeneutical notion. Leaning heavily on one particular aspect of the so-called "doctrine" of ideas, he detects the first traces that the originary Greek conception of truth as dis-closing has become distorted. If we are to understand Gadamer's profound debt to Plato, therefore, and begin to see how it serves as our second point of simultaneous proximity to and departure from the Heideggerian thought-path, we should look at Heidegger's own limited engagements with Aristotle's master. But let us first examine the intellectual and scholarly soil out of which Gadamer's unique brand of Platonism grew.

TWO

Platonic Methexis: *Heidegger's Aristotelian* Destruktion *and Gadamer's Heideggerian* Wiederholung

Gadamer, Neo-Kantianism, and Hermeneutics

A Young Scholar at Marburg

Gadamer came to intellectual maturity in the 1920s at the University of Marburg where he studied both philosophy and philology during a time of significant transition from a scholarly establishment dominated by the neo-Kantian philosophy of Hermann Cohen and Paul Natorp and the systematic classical philology of Ulrich von Wilamowitz-Moellendorff and Werner Jaeger to a new cadre of more radical young thinkers such as Ernst Robert Curtius, Paul Friedländer, Rudolf Bultmann, and Martin Heidegger. In 1922, Gadamer wrote his doctoral dissertation[1] under Paul Natorp—a man whom Gadamer would later characterize as "the strictest method fanatic and logician in the Marburg School."[2] Although firmly situated in the neo-Kantian tradition, Natorp, in his late thinking, went beyond the "transcendental method" of the nineteenth-century neo-Kantians to postulate a "transcendence of method," or what he called "general logic," which was, as Gadamer says, "no longer restricted to the fact of the sciences and its a priori foundations."[3] According to Gadamer, "life," for Natorp, "created in ethical action and artistic creation, in *praxis* and *poiēsis*, not in its objectivizing within the human sciences, should be grasped in unity with science rather than with the objectification inherent in willing and creating themselves."[4] This elaboration of the Kantian unification of theory and practice allowed Natorp to propose in his 1902 book, *Platos Ideenlehre*, the radical notion that Plato had no "doctrine of ideas" in the conventional sense. The ideas, rather than having their own independent existence, were, as Robert Sullivan puts it, "more or less like hypotheses, or mental configurations . . . and this meant that they were subjective conjectures to be tested for fit against perceived reality."[5] This notion had profound implications for the young Gadamer; for, as he now began to realize, if the ideas have no separate and absolute existence, then meaning in Platonic philosophy must be delimited by context, and Plato must be seen as an interpretive or hermeneutic philosopher rather than a systematic one.

After Natorp's retirement in 1923, Gadamer began to study philology under Paul Friedländer (a student of Wilamowitz) and philosophy under Natorp's successor, a young professor by the name of Martin Heidegger. Friedländer had a tremendous influence on Gadamer, and had it not been for the powerful figure of Heidegger, Gadamer might possibly have chosen to pursue classical philology rather than philosophy. Gadamer himself gives us a clue to the extent of his philological inclinations when, in his autobiographical *Philosophical Apprenticeships*, he invokes Nietzsche's famous declaration: "I have long been accustomed to judging philosophy professors according to whether or not they are good philologists."[6] Even without such direct testimony, Friedländer's impact is easy enough to discern in virtually all of Gadamer's work, but it is especially apparent in the early years as Gadamer begins his serious engagement with the Greeks.

Of particular importance for this early work was Friedländer's break (in 1922) with the plodding "scientific" classicism of Wilamowitz to embrace the holistic and unsystematic historical approach of the poet Stefan George and his circle. For the Georgians (and Friedländer) Plato's dialogues held no secret unwritten doctrines that needed to be ferreted out or exposed. Plato was to be taken at his word. But one had to recognize that Plato's "word" was saturated with irony and playfulness—a kind of serious playfulness, however, born of a desire to imitate the seriousness of live dialogical encounters.[7] As with Natorp, the dialogues were not to be seen merely as didactic statements of philosophic doctrine rendered in dramatic form—as if Plato had not yet understood the "proper" method of philosophical discourse. They were, instead, literary or dramatic works intended as inducements for the reader to take up the task of "cultivating wisdom in the soul"[8] through actual participation in Socratic philosophy.

Friedländer's pedagogical/propadeutical reading of the dialogues allowed Gadamer to make sense of a great many problems that went unaccounted for in the standard Aristotelian, neo-Platonic, and neo-Kantian "methodological" interpretations of Plato. Gadamer could now, for instance, take Plato seriously when, in the *Seventh Letter*, the *Phaedrus*, and elsewhere, he takes the written word to task for being too static and sings the praises (in writing!) of the dynamism and ultimate value of the spoken word. And—as we shall see—Plato's "illogical" and inconclusive discussions, his apparently disingenuous professions of ignorance, the docility of his interlocutors, and his ironic protestations against *mimesis* all become indispensable for Gadamer as he places language and the priority of the question at the very center of his Plato interpretation. Friedländer's philological treatment of the Platonic texts, in fact, plays a large part in determining Gadamer's overall approach to philosophical hermeneutics. We can therefore attribute Gadamer's ironically Heideggerian turn away from Heidegger and toward Plato in large part to the influence of Paul Friedländer.

Friedländer taught Gadamer to read Plato as a literary figure, and, as he was to reminisce in 1977, "Under Friedländer one learned in an incomparable way to discipline one's feel for language, that inner ear without which literary judgment is impossible."[9] This statement—with its references to "discipline" and "feel," "language" and "literary judgment"—reveals a great deal about Gadamer's early disdain of the traditional methodological mode of philosophizing. Here we begin to see that, although scientific (or, more properly, *wissenschaftlich*) rigor remains the cornerstone of good scholarship for Gadamer (as it did for Heidegger as well), even in the earliest stages of his career he is not afraid to look beyond conceptual analysis to focus on the text, and beyond the text itself to account for its "situatedness" both in the world and in the medium of language. As we proceed, it will become increasingly apparent how two traditionally incompatible words like "discipline" and "feel" can be used by Gadamer in such a context without the slightest hint of irony.

What should be fully apparent to us by now is that in his aversion to methodology, his criticism of the doctrinal interpretations of Plato, and his overall philological approach to philosophical questions, Gadamer's early thought was deeply influenced by the work of Natorp, Friedländer, and (to a certain extent) the Stefan

George circle.[10] As for his general philosophical orientation, however, Gadamer's Heideggerian roots, as we have seen, are quite obvious and frequently acknowledged by him. What is not commonly understood is how Heidegger's reading of Aristotle allows Gadamer to get beyond the neo-Kantian distinction between "Plato, the idealist" and "Aristotle, the realist,"[11] thus allowing him to posit what he calls the "Platonic-Aristotelian unitary effect"—the idea that Plato and Aristotle are not at all at odds, but are simply expressing the same truths in different ways.[12]

In the standard Plato and Aristotle interpretations, the specific occasions for their works and the problem of their divergent literary forms are, according to Gadamer, virtually ignored. By engaging in Husserlian/Heideggerian phenomenological description—instead of simply reducing the Platonic and Aristotelian texts to individual statements and pitting them against one another to demonstrate their inconsistencies—Gadamer attempts to look behind the written works to discover the questions for which they were the answers.[13] That is to say that a complete "analysis" of any text must examine not only what is said, but why, how, when, and where it is said. This kind of approach becomes especially important when reading someone like Plato, whose dramatic fictions are not easily reduced to propositional statements.

Having thus found neo-Kantian idealism too limited,[14] particularly with its failure to adequately account for Aristotle's critique of Plato, Gadamer dissociates himself from the neo-Kantians and looks to contemporary French and English research in his attempt to "penetrate Aristotle's thought."[15] It is not until he encountered Heidegger, however, that Gadamer comes to terms with the "unity in the logos philosophy, which started with Socrates' questioning and . . . permanently determined the entire conceptual apparatus of Western thought."[16] Again eschewing method and traditional analysis, Gadamer describes why at this stage Heidegger became decisive for him:

> Heidegger had worked his way through both the Catholic-Aristotelian and neo-Kantian traditions, and in appropriating Husserl's minutely detailed art of conceptualization, he had steeled the endurance and power of intuition, which are indispensable for doing philosophy with Aristotle. Here, then, was an advocate of Aristotle who, in his directness and the freshness of his phenomenological insights, far surpassed all the traditional shadings of Aristotelianism, who surpassed Thomism

> and, yes, even Hegelianism. To this day hardly anything has been made of this event, but it has had its effect on academic teaching, and my own path was defined beginning there. By the time I published my first book in 1931 [*Platos dialektische Ethik*], the convergence, at least in the area of practical philosophy, of the aim of Plato's thinking with Aristotle's conceptual distinctions had become evident to me.[17]

And it is precisely, as he says, "in the area of practical philosophy," that Gadamer will ground not only his unitary interpretation of the Greeks, but the theoretical aspects of philosophical hermeneutics as well. A practical philosophical approach grounded in ontology, in fact, is what distinguishes Gadamer's Heideggerian reading from the standard theoretical/metaphysical interpretations of Plato, and even, as I will argue, from Heidegger's own.

Though generally considered a "conservative" Heideggerian, Gadamer's earliest work with Natorp and Friedländer is precisely what allows him to depart significantly from Heidegger toward a rehabilitation of Plato's role in the so-called history of being. As Gadamer points out, for Heidegger, Plato's doctrine of ideas signaled "the first step in the transformation of truth from unconcealedness to the appropriateness and correctness of statements."[18] Plato, in other words, by conceiving truth epistemologically (as *orthotes*) rather than phenomenologically (as *a-lētheia* or un-concealing) becomes the pivotal figure in Western philosophy. The doctrine of ideas posits a radical separation (or *chōrismos*) between the physical realm of the senses and the noetic realm of the intellect, and thus initiates the long period of metaphysical speculation which, because of its emphasis on epistemology at the expense of ontology, Heidegger refers to as the history of "*Seinsvergessenheit*" or "the forgetfulness of being."

Gadamer, of course, tends to accept Heidegger's overall interpretation of the history of being.[19] Through his own intimate acquaintance with Plato, however, he eventually comes to ask the question of whether

> Plato himself did not attempt to think the realm of unconcealedness, at least in the idea of the good, and not merely because of certain complications and internal difficulties in the doctrine of the forms; but rather whether from the very beginning he had not questioned behind this doctrine and thereby behind *aletheia* as correctness.[20]

In raising this possibility, Gadamer is essentially taking Heidegger to task for reading "Plato's works through the eyes of Aristotle's critique"—a critique that "aims relentlessly at the refutation of the *chōrismos* of the ideas" but which does not account for the later dialogues, wherein Plato himself "dealt with *chōrismos* in a radical way and critically rejected it."[21]

As our encounter with Gadamer unfolds, we will see how he both agrees with Heidegger's occasionally (and ironically) unphenomenological Aristotelian reading of Plato and how he criticizes it—how, as P. Christopher Smith points out, he "goes beyond Heidegger's interpretation of Plato, but in a Heideggerian way."[22] At this point, however, it becomes important for us to recognize not just Gadamer's indebtedness to Heidegger, but also that his first (and, perhaps, most fundamental) hermeneutical work is thoroughly grounded in the Heideggerian critique of metaphysics. Indeed, throughout his career, Gadamer rarely loses sight of his roots in both Heidegger's phenomenological and Friedländer's philological interpretations of Greek philosophy. His entire career, in other words, can be seen as a constant and simultaneous turning away from and turning toward his Heideggerian provenance.

Developmental Constructs

If, however, Heidegger and Friedländer were positive sources for Gadamer's distinctively holistic reading of Plato and Aristotle, Werner Jaeger, who embodied the established interpretation of the Greeks with his developmental view of Aristotle, represented the model against which he was reacting.[23] Gadamer found Jaeger's theory of Aristotle's development "from Platonist to critic of Plato's doctrine of ideas and, finally, to empiricist" to be embarrassingly simplistic.[24] He found Jaeger's claim to having detected a clear-cut progression in Aristotle's ethical thought particularly annoying:

> Aristotle's presumed evolution from a "politics of ideas" (in the *Protrepticus*) through a still hesitant distancing of himself from Plato in the *Eudemian Ethics* to the "mature" and self-confident position of the *Nicomachean Ethics* is an arbitrary and contradictory construction of Jaeger's. It is particularly unconvincing if one also brings Plato's late dialogues to bear on the issue, for the *Philebus* and the dialogue on the statesman would be so far in advance of the supposedly Platonizing beginnings of Aristotle's ethics that one can properly ask

> oneself just who is criticizing whom here. The development schema—the postulation of the ideas apart by themselves, then participation of the appearances in the ideas, then dialectic of idea and appearance, and then, at the end, the equating of idea and number—slowly begins to come apart.[25]

And it is not only Jaeger's developmental reading of Aristotle that Gadamer finds lacking. When it comes to the prevailing consensus regarding Plato, Gadamer is also highly critical of the "naive chronological ordering of Plato's dialogical fiction, which in the end was tantamount to a veritable game of running back and forth from one home base to another."[26]

We should bear in mind, however, that Gadamer's criticisms are not directed specifically at the scholarly competence of these attempts to organize the classical texts. In fact, he tends to accept Jaeger's overall ordering of the Aristotelian corpus. And he does not wish to contend that Plato and Aristotle are consistently and pedantically saying the same things throughout their respective writings—far from it. Gadamer takes issue, rather, with the kind of reductionist scholarship that tries to compartmentalize the thought of the two most important and complex figures in the history of philosophy by offering a model based on a simplistic progression of conceptual "periods" and "phases."

Not to address a given text in all of its complexity and depth, not to place it in its cultural, historical, linguistic, and philosophical contexts is, for Gadamer, to treat it as a thing rather than an event; not to consciously take into account the entire history of its interpretation and not to recognize the historical nature of all interpretation is to fall into the very trap that Plato warned about 2,500 years ago. For Plato, living in a still predominantly oral culture, writing language down rendered it static, calcified, unable to defend itself against the queries of its critics—the written word, that is, could not be engaged in dialogue. For Gadamer, living in a culture dominated by writing, to reduce written language to its bare conceptual elements is tantamount to the same thing—it denies the text its temporal character as a phenomenon that demands to be engaged dialectically. And, in one way or another, dialectic reveals itself throughout Gadamer's entire corpus (as do contextuality and historicality) as a fundamental phenomenon of the hermeneutical situation—an extremely un-Heideggerian bit of greenery emerging ironically from profoundly Heideggerian soil. Let us now turn to that soil itself (i.e., Gadamer's *oeuvre*) in order to see how such an apparently anomalous plant as the dialectic could not only grow there but thrive.

Truth and Method and the History of Hermeneutics

Between 1927 and 1942, Gadamer wrote at least six essays, more than a dozen review articles, and one book, all bearing directly on the question of ancient Greek philosophy.[27] Since the publication of *Wahrheit und Methode* in 1960, Gadamer has published another book and no fewer than twenty major essays dedicated specifically to the same topic.[28] Although these works do not account for all or even the bulk of his *oeuvre*, throughout his entire career Gadamer has never abandoned his enthusiasm for the Greeks, and *Truth and Method* itself stands as testimony to the fundamental importance of Plato and Aristotle for the entire Gadamerian project. Although it is obviously not the central theme of *Truth and Method*, one of our primary tasks here has been to show how Gadamer's interpretation of Greek philosophy nevertheless determines the fundamental path of his hermeneutic theory—a path that converges with Heidegger's only after it has already journeyed through the dialogical/dialectical realm of Platonic thought.

Truth and Method is undoubtedly Gadamer's longest and most singularly significant work. And, as such, it is usually looked on as the primary practical example and the definitive theoretical statement of Gadamerian hermeneutics. But if we consider the extraordinary fact that Gadamer was born in 1900, began his professional career in the 1920s, finished *Truth and Method* in 1960, and is still alive and working in the late 1990s, we begin to realize how problematic it is to focus on even so important a book as *Truth and Method* to the virtual exclusion of an entire body of work spanning nearly seventy years.[29] This is why, except that he tends to overlook Aristotle's effect on Gadamer,[30] I agree with Francis Ambrosio's assessment that

> Too little heed is given to the formative role played by Gadamer's interpretive encounters with major figures in the philosophical tradition, especially Plato, Hegel, and Heidegger, both in *Wahrheit und Methode* itself and, more importantly, in his hermeneutic essays on these figures. Without this expansion of interpretive scope our understanding of the meaning Gadamer has succeeded in giving to these reflective notions in *Wahrheit und Methode* necessarily remains incomplete.[31]

I think it is a mistake to see *Truth and Method* as Gadamer's intellectual apogee before which he is only developing his theory of hermeneutics and after which he is merely commenting on it. One should bear in mind that *Truth and Method* is by no means a comprehensive and complete statement of the Gadamerian project.[32] Although it is more theoretical and self-reflexive than much of the rest of his work, it too is only (as Heidegger might have put it) "on the way" toward an understanding of the hermeneutical process. And to extract it completely from the context of Gadamer's entire corpus is to miss the very point of hermeneutics.

However, we would also fail to do justice to Gadamer if we were to emphasize any other aspect of his work without at least acknowledging its proximity to *Truth and Method*. Though it seems to refer to Plato and Aristotle only in passing, *Truth and Method* becomes important for this particular discussion because it situates them at the very heart of the question of understanding as an ontological as well as a hermeneutical phenomenon. We have already seen how Aristotle comes to play this role through Gadamer's Heideggerian interpretation. His appropriation of Plato, however, is considerably more complicated. The dialectic and dialogical aspects of philosophical hermeneutics to some degree predate Gadamer's tutelage under Heidegger and permeate his entire body of work. Before we can engage Gadamer on this point, therefore, we should also take a closer look at *Truth and Method* itself and see how Gadamer situates his own project within the history of hermeneutics.

In the first section of *Truth and Method*, Gadamer looks to the phenomenon of art in order to set the stage for a nonobjective approach to understanding that distinguishes modes of interpretation in the human sciences from the theoretical-objective model of the natural sciences. In the arts, he writes, "There is no unequivocal objectivity and . . . every interpreter submits 'his own' interpretation, which is nevertheless by no means arbitrary but may attain, or fail to attain, a definable degree of appropriateness."[33] Aesthetic interpretation, in other words, although relative to the individual interpreter, is not totally unbounded; its subjectivity is limited by a recognition of its own historical and cultural contexts. Beginning with Schleiermacher and culminating in Dilthey's aporetic attempt to reconcile a *lebensphilosophisches* approach to the human sciences with the rigor and certitude of scientific method, the modern hermeneutic tradition, however, has recognized this necessity for self-understanding while paradoxically maintaining an ideal of scientific objectivity. Hence Gadamer begins his effort to give hermeneutics a means of avoiding Dilthey's *cul-de-sac* by describing a process of textual interpretation that is grounded in the reflexive critical understanding of the interpreter but does not try to step outside the hermeneutic circle in search of universal truths. And just as Gadamer himself does not simply *assume* his hermeneutical perspective, we too should briefly trace the historical development of hermeneutics from its beginnings as a conceptual tool to its Gadamerian incarnation as a fundamental phenomenological *ethos*.

The fundamental innovation of modern hermeneutics was to appropriate the exegetical methods of biblical and classical scholars and expand them to account for interpretation not only in all written texts but "wherever thoughts come into words, as in conversation and the matters of daily routine."[34] Schleiermacher, whom Dilthey called the "Kant of hermeneutics," expanded the hermeneutical circle beyond the internal relationships of textual analysis toward a general theory of human understanding such that in any given situation, as Michael Ermarth puts it, "the interpreter must already have a preliminary sense (*Vorkenntnis*) of the whole matter and context being presented, if he is to grasp the particular meaning at hand."[35]

Already, in Schleiermacher, we begin to see certain affinities with Gadamer's own approach to interpretation. But the historical aspect of hermeneutics that Gadamer both embraces and criticizes in *Truth and Method* is not fully thematized until Johann Gustav Droysen, later in the century, offers his theory of hermeneutics as an "organon" of historical thought. For Droysen, to understand is to understand historically.[36] Human consciousness, in other words, is historical insofar as we tend to actively impose a coherent continuity onto the events that we perceive. Thus, for Droysen, hermeneutics becomes "historics," and interpretation is subsumed under the larger science of history.[37]

On the other hand, in spite of their much more expansive ideas about interpretation, both Schleiermacher and Droysen restricted the application of hermeneutics mainly to philological or historiographical texts. Dilthey, on the other hand, projected their work into a theory of understanding and interpretation as conditions of lived experience—a theory that was applicable to all of the so-called human sciences. As Ermarth explains,

> Even more than his predecessors, Dilthey insisted that there is a special relation between our immediate awareness of being alive and the interpretive knowledge we have of these manifestations. This continuity between our ordinary "sense" of the world as given in concrete lived experience (*Erlebnis*) and the methodical cognition of the human sciences remained the armature of Dilthey's reflections. The critical foundation of the human sciences seemed to entail a "phenomenology of consciousness" or a reflective anthropology which would explicate the various structures, patterns, and categories of the human-historical world of lived experience. *In this world our way of being is involved in our way of knowing.*[38]

Dilthey's connection between being and knowing comes very close to a Gadamerian way of approaching hermeneutics, and indeed, in many ways Gadamer is assuming Dilthey's unfinished project as his point of departure. Dilthey's problem, however, was that he aspired to develop hermeneutics into a methodology applicable to the human sciences in the same way that the so-called "scientific method" is applicable to the natural sciences. Gadamer, in fact (who does not share this Diltheyan desire to put the *Geisteswissenschaften* on a systematic par with the *Naturwissenschaften*) makes the leap into what John Caputo calls twentieth-century "radical" hermeneutics[39] precisely by obviating Dilthey's reliance on the role of method in achieving scientific understanding.

Finding the methodological (and still primarily epistemological) model of the nineteenth-century "romantic" tradition inadequate for a genuine confrontation with hermeneutical truth, Gadamer looks again to Heidegger for a way of grounding the hermeneutic question. Heidegger's existential analytic of *Dasein* becomes pivotal for Gadamer insofar as it rethinks Dilthey's notion of "*Verstehen*" or understanding. In construing understanding as a mode of experience within the context of *Lebensphilosophie*, Dilthey takes an important step in the right direction, but he still does not manage to break out of the epistemological mold. With Heidegger, however, *Verstehen* becomes a fundamental mode of human existence.[40] Following Heidegger's move away from the Diltheyan emphasis on the scientific method, Gadamer suggests that if "*Verstehen* is the basic moment of human *in-der-Welt-sein*, then the human sciences are nearer to human self-understanding than are the natural sciences," and as such "the human sciences thereby attain an 'ontological' valence which could not remain without consequences for their methodological self-understanding."[41] If understanding, in other words, is essential to human existence, then the hermeneutic process (which engages the project of understanding) can turn away from the metaphysical and epistemological structures of mathematics and the natural sciences and gain a phenomenological foothold in the world.

In *Truth and Method*, of course, Gadamer goes on to describe his nonmethodological theory of hermeneutics in great detail. What is directly relevant to our discussion, however, is this Heideggerian notion of understanding as an ontological phenomenon. For until the advent of phenomenology understanding had been conceived of almost exclusively as an abstract epistemological structure. But, as is evident in *Truth and Method* and inherent (I would argue) in all of his writings on the Greeks, Gadamer's interpretation of Plato and Aristotle, although immersed in the language of philology, literature, history and ethics, is fundamentally ontological; that is to say, these interpretations (albeit implicitly) are grounded thoroughly in and guided by a Heideggerian phenomenology of being. We have already seen how Gadamer follows Heidegger into an ontological reading of Aristotle's concept of *phronēsis* only to appropriate that very reading as one of the central moments in his own markedly different project. Let us now examine Heidegger's interpretation of Plato, not in order to establish it as just another point of departure for Gadamer, but to mark it as a key point of distanciation—a place into which Gadamer's explicit and already well-developed dialectical orientation will not allow him to follow his teacher.

Heidegger's "Problem" with Plato

Heidegger's preference for retrieving Aristotle from the tradition rather than Plato may be a simple function of his own Thomistic background, but whatever the case, very early in his career he offers us a rationale of sorts in the form of a hermeneutical principle. In his *Platon: Sophistes* lectures, he insists that there can be no "*scientific understanding, i.e., [no] historical going-back to Plato without a passage through Aristotle.* Aristotle," he continues, "initially blocks, as it were, every entrance to Plato."[42] This is clearly why he introduces these Plato lectures with a nearly 200-page discussion of the *Nicomachean Ethics*. In the opening pages of the text, Heidegger explains it this way:

> Until now it has been customary to interpret Platonic philosophy by proceeding from Socrates and the Presocratics up to Plato. We wish to blaze the inverse path from Aristotle back to Plato. This path is not unheard of. It follows the old proposition of hermeneutics that one should go with one's interpretation from the light into the darkness. We will make the presupposition that Aristotle understood Plato. Indeed, whoever knows Aristotle even roughly, will see from his standard of work that it is nothing bold to suppose that Aristotle has understood Plato. . . . If we wish to penetrate Platonic philosophy, then we do this along the guiding thread of Aristotelian philosophy. This is no value-judgment of Plato. What Aristotle says is that which Plato put into his hand, only more radically, more scientifically developed.[43]

Gadamer does much the same thing. He, too, argues that Plato and Aristotle are saying essentially the same thing only in different ways.[44] Heidegger, however, in his contention that going from Aristotle to Plato is like going "from the light into the darkness," tells us that Aristotle somehow radicalizes Plato's thinking and develops it more scientifically—the implication being that the clarity and force of Aristotle's treatises can render Plato's dialogues less obscure.

In Gadamerian terms, opting for such an Aristotelian entry into Plato's texts could be seen as a fine example of *wirkungsgeschichtliches Bewußtsein*, that is, an acute awareness of both the historical, palimpsestic layering of interpretations and the unavoidability of the first and foremost interpreter of Plato. I want to suggest, however, that in adopting this framework Heidegger traps himself in much the same kind of (in my view) limited and rather one-sided reading of Plato that Aristotle himself offers—a reading that, while philosophically and even phenomenologically "accurate," fails to take into account many of the larger contextual elements of Plato's hermeneutic situation. By this I mean such factors as the social and political situation of fifth-century Athens, the dramatic settings of the dialogues, and the constant religious and mythological allusions that suffuse Plato's writings—all of which one would perhaps expect of a truly Heideggerian interpretation and which Gadamer, as we shall see, takes great pains to develop. Let us first, however, take a slightly closer look at Heidegger's Plato.

Our standard source for determining Heidegger's interpretation, "Platons Lehre von der Wahrheit,"[45] initially offers a reading of the Allegory of the Cave as a progressive movement from truth as *hidden* un-hiddenness, if you will, toward *essential* un-hiddenness according with Heidegger's usual reading of *alētheia* as *Unverborgenheit*. He frames his reading of the cave allegory thus:

> The essence of truth, thought in the originary [*anfänglich*] Greek sense of *alētheia*, unhiddenness in relation to the hidden (the pretended and the disguised)—and only this—has an essential relation to the image of the cave underground. Wherever truth is of an essence other than or is not at least co-extensive [*mitbestimmt*] with unhiddenness, there an "allegory of the cave" has no basis for clarification.[46]

The images which occur in such an "allegory of the cave," in other words, by their very structure—insofar as any cave metaphor would tend to imply a moving from obscurity to clarity—demand clarification in terms of *alētheia* as *Unverborgenheit*. Thus we can see that Plato's *muthos* of progressive revealing accords very well with Heidegger's own conception of aletheic phenomenology. It is precisely in the cave allegory, however, that Heidegger locates the crux of the problem. "But still," he writes, "even if *alētheia* in the 'allegory of the cave' may be specifically experienced and named at emphatic points, another essence of truth besides unhiddenness forces its way into the foreground."[47] This "other essence of truth" shows itself, without being thematized in the allegory, as *orthotes* or "correctness." In order to demonstrate this, Heidegger zeroes in precisely on the phenomenality of the images in the allegory. The problem is not that the truth of phenomena occurs in and as the shining forth of the ideas—this, in fact, accords quite well with the originary Greek notion of truth—but that the ideas as "what can be seen" (*idea*) shine through and are specifically responsible for the visibility of phenomena. What he finds problematic, in other words, are the ideas themselves rather than *alētheia* per se. The focus of the allegory becomes not the phenomenon of *alētheuein* or "truing" but the presence, the *ousia*, of the ideas, and the Idea of the Good (*idea tou agathou*), in particular. Thus, according to Heidegger, even though Plato refers to *agathon* (at 518c, 9) as "the most phenomenal (apparent) of beings" (263, 134), whatness, *essentia* rather than *existentia*, becomes the hidden focal point of Plato's *paideia*. And precisely in this focus truth gets transformed. Thus Heidegger can ask,

> doesn't the "allegory of the cave" deal particularly with *alētheia*? Certainly not. And nevertheless the fact remains: this "allegory" contains Plato's "doctrine" of truth. For it is based on the unstated occurrence whereby the *idea* became the master of *alētheia*. The "allegory" gives an image of what Plato says about the *idea tou agathou*: *aute kuria alētheian kai noun paraschomene* (517c, 4), "it is itself master, dispensing both unhiddenness (to what emerges) and the ability to perceive (the unhidden)." *Alētheia* comes under the yoke of the *idea*. When Plato says that the *idea* is the master permitting unhiddenness, he banishes to something left unsaid the fact that henceforth the essence of truth does not unfold out of its own essential fullness as the essence of unhiddenness, but shifts its abode to the essence of the *idea*. The essence of truth relinquishes the basic feature of unhiddenness.[48]

Even if, in other words, *alētheia* is not the primary thrust of Plato's *muthos*, there is an implied or unsaid "doctrine" of truth to be found there, one which comes under the sway of the Idea of the Good. Truth itself no longer harbors the phenomenon of revealing. The occurrence of truth becomes but an epiphenomenon subordinated to the overarching permanence and mastery of the Good. The education of the philosopher thus becomes a question of "making one's glance more correct. Everything depends on the *orthotes*, the correctness of the glance."[49] The shift is one of location. The "place of truth," as Heidegger refers to it, shifts from the unhiddenness of the beings themselves—a feature that nevertheless still resounds in the allegory—to a question of the adequacy of human comportment toward those beings. Because the allegory is cast in terms of beings (the objects of human comportment) and knowing (the subjective beholding of these objects) rather than the phenomenality of the event itself, truth as an instrument of *paideia* becomes effectively, if not thematically, a question of the degree to which the philosopher is able to accurately perceive the unchanging essence of the *idea*.

Heidegger, however, does not (contrary to some interpretations) insist that this shift from *alētheia* to *orthotes* should be seen as determinative of how one reads Plato, that Plato, in other words, should be seen henceforth as the pure and original metaphysician. On the contrary, he sees the shift as signaling a clear ambiguity in Plato's so-called doctrine.[50] Plato still speaks of *alētheia* and uses the word in its appropriate and originarily Greek sense of unhiddenness, but the *context* of his theoretical employment of the word belies a shift in emphasis from the phenomenality of truth itself to a perceiving of phenomena for which unhiddenness becomes merely a mode or a means through which to achieve its end—that is, adequacy or correspondence.

One must be careful, however, not to hypostatize Heidegger's interpretation by placing too much weight on this particular essay. In the *Nietzsche* texts, particularly in Volume I, chapter 20 and following, which were taken essentially from his 1936–1937 lecture course at the University of Freiburg-im-Breisgau,[51] we are presented with a slightly more complicated view which takes great pains to distinguish between Plato's actual writings and Platonism as a tradition. Here he tells us explicitly that "Plato's work is not yet Platonism."[52]

At issue in this volume is Nietzsche's overcoming of Platonism and to what extent his inversion of the "true world" and the "apparent world" is a simple overturning of a "two worlds" doctrine that can be found in Plato. Heidegger's interpretation of Platonic truth here does little or nothing to contradict his interpretation in "Platons Lehre von der Wahrheit." The larger context, however, concerns itself with "the will to power as art," and this particular section focuses on the parts of the *Republic* and the *Phaedrus* dealing with *mimesis* and the Beautiful as manifestations of truth rather than the Good as presented in the allegory of the cave. Consequently, as Heidegger takes great pains to provide a "Greek-Platonic" view of truth rather than a Platonistic one, we find a greater emphasis on the self-showing of phenomena and being as emergence, as *phusis*, rather than beings as *ousia* or presence. And the larger scope of the discussion here becomes hermeneutically significant for our inquiry, for here we find certain revealing remarks about Plato's "method" which bring Heidegger's quotation marks around the word "doctrine" into better focus for us. "Method," Heidegger says,

> the manner of inquiry, was never for [Plato] a fixed technique; rather, it developed in cadence with the advance toward Being. If therefore at our present position method is formulated in an essential statement, such a designation by Platonic thought concerning the Ideas corresponds to that stage of the Platonic philosophy which is reached when Plato composes the dialogue on the state. *But that stage is by no means the*

> *ultimate one.* In the context of our present inquiry this account of method is of special interest.[53]

Thus we get a more phenomenologically and hermeneutically viable Plato whose method or path is neither predetermined by nor completed in the so-called theory of the Forms. He warns us, in fact, to be wary of reducing Plato's thoughts to mere "doctrines" (taken in the traditional metaphysical sense): "Whatever Plato says about truth and knowledge, or beauty and art, we may not conceive of it and pigeonhole it according to the later epistemology, logic, and aesthetics."[54] This general recognition of the unsystematic and contextually specific orientation of the dialogues, however, does not prevent Heidegger from seeing a specific and determined *telos* to Plato's thinking: "Nevertheless," he points out, "a certain basic way of proceeding prevails in Plato's thought. Everything is gathered into the guiding question of philosophy—the question as to what beings are."[55] Heidegger, therefore, seems to view Plato ultimately as a philosopher whose main impetus carries him—to put it in terms of fundamental ontology—toward the ontic rather than the ontological. He also sees Aristotle, however, as essentially an ontically oriented thinker, and yet, as we have seen, he manages to extract or retrieve from Plato's student an important insight—the phenomenological value of *phronēsis*—in spite of Aristotle's own elevation of *sophia* to the status of the highest mode of *alētheuein*. Why, one might ask, does Heidegger not attempt a similar *Wiederholung* of phenomenological themes from out of Plato?

Heidegger, of course, is under no obligation to retrieve Platonic thinking for his own project. But I would argue (as Gadamer does with respect to Aristotle) that Heidegger's *Destruktion* of the theory of the Forms, though certainly phenomenologically powerful and hermeneutically accurate in its own terms, becomes rather too Aristotelian (and so, I would argue, still too doctrinal in the traditional sense) in that it addresses primarily the theoretical structure of *Socrates'* "spoken" arguments while largely ignoring the dialogical and literary contexts provided by Plato himself. Gadamer, on the other, by taking a considerably broader view, does manage to appropriate a number of hermeneutically important themes from Plato's dialogues, including the thought of *methexis* or participation. Here we arrive at yet another counter-turning moment: Aristotle's (and essentially Heidegger's) main bone of contention with Plato is that Plato provides no real solution to the problem of how the Forms are supposed to participate in their corresponding physical objects (and vice versa). But not only does Gadamer not see this as a problem at all, he finds *methexis* to be the phenomenological key to a Heideggerian appropriation of Platonic dialectic for his own hermeneutical project. Therefore, we would do well to turn now to what P. Christopher Smith calls "H.-G. Gadamer's Heideggerian Interpretation of Plato."[56]

Gadamer and Dialectical Participation

One of the most difficult problems facing any interpreter of Plato is how to account for the apparent multitude of inconsistencies, paradoxes, dead-ends, and just plain errors that seem to permeate the dialogues. Why, for instance, every time we think we understand something about Plato's methodology, does he seem to shift the ground beneath us? Or, how is it that we are constantly finding flaws in the logic of the dialogues, yet we can rarely find grounds to discount their conclusions? And how is it that whenever we arrive at the "definitive" interpretation of a particular dialogue, someone else invariably comes along with an equally valid reading? Why, in other words, after nearly two and a half millennia, have we yet to "figure Plato out"?

For Gadamer, the problem with this question would be that it assumes that there are indeed "answers" hidden somewhere in the works of Plato that we can arrived at if only we can find the correct method. The question itself arises from our habit of paying minute attention to the content of the dialogues while all but ignoring their various contexts. The Platonic dialogues are so problematic for us because we have conditioned ourselves to read them as though they *were* Plato's philosophy, while ignoring his own perfectly lucid statements to the contrary. Even Aristotle and Heidegger, as we have seen, seem to remain trapped within this "interior" mode of analysis.

Why do we have so much trouble understanding Plato? Because, Gadamer would argue, we rarely ever take him seriously. Whenever most modern readers run across something in Plato that does not fit neatly into the conceptual framework they have imposed on him, they either ignore it or explain it away as just another example of his famous ironic wit. Gadamer's reading, on the other hand, begins to understand Plato in a way that not only accounts for the many ironies and inconsistencies, but positively embraces them as the most essential components of the Platonic texts. And he can do this precisely because he takes Plato's playfulness seriously.

In the course of his Plato studies, Gadamer has confronted some of the most difficult textual questions: Why, for example, do the arguments in the dialogues rarely seem "dialectical" according to Plato's own descriptions of the technique? How can we take Socrates' professions of ignorance seriously when Plato so often supplies him with the weakest possible interlocutors and so many of the arguments seem to arrive at predetermined conclusions? Why should we believe Plato's apparent condemnations of *mimesis* and the written word, when his own writings are so obviously mimetic? And how do we reconcile the fact that in several places Plato seems to contradict his own "doctrine of Ideas"? Gadamer does not offer one simple systematic or comprehensive answer to any or all of these questions. He does, however, offer various highly coherent readings of Plato that take into account the context, the form, and the content of individual dialogues, as well as their author's own historical situation, while never losing sight of Plato's one overarching dictum that philosophy, by its very nature, is dialectical. But how does Gadamer interpret the Platonic conception of the dialectic? Plato's own utterances on the subject (at *Phaedrus* 266b, e.g.) sometimes involve the terms *sunesis* or *sunagōge* (collection) and *diairesis* (division). Hence traditional definitions tend to formulate the dialectic as a logical or rational technique or a epistemological method of combining and dividing hypotheses and opinions aimed at achieving at least an approximation of absolute truth. Gadamer's Plato, however, is no epistemologist. So, before embarking on a detailed discussion of Gadamer and Platonic dialectic, I want, first of all, to try to place the primary source for many of these systematic interpretations—Plato's "divided line"—in its proper context.

In a number of places in the *Republic*, but especially in Book VII (522c–535), Socrates places great emphasis on the importance for the philosopher of learning mathematics and thinking geometrically, but only as a *prelude* to philosophy. Such references clearly echo the third level of the divided line where Socrates describes the method of inquiry here as that of the geometer—a method that begins with "the kind of assumptions that lead to conclusions and not to first principles" (510c).[57] At this level, the soul is "necessarily dependent upon hypotheses," and "because it is unable to go beyond these hypotheses, it is also unable to attain the level of first principles and new beginnings" (511a).[58] At the highest level, however, the level of the dialectic,

> Assumptions are not treated as first principles but as real hypotheses. That is, they are not employed as beginnings [*archas*], but as ladders and springboards, used in order to reach that realm that requires no hypotheses and is therefore the true starting point for the attainment of unobstructed knowledge. When reason attains that level and becomes aware of the whole intelligible order, it descends at will to the level of conclusions but without the aid of sense objects. (511b–c)[59]

Dialectic, in other words, treats hypotheses as mere opinions and not as truths in themselves. The hypotheses do get the discussion started, but they themselves are questioned rather than assumed as conclusions in their own right. Only after thoroughly interrogating these assumptions, then, does the dialectical soul willingly go back down to the level of conclusions or ends.

Let us draw back for a moment and look at this image from a wider perspective. The entire divided line is presented in geometrical terms, and geometry, though a necessary pedagogical prelude to the dialectic, is not itself strictly dialectical. In other words, when we look at the divided line within the larger context of the dialogue as a whole, we discover that, rather than the ultimate philosophical statement, the divided line shows itself to be but a geometrical *analogue* of philosophy. The divided line itself belongs not to the highest level, the level of the Forms, but to the *third* level, the level of discourse that remains unable to go beyond its own hypotheses. We might even say that the divided line is precisely *metaxu*, between ignorance and knowledge.[60] That is, from the immediate perspective of Socrates, the fictional character, the divided line in and of itself (in spite of over two thousand years of metaphysical interpretations) cannot qualify as true philosophy—and certainly not Plato's philosophy; rather (as Gadamer tries to show), from the wider perspective of Plato, the serious writer of playful dialogues, philosophy cannot be contained within the bounds of doctrinal formulations anyway. In other words, the geometrical description of the dialectic in Book VI and the divided line itself (with its air of geometrical precision) are both mere assumptions that must themselves be questioned in the course of actual conversation between people or in the living dialectical interaction between a reader and the text.

In Book VII of the *Republic* (at 534d), as well as in other dialogues such as the *Cratylus* (at 390c), the etymological relationship between the words "dialectic" and "dialogue"[61] becomes evident as Socrates characterizes the dialectic in terms of asking and answering questions. This strikes much closer to home for Gadamer; but in order to see that such a "dialectic of question and answer" need not be construed as yet another epistemological technique, we should look at how Gadamer pursues an ontological (and ultimately phenomenological) interpretation of dialectic as a form of "participation" or *methexis*—one of the terms Plato employs for the relationship between the phenomenal and noumenal realms and, along with *chōrismos* or "separation," the main focus of Aristotle's critique of the theory of the Forms. If, however, we are going to discuss how Platonic participation informs Gadamer's view of interpretation—that is, how the dialectic is at once linguistic and ontological—we should do so hermeneutically. That is, we should first look into how Gadamer sees Plato as *participating* in his own cultural and historical context, and, furthermore, how he sees this context as affecting Plato's philosophical development.[62]

Plato and the Sophists

Unlike some philosophers and classicists, Gadamer accepts the authenticity of Plato's *Seventh Letter*. It becomes, in fact, very important for Gadamer because it illustrates, more clearly than even the *Phaedrus*, Plato's antipathy to any and all attempts to "do" philosophy by simply writing it down. Just before the so-called "excursus" in the *Seventh Letter*, Plato expresses his indignation at the fact that Dionysius II of Syracuse has had the audacity to write a "philosophical" treatise, especially after having had but one encounter with Plato himself:

> But this much at any rate I can affirm about any present or future writers who pretend to knowledge of the matters with which I concern myself, whether they claim to have been taught by me or by a third party or to have discovered the truth for themselves; in my judgement it is impossible that they should have any understanding of the subject. *No treatise by me concerning it exists or ever will exist.* It is not something that can be put into words like other branches of learning; only after long partnership in a common life devoted to this very thing does truth flash upon the soul, like a flame

> kindled by a leaping spark, and once it is born there it nourishes itself thereafter.[63]

This passage from the *Seventh Letter* is grounded in what Gadamer sees as the crisis of ethical and pedagogical norms that, although coming to a head in fifth-century Athens, began more than three hundred years earlier (around 750 B.C.) with the reintroduction of writing into the Greek world. Both before and long after the introduction of the Greek alphabet, however, military, agricultural, religious, moral, and political instruction were conveyed mainly through the epic poetry of Homer and Hesiod as recited by the rhapsodes.[64] As Gadamer points out in his essay "Plato and the Poets," "It was the practice then to justify the whole of one's knowledge by recourse to Homer (just as Christian writers justified their knowledge by recourse to the Bible)."[65] The tradition of education in ancient Greece, in other words, was an oral one transmitted through the media of poetry and myth. Embodying the entire ethos of a culture, this pedagogical mode lasted almost completely intact for nearly three hundred years after the advent of Greek literacy. However, even though Homer and Hesiod would always retain some degree of educational authority (as they do even today), by the middle of the fifth century, as literacy began to take hold among the Athenian elite, epic poetry began to lose its pedagogical hegemony over the youth of Athens.

Eric Havelock offers a cogent (though controversial) argument for the nature and extent of this impact of literacy on Greek culture that in many ways is compatible with Gadamer's own view. The Greek alphabet, writes Havelock, "converted the Greek spoken tongue into an artifact, thereby separating it from the speaker and making it into a 'language,' that is, an object available for inspection, reflection, analysis."[66] While it may or may not be true that the advent of Greek writing was, as Havelock seems to suggest, single-handedly responsible for the subject-object dichotomy that dominated Western thought for the next 2,500 years, Gadamer would no doubt find himself in general agreement with Havelock's assessment that, in writing,

> [a] visible artifact was preservable without recourse to memory. It could be rearranged, reordered, and rethought to produce forms of statement and types of discourse not previously available because not easily memorizable. If it were possible to designate the new discourse by any one word, the appropriate

> word would be *conceptual.* Nonliterate speech had favored *discourse describing action*; the postliterate altered the balance in favor of *reflection.* The syntax of Greek began to adapt to an increasing opportunity offered to *state propositions* in place of *describing events.* This was the "bottom line" of the alphabetic legacy to postalphabetic culture.[67]

Havelock is suggesting here that, prior to the introduction of writing, propositional discourse was essentially impossible. Before the advent of writing, that is, because language was confined to the realm of speech, it was limited to expressing itself in terms of actual or potential events or phenomena. Writing, however, allowed speech to become separated from the concrete world of verbal interaction. Language could now be objectified; it thus became capable of self-reflexiveness and abstraction. And metaphysics, science, and theoretical thinking in general become possible only with the writing down of language.

Although Gadamer's Plato would no doubt take issue with Havelock's *positive* evaluation of the effect of writing on Greek culture,[68] he would certainly concur with his assessment as to the principal locus of this innovation. As Havelock points out a little later in the same discussion,

> With literacy there also arrives the literate consciousness. Poetry becomes increasingly segregated from the mainstream of cultural record and custom, and is converted into an exercise in aesthetic sensibility and private insight. In parallel, the intellectual man tends to be recognized as a type participating in the body politic but not of it. His conceptualized written language no longer expects to command the direct sympathy of nonliterate listeners. He ceases to be a bard and becomes a "thinker." The first beginnings of this latter process become perceptible before the end of the fifth century, in the era of the early Sophists.[69]

The Sophists themselves did not pioneer the art of writing; the Greeks, of course, had been writing for several hundred years already, and even Socrates, the arch nemesis of sophism, was literate. As rhetoricians first and foremost, however, the Sophists saw it as their mission to explore, exploit, and codify all of the possibilities inherent in language, and the written word became at once the primary medium and the indispensable tool of their craft. But writing at this time—perhaps because of its implicit claim to authority—was still widely distrusted, even by such prominent literary Greeks as Aeschylus, Herodotus, Thucydides, and Aristophanes.[70] And there is at least one (perhaps apocryphal) story about the Athenians gathering all the books of Protagoras together in the Agora to be burned because of his alleged impiety—the books themselves being thought especially hateful.[71] Plato's attacks on the Sophists and writing in general, therefore, though certainly more vehement and persistent than most, were not merely the idiosyncratic ravings of a philosopher trained in the verbal dialectic of Socrates. Perhaps we would do well to take seriously Rudolf Pfeiffer's (somewhat oversimplified) conclusion that "The Socratic and Platonic arguments are the expressions of a general, deeply rooted Greek aversion against the written word."[72] At any rate, one need only look to *The History of the Peloponnesian War* and Thucydides' deeply pessimistic view of the misuses of rhetoric for corroboration of the debilitating effects of propositional language on a still primarily oral culture—and this from a devotee of sophistic discourse.

In the course of his own philological and philosophical endeavors, Gadamer comes to view Plato's Athens in terms of this clash between oral and written cultures. For Gadamer, in fact, Plato's entire project can be seen as participating in a dialectical intercourse with Athenian culture—a culture besieged by relativism and the corruption of language. And, having himself participated in an interminable war that resulted in the evisceration of the most powerful political entity in the Mediterranean world, is it any wonder that Plato might have been preoccupied with the potential destruction of an entire cultural ethos? But Gadamer's Plato is no simple reactionary trying to resurrect an outmoded way of life. And his elaborate and scathing critiques of mimetic poetry and myth cannot be reduced to their metaphysical incompatibility with a philosophical system rooted in an inflexible doctrine of Ideas. If we accept (as Gadamer does) the authenticity of Plato's *Seventh Letter*, it becomes clear that Plato's position "is the quite conscious expression of a decision—a decision made as a result of having been taken with Socrates and philosophy, made in opposition to the entire political and intellectual culture of his time, and made in the conviction that philosophy alone has the capacity to save the state."[73] Whether or not he ever had serious hopes of actually implementing the so-called city in *logos* that we find in the *Republic* is beside the point. It was philosophy itself—as an ethical and pedagogical paradigm, as a fundamental way of comporting oneself, as a mode of being in the world—that carried this potential. He therefore finds himself compelled to put forward the dialectic in opposition to other modes of discourse.

Gadamer's Plato attacks the myths of the epic tradition because they demean the gods by representing them as fallible, scheming, and petty imitations of humans, and because Homer's image of Hades arouses in men the fear of death. According to Gadamer, Plato objects "to the excessive bewailing of the dead, the excessive scorn and ridicule, and the wanton passion and desires in Homer's gods and heroes."[74] Indeed, although Plato reserves some of his harshest criticisms for contemporary poets and tragedians, he is of one mind with them in his motivation for indicting Homer and Hesiod. As Gadamer puts it, "Both Plato and the poets reject what is false, not just because it is false, but for pedagogical reasons."[75] Education, then, *paideia*, emerges as Plato's paramount concern, and the Homeric myths, because of their poetic greatness and their traditional pedagogical authority, demand the utmost of Plato's ethical scrutiny. But the contemporary poets themselves were well aware of their own persuasive power over the young minds of the Athenian elite, and this is precisely why Plato excludes their poetry from his utopian state.

Gadamer, however, does not entirely approve of Plato's attitude. He is quite critical, in fact, of Plato's decision to censor poetry in the *Republic*, which, he contends,

> amounts to an overburdening of the pedagogical function of poetry, an overburdening which is to be accounted for only by the critical motive behind what Plato says. Plato's Socratic insight was that a binding political ethos, which would assure the proper application and interpretation of poetry, no longer existed once sophism had come to define the spirit of education.[76]

In other words, by placing too much emphasis on poetry itself as the medium of education, Plato exaggerates the potential for sophistic textual manipulation to infect the young. He thus fails to account for the ability of the "existing ethos in the communal life of young and old to guide and define the effect of the poetic word."[77] In other words, though he displays a distinctly hermeneutical concern about "the proper application and interpretation of poetry," Plato very unhermeneutically ignores the overall cultural *context* in which the Sophists are operating. But Gadamer recognizes in this overestimation of the dangers of sophism the essence of Plato's motivation for writing the dialogues. In his own myths and ironically poetic style, Plato wants to offer a new kind of pedagogy that is no longer subject to sophistic manipulation—a pedagogy grounded, as we shall see, in an inducement away from the texts themselves toward actual participation in philosophical dialectic.

When we turn to the dialogues themselves, however, we are immediately confronted with a problem: they are obviously dia*log*ical, but are they themselves dia*lect*ical? It is often difficult, in spite of the considerable irony and humor of these works, for the late-twentieth-century reader to come away from them—particularly the later dialogues and the middle part of the *Republic*—with the impression that Plato's works could be anything other than cleverly framed but nevertheless expository disquisitions on philosophical topics. And yet, as we have intimated a number of times so far, according to Gadamer the dialogues are not to be thought of as philosophical in and of themselves but only as *propadeutical* to actual dialectical engagement or participation in philosophy. We have even quoted Plato himself as denying that he ever wrote a philosophical treatise of any kind. But we have also alluded to the idea of "play" in connection with Plato's written works, just as we have stressed the hermeneutical value of the specific dramatic context of each dialogue. And, as we shall see, the play of language and the situatedness of any conversation are important components of Gadamer's view of the dialectic. But in order to deal with these in a meaningful way, we need to approach them through the more specific problem of Plato's ironic condemnation of *mimesis*.

Plato and the Apparent Irony of Mimesis

Mimesis is usually thought of as a metaphysical problem for Plato. That is to say, in the generally accepted view of Plato's "doctrine of the Forms," the further removed an entity is from the eternal Forms, the less real it is and the less value Plato places on it. Like the other mimetic arts, poetry, because it exists only in imitation of the phenomenal world of human interaction (which is already only a reflection of the noumenal world of the Forms), is at the very bottom of the ontological hierarchy. Thus, insofar as it draws the human soul away from its ultimate object, the Form of the Good, mimetic poetry is to be scorned as antithetical to the Platonic project.

This traditional account is no doubt accurate, and it can be amply supported by textual evidence. But, if we rely in this matter on a view of Plato's metaphysics gleaned almost exclusively from the scientific-sounding portions of the texts, leaving the drama and irony to the literary specialists (an approach which—as an approach—runs into its own problems of consistency), then we are left with an irresolvable contradiction. As we have seen, Plato is very critical of the dramatic forms used by the epic poets and the tragedians precisely because they are mimetic. What, then, are we to make of Plato's own mimetic dramas? Does he not, after all, employ the same direct discourse in his dialogical fictions for which he criticizes Homer's *Iliad*?[78] It would seem that in his tirades against *mimesis*, Plato is doing himself a philosophical and rhetorical disservice.

All *mimesis*, however, is not the same. Plato, as we have already indicated, concerns himself primarily with the moral and pedagogical *effect* of mimetic poetry on the human soul. "The poet," writes Gadamer, "creates disconcertion and enervating lassitude in the soul of the spectator when he conjures up outbursts of the volatile human passions."[79] Gadamer refers to this "aesthetic" form of *mimesis* as "mere" imitation and contrasts it to a properly pedagogical form whereby I, for example, would learn by *intentionally* imitating others. What I would learn in this way is, according to Gadamer, "not so much something which belongs to the other as something which I can appropriate for myself. The purpose of such imitation is thus not to imitate but to learn how to do something myself."[80] I am, therefore, not subject to and at the mercy of inadvertent and arbitrary mimetic influences, but am myself intentionally immersed in imitation of that which I consciously perceive to be beneficial to me, like philosophical dialogue, for example.

Gadamer's teacher, Paul Friedländer, reminds us that until Plato encountered Socrates and philosophy he aspired to be a tragic poet, and thus the dramatic form seems to have emerged naturally as his mode of expression. But unlike the art of the tragedians, Plato's new mimetic art, says Friedländer, "is not the kind of imitation that aims at pleasure. It aims at truth and, therefore, it will not only be pleasant as the old art was but also *useful* for the state and the life of man."[81] Thus the dramatic *mimesis* of the dialogues is meant as a practical pedagogical guide to moral behavior—a sort of "how-to manual" for living the life of Socrates—and as such it is to be sharply distinguished from artistic *mimesis*, which exists for the sheer pleasure of imitation. The great problem with this latter purely aesthetic mode of *mimesis* is that it turns the actors and the spectators away from themselves. And, in so doing, it engenders a self-forgetfulness or a self-alienation that is dangerous to the soul. For Gadamer, then, Plato's critique of mimetic poetry is at the same time a critique of the moral consequences "aesthetic consciousness," and such aesthetic self-forgetfulness, he contends, "opens the way for the sophists' game with the passions to infiltrate the human heart."[82]

Friedländer, however, goes on to qualify his remark about the practicality of Plato's *mimesis* by pointing out that no matter how useful it is "it is still mimesis, occupying 'the third place as seen from the king and truth.' However much it approaches seriousness, it is still play."[83] The dialogues, then, despite whatever practical intent Plato has for them, because they must inevitably remain in the vulnerable mimetic realm of the written word, ultimately cannot be taken seriously. Plato's dialogical fictions, in other words, as a truly philosophical form of poetry, point *beyond themselves* to what is of real consequence. They are, says Gadamer, "nothing more than playful allusions which say something only to him who finds meanings beyond what is expressly stated in them and allows these meanings to take effect within him."[84]

Dialectic, Hermeneutics, and Play

By now we have alluded to the "playfulness" of the dialogues a number of times, but we have yet to deal explicitly with the Gadamerian concept of play. By looking closely at what Gadamer means by play, both hermeneutically and with direct reference to the works of Plato, we can begin to provide the phenomenological grounding for our notion of dialectic as a form of *methexis*.

For Gadamer's Plato, because they are written down, the dialogues taken by themselves are not, strictly speaking, dialectical. Any attempt to restrict dialectic exclusively to either written or verbal forms would be itself unhermeneutical and thus undialectical.[85] When Gadamer talks about dialectic, however, he is talking about conversation, dialogue; for Gadamer, all genuine dialogue is inherently dialectical and, as such, takes on the structure of a game. In any true game, it is not the players who are the subjects of the game, and they do not really control it. Rather, the game becomes its own subject, and the course of the game to a large degree controls the actions of the players. When players get caught up in play, in other words, they find their individuality subsumed by or subordinated to the larger phenomenon of the game. In much the same way, the course of a dialogue is determined by the verbal play of the speakers, and not by the speakers themselves. But in order for the play of conversation to take over, the speakers must be willing to yield to its movement. In Gadamerian terms, they must be genuinely interested in coming to agreement (or at least an understanding of each other's position), and this means that for either of them to learn anything or for any degree of truth to emerge from the dialogue both partners must be able to put their own preconceptions at risk; they must remain open to the possibility of being wrong. The concept of "openness," therefore, become central to the hermeneutic project, and dialectic is the hermeneutical instantiation of what Gadamer calls "the logical structure of openness." In *Truth and Method*, he explains that the important thing in human discourse is

> to experience the Thou truly as a Thou—i.e., not to overlook his claim but to let him really say something to us. Here is where openness belongs. But this openness is, in the end, not there only for the person from whom we wish to be told something; rather whoever in general allows something to be told to him is, in a fundamental way, open. Without such an openness to one another there is no genuine human bond . . . Openness to the other, then, involves recognizing that I, within myself, must admit something against myself, even though there were no other who claimed it against me.[86]

Thus openness to the other and a willingness to put one's own prejudices at risk constitute the principal modes of comporting oneself in a genuinely dialectical hermeneutic. Furthermore, for Gadamer, "the passageway of all knowing leads through the question," and then, in true Socratic fashion, he tells us that "in order to be able to ask, one must want to know, but that means: knowing that one does not know."[87] In terms of dialogue and dialectic, then, openness takes the form of *questioning*. The Platonic Socrates thus becomes the paradigmatic dialectician not by following a specifically discernible methodology but by virtue of his profession of ignorance and his persistent questioning.

But the play of conversation in the Platonic dialogues is at once dialectical and *didactic*. It is dialectical because, through his *docta ignorantia*, Socrates constantly maintains an attitude of openness toward his interlocutors and toward the question at hand, and hermeneutical openness is what allows the conversation to develop according to its own dynamic, to develop, that is, according to what Gadamer will call (following both Hegel and Heidegger) *die Sache selbst.* Platonic dialogue is didactic not because Socrates intends to convey some prior knowledge of a subject to his conversation partner(s) or to the reader—in fact the least didactic of all the dialogues are those in which the interlocutors seem the weakest; the didacticism of the Platonic texts arises in Socrates' encounters with the most opinionated interlocutors (usually the Sophists), as he dismantles their preconceived ideas on a particular topic and thereby teaches them to recognize their own ignorance—teaches them, in other words, to remain open to the possibility of being wrong. The dialectic cannot proceed in the face of dogmatic opposition. Thus Gadamer effectively undermines another traditional view of the dialectic—that it consists primarily and/or essentially in the logical refutation of untenable opinions. Such refutation would certainly constitute an aspect or a mode of Platonic dialectic for Gadamer, but only after Socrates has destroyed the illusion of knowledge in everyone present can the dialectical play of conversation truly take over.[88] This is why in most of the dialogues Plato assigns to Socrates the initial task of creating an environment of openness wherein dogmatic pronouncements give way to the genuine play of conversation—an environment in which it becomes possible, as Gadamer says, "to experience the Thou truly as a Thou."

In the later dialogues, as P. Christopher Smith points out, "Plato is careful to select interlocutors in whom there is a minimum of spoil-sport contentiousness and a maximum of willingness to follow where the discussion may take them."[89] Thus for Smith as for Gadamer, what is of primary importance for understanding the process of dialectic (and hence the dialogues themselves) is not the speech acts of the individual speakers, but "the action of language itself upon those who are involved in speaking it."[90] Whether or not they actually do agree with each other in the end, whether one or the other wins, or whether they just agree to disagree, the results of a dialogical encounter are much less important to the play of conversation than the willingness of the participants to put themselves and their opinions at risk. It is the actual movement back and forth between them, the process of give and take that is important for a successful conversation. As Gadamer sees it, Platonic dialectic has no rigidly defined structure or rules,[91] but is simply the act of yielding to the movement of genuine conversation, and the dialogues are meant as mimetic representations of this dialectical process. But ultimately for Gadamer,

> these dialogues are more than philosophical dramas and Socrates is not the hero of these poetic compositions. Even the representation of Socrates is meant as an inducement to philosophize. The intent and purpose of these discussions are neither to portray human beings nor to recount statements and responses. It is not coincidental that Plato is fond of representing these discussions in a recapitulation and he does not even hesitate to have Socrates repeat the ten-book-long discussion of the *Republic* on the following day. Plato is not concerned with vivid and forceful accounts but with what makes any such repetition worthwhile: the maieutic power of these discussions (*Theaetetus* 149 c ff.), with the movement of philosophizing which redevelops in every repetition.[92]

By their "maieutic power," Gadamer refers to the productive and reproductive possibilities inherent in the dialogues, the potential for them to have an effect in the world beyond the confines of their specific arguments and their ability to induce the painful labor, if you will, of actual philosophical engagement. And in the process of recapitulation and repetition, in the repeated inducement to participate in the movement of dialectical discourse, the dialogues perform their ethical and pedagogical task—a task carried out via a maieutic or (re)productive *mimesis*.

But the environment of the Platonic dialogue is not simply determined by word play. It is necessarily characterized by what Gadamer calls "the Doric harmony of deed and speech, *ergon* and *logos*."[93] The dialogues are works of drama rather than treatises precisely because, for Plato, language can never be divorced from the concrete world of action. Thus the dialogues only begin to make sense when we acknowledge the situatedness of the conversations. Plato is quite careful to set his dialogical fictions in recognizable, concrete circumstances, and, with a few exceptions, his characters are usually real (that is, historical) people with their own unique personalities and problems. The course of each dialogue, and thus the play of each conversation, is determined to a large degree by the uniqueness of these encounters. In the *Symposium*, for example, Socrates' response to his drunken and wily ex-lover Alcibiades on the topic of love is quite different from his discussion of the same subject with his naïve young friend in the *Phaedrus*. This is why purely analytical approaches to Plato have had so much trouble with the "logic" of the dialogues. As Smith points out, "many interpreters of Plato, indeed most within the English speaking world, Cornford, Crombie, Vlastos, Hackforth, to name a few," have traditionally applied a "logical-methodological" approach that is based on a mathematical model of analysis and ignores the contextuality of the Platonic texts. "The principal issue which they raise," he writes,

> though certainly not the only one, is in regard to the *logic* of the argument made in the dialogues. They look for a methodical demonstration in which each point is expected to follow from the previous one and the appropriate conclusion to be drawn. Their tacit assumption is that the spokenness of what is said can be stripped away baring the essential logic of what is meant. . . . What they discover, of course, is that either Plato's logic or his method is faulty, or both: the arguments which his Socrates presents are full of fallacies and his demonstrations elliptical at best and sophistic at worst.[94]

If we, on the other hand, imagine the dialogues to be actual verbal discussions, we no longer expect such exactitude and precise argumentation. In a *living* dialogue, physical, emotional, psychological, historical, and cultural factors all come to bear on the play of the conversation. Insofar as Plato explicitly disavows the writing of systematic philosophical treatises, then, the dialogues seem to exhibit a higher degree of "logic" and certainly a great deal more consistency if we read them rather for what they appear to be on the surface—dramatic representations (or perhaps demonstrations) of live dialogical encounters. And as such we can begin to see how they are "playful" both in the sense of lacking the "seriousness" of what Plato would consider real or live philosophizing and in the sense of following the playful movement of actual conversations rather than systematic, apodictically determined philosophical treatises.

Ultimately, however, even Plato's verisimilitude cannot overcome what Gadamer (following Plato) refers to as the weakness of all writing: namely, that "no one is able come to the aid of written discourse if it falls prey to misunderstanding, intentional or unintentional."[95] Once language is committed to writing, it becomes detached from its author and effectively decontextualized. This is why the dialogues are, as Gadamer says, of the genus *protreptikon*: they are not philosophy per se, but exhortations to philosophize.[96] Insofar as they playfully illustrate the movement of dialogical interaction, and insofar as they actively engage us in this movement by raising so many difficult and challenging questions, the dialectical intention of the dialogues—the protreptic inducement to philosophize—is ultimately fulfilled by every scholar who participates in his or her own dialogue with the Platonic texts. In *Truth and Method*, Gadamer succinctly captures this hermeneutical relationship between written and spoken dialogue:

> What precisely characterizes dialogue, over against the rigid form of expression that demands to be fixed in writing, is this: that here, in questioning and answering, in giving and taking, in talking past one another and agreeing with one another, language accomplishes each communication of meaning which it is the task of hermeneutics to skillfully work out vis-à-vis the literary tradition. *It is, therefore, more than a metaphor—it is a memory of what is originary, if the hermeneutic task conceives of itself as a coming-into-dialogue with the text.* That the interpretation which this carries out accomplishes itself linguistically does not signify a transposition into a foreign medium, but rather, on the contrary, *a restoration of the original communication of meaning.* That which is handed down in literary form is thereby fetched back out of the alienation in which it finds itself into the living present of dialogue, which is continually the originary accomplishment of question and answer.[97]

In the act of interpretation, therefore, written language is reconstituted and recontextualized into what Gadamer calls the "living virtuality of speaking" (*die lebendige Virtualität des Sprechens*), a concept which (as we shall see in chapter 3 below) finds its true expression in Gadamer's appropriation of that other great dialectician, G. W. F. Hegel. We have yet, however, to fully trace out the guiding thread in our discussion of Gadamer and Plato—that is, the role of dialectical participation in philosophical hermeneutics. More specifically, we have yet to see exactly how the Platonic dialectic that we been describing here is, for Gadamer, no mere technique but every bit the ontological phenomenon that Aristotelian *phronesis* is for Heidegger.

Plato's Dialectical Ontology

Now that we have established an interpretation grounded in a nonmethodological, nonsystematic approach to the dialogues—an approach alien to Aristotle and one that Heidegger, in spite of his hermeneutical affinities and because of his Aristotelian reading of Plato, does not really enter into—what are we to make of the theory of Ideas itself? Can we simply ignore Plato's elaborate ontological discussions in the *Republic*, the *Philebus*, the *Sophist*, and the *Parmenides*, because they are "mere" play or "merely" propadeutical and thus not to be taken as "serious" theoretical statements?[98] Can we simply dismiss two thousand years of metaphysics as being founded on an elaborate jest? It becomes very important at this point to remind ourselves that, although Gadamer interprets the dialogues as mimetic *reflections* of actual engagements in philosophy, they are mimetic reflections of *Plato's* engagements in philosophy. That is to say that although they are meant propaedeutically and are, therefore, incomplete as philosophical statements, they do, nevertheless, illustrate at least some of Plato's actual philosophical thinking. If we take this simple fact into account, it becomes clear that, even though our hermeneutical reading precludes finding any systematic exposition of Plato's metaphysics in the dialogues, underlying these fictional compositions is a series of profound—if profoundly antidogmatic—metaphysical assumptions.

The main issues raised by Gadamer with respect to the doctrine of Ideas are precisely the ones raised by Aristotle as he criticizes Plato's theory in the *Nicomachean Ethics* and elsewhere. They have to do primarily with the problems of *chōrismos* (separation) and *methexis* (participation). The gist of Aristotle's criticism is that because of the profound *chōrismos* between the two realms, any notion of *methexis* becomes effectively impossible. Gadamer, of course, will argue against such a radical separation within Plato's theory and point out that the participation between the ideas and their manifestations as objects is essentially dialectical in character by seeing the *chōrismos* as directly analogous to *diairesis* and, in so doing, showing how Platonic dialectic can then be viewed ontologically. He will thus retrieve *methexis* from the Aristotelian critique and appropriate it as a "model" for how live hermeneutical encounters occur as ontological phenomena in much the same way that—following Heidegger—he appropriates Aristotelian *phronēsis* as a "model" for the universality of hermeneutic application.[99]

Aristotle's complaint is specifically that the Ideas, because they are supposed to exist in a separate and inaccessible realm, effectively duplicate the world and are thus redundant and meaningless abstractions. He attempts to remedy this ontological anomaly by bringing the Ideas or the Forms back into the sensible world to serve as transcendental rather than transcendent principles of organization and classification. The word "horse," for instance, rather than referring to the "real" and perfect metaphysical entity of which all physical horses are mere reflections or approximations, is for Aristotle a class or a categorial designation of sorts that describes the immanent and essential characteristics of which all horses partake. The problem that Aristotle sees in the Platonic doctrine is that the *chōrismos* between the intelligible and the sensible *precludes* any such participatory relationship between the two. How, in other words, can two things participate across an unbridgeable chasm? Aristotle pursues this critique in all three of his ethical treatises because he also sees it as a serious flaw in Plato's ethical thinking, which is grounded in the human soul's participation in the Idea of the Good. Obviously, living the good life will be very difficult if it is predicated on gaining knowledge from an inaccessible realm. Thus, the core of Aristotle's argument, P. Christopher Smith explains, is that "Plato improperly fuses the ontological and the practical in his applications of the idea of the good."[100] Aristotle simply cannot reconcile his own practical ethical theories with the notion of the Good as something separable (*chōriston*), an individuated thing in itself. But significantly for Gadamer (and unlike Aristotle), Plato feels no such compunction to make explicit categorial distinctions between things practical, ontological, or (for that matter) epistemological. It is often difficult to identify precise transitions in the dialogues between and among the various philosophical disciplines because Plato himself had neither a conception of nor saw any need for such distinctions—which, incidentally (and perhaps a little ironically), would seem to be why Heidegger prefers Aristotle.

The upshot of Gadamer's argument is that Aristotle is philosophically correct but hermeneutically wrong. That is, his ontological critique of Plato is essentially correct, but the original interpretation itself misses certain crucial points. The *chōrismos*, in fact, far from disallowing the possibility of *methexis*, actually provides the theoretical mechanism whereby physical entities participate in the Ideas dialectically—or vice versa. For how can one thing be said to participate in another unless those two things are distinguished from each other in the first place?[101] Phenomenologically speaking, in other words, *methexis* is not really a participation of discrete "things" at all. As John Sallis points out in *Being and Logos*, the divided line is divided, but it is still a line, "It represents the visible and the intelligible as segments of a single continuous line rather than as two separated domains."[102] For Sallis, the line represents a continuum along which the human soul travels by means of the dialectic, and, pointing out that Socrates names the *objects* of the soul's affections only at the two lowest levels, he concludes that the four levels of the divided line are not distinct regions at all, but "different levels of showing, four modes in which the same things can show themselves, just as on the side of the soul, one and the same soul can apprehend things with different degrees of clarity."[103] In much the same way, Gadamer maintains that "The *chōrismos* is not a doctrine that must first be overcome. Rather, from beginning to end, it is an essential component of true dialectic."[104] He thus associates the *chōrismos* with the dialectical principle of differentiation, *diairesis*, rather than, as traditional Platonism would have it, a radical metaphysical separation.

For Gadamer's Plato, while it may not constitute an "art" in the strict sense of a set of rules or a technique, as we have already pointed out, the dialectic can be characterized as a hermeneutical principle comprised of the differentiation (*diairesis*) between various possibilities and the subsequent choice or judgment (*proairesis*) between the distinguished alternatives, choices that, in turn, are always subject to further differentiation. But while the dialectic is also marked by the steadfast determination of the interlocutors not to be dissuaded from a chosen path of discussion by pseudo-dialectical sophistic techniques, the participants must always remain open to properly articulated alternatives—even if it means reiterating certain points in the discussion. In other words, the dialectic describes an oscillating movement of give and take, back and forth, question and answer, that follows the immanent flow of the topic at hand. As long as the dialogue is underway, then, there is no moment of radical division, there is no halt in the flow of *die Sache selbst*. Therefore, in Gadamer's dialectical notion of *chōrismos* as a form of or at least analogous to *diairesis*—as opposed to Aristotle's strictly metaphysical conception of it—there is no unbridgeable gap. Gadamer reads Plato's division between the physical and noetic realms not as a radical metaphysical divide but as the very phenomenological distinction that allows the dialectical interaction between phenomena and noumena to occur at all. On this reading, in other words, Plato's dialectic becomes much more than a rhetorical technique for interrogating and destroying people's opinions (if it ever was that at all). The adverb, "dialectically," also describes, at least analogically, how the noumenal participates in the phenomenal, how the ideas, in other words, reveal themselves. To put it in terms of Heidegger's essay, "Platons Lehre von der Wahrheit," one could say that the dialectic is closely akin to the originary "Greek-Platonic" notion of *alētheia* as self-showing or unhiddenness. Thus we can start to see how dialectic not only entails but depends on an ontological rather than an epistemological notion of participation—one that is neither metaphysically or rhetorically overdetermined. Gadamer retrieves Platonic *methexis* precisely as a phenomenological component of the dialectic and thereby appropriates it as a model for the ontological aspect of hermeneutical engagement in living dialogue (the word "*dialektos*," as we have already mentioned, being very closely related, etymologically, to "*dialogos*"). For Gadamer, then, all genuine dialogue is dialectical insofar as the interlocutors participate in the conversation in the same way that the phenomenal realm participates in the noumenal. That is to say, understanding occurs through the dialogical interaction of the participants just as the ideas reveal themselves through the dialectical interaction of the two realms. In other words, by reading the theory of the forms dialectically—interpreting the *chōrismos* as an instance of *diairesis*—one can view dialogue ontologically—interpreting verbal engagement as an instance of *methexis*.

A question arises, however, with regard to this hermeneutical appropriation. If, in ontological terms, separation is a phenomenological prerequisite to participation rather than a metaphysical obstacle, then exactly how does the idea of *chōrismos* fit into this *dialogical* rendering of *methexis*? Although Gadamer does not thematize it in these terms, I would suggest that, just as *methexis* serves a model for participating in the hermeneutic situation, *chōrismos* could be seen as a model for the interdiscursive space between "I" and "Thou" that makes this participation possible. In this case, *chōrismos* would perhaps coincide with what Gadamer refers to as "die Mitte der Sprache," a spatial metaphor that describes the phenomenological role of language in understanding.[105] But, as we shall discover in the second half of our inquiry, such an interpretation can only be carried out in the course of a thorough analysis of Gadamer's encounter with Hegel.

Part 2

Hegelian Dialectic and Hölderlinian Poetics

Even given the rather narrow and incipient nature of our endeavor so far, I would argue that what we have found here is highly indicative (perhaps even paradigmatic) of Heidegger's and Gadamer's philosophically contiguous and yet decidedly different projects. Our purpose to this point has been to explore their respective interpretations of Plato and Aristotle and discover to what extent they coincide with and depart from one another—that is, to what extent they turn away while simultaneously turning toward each other. On the one hand, we have their nearly identical readings of Aristotle. Heidegger appropriates Aristotelian *phronēsis*, albeit implicitly, as a phenomenological prototype of sorts for *Dasein*'s originary [*ursprünglich*][1] comportment toward being and the world. He effectively incorporates *phronēsis* (or at least a "phronetic" comportment toward being) into his project by way of dismantling the traditional reading of Aristotle and even by reading Aristotle to some degree against himself. Aristotle thus enters into *Being and Time* and fundamental ontology at the very core and inception of this new phenomenology. Gadamer's relation to Aristotle, however, while clearly indebted to Heidegger's early seminars, takes him in a markedly different direction. Rather than operating implicitly, *phronēsis* re-emerges from the Heideggerian project to serve, for Gadamer, as an explicit model not for phenomenology itself, which he no longer feels compelled to thematize, but for recasting the notion of *Anwendung*, or application, as a fundamental moment of the hermeneutic experience. As with Heidegger's original reading of *phronēsis*, Gadamer's notion of application is thereby released from its traditional epistemological role as a term for subject-object interaction and allowed to show itself as an ontological occurrence. As a model for hermeneutic application, however, *phronēsis* now helps illuminate, not phenomenology per se, but the phenomenon of interpretation as it occurs within the human sciences and within any genuine conversation. On the other hand, while Plato does indeed become important for Heidegger's Nietzsche interpretation and (to a lesser extent) his reading of Parmenides, the course of Heidegger's larger project is never really determined by Plato with the pervasiveness that Gadamer's is. Ultimately, Heidegger's encounters with Plato, though certainly not as metaphysically overdetermined as some make them out to be, remain significant primarily for locating what Heidegger sees as the first indication of a transition in Greek thinking from *alētheia* to *orthotes*. Gadamer, however, does much the same thing with Plato that he does with Aristotle, although in a much more elaborate and detailed way. Whereas he places *phronēsis* literally at the center of *Truth and Method* and stresses its importance for the project as a whole, Platonic dialectic and, by implication, *methexis* suffuse almost his entire body of work. As we have seen, Gadamer recruits *methexis* (much as he does *phronēsis*) to help describe a central element of the hermeneutic phenomenon—the element of participation. But here we get much closer, as we shall soon discover, to a more direct and overarching phenomenon for philosophical hermeneutics, and one which will show much more dramatically where Gadamer departs from his teacher. For the dialectic is not simply a model for one particular aspect of understanding; it describes for Gadamer precisely the way in which understanding occurs—a contention that Heidegger would certainly have rejected.

Their respective relationships to Aristotle, therefore, would seem to display a moment of nearly complete intellectual convergence that turns out to be the beginning of a crucial divergence, and their readings of Plato show them at once at a distinct philosophical distance while maintaining a profound hermeneutical proximity. Could, then, what looks like their most drastic point of departure (i.e., their almost diametrically opposed attitudes toward the dialectical thinking of the later metaphysical tradition) somehow reveal an even deeper and more pervasive proximity—an even more dramatically counter-turning moment—in this dialogue between Heidegger and Gadamer? As a way of entering into this question, the second half of our project will try to show that in his very turn away from the strictly philosophical toward the poetic, Heidegger's appropriation of Friedrich Hölderlin's tragic poetry brings him ironically close to Gadamer's embracing of Hegelian dialectic.

THREE

Heidegger, Hölderlin, and Tragic Intensification

In abandoning Heidegger's history of *Seinsvergessenheit*, Gadamer has sometimes been accused (perhaps even by Heidegger himself)[1] of abandoning altogether the question of being as the centerpiece of philosophical inquiry—falling, in other words, back into the oblivion of being. Such charges often refer to Gadamer's refusal to acknowledge the existence of a "language of metaphysics" that is somehow to be "overcome," to his reintroduction of the problem of consciousness as an integral component of philosophical thought, and his criticisms of Heidegger's "poetizing." This alleged backsliding is also typified by his insistence on remaining in the domain of hermeneutic phenomenology—a philosophical realm that Heidegger apparently renounced along with *Being and Time* and fundamental ontology. What Gadamer seems to overlook is nothing less than being itself. Gadamer, in other words, seems to turn away from the question that lies at the very heart of Heidegger's lifelong project. For what could be more anathema to Heidegger's persistent attempts to de-subjectify the phenomenon of human being-in-the-world than the notion of "*wirkungsgeschichtliches Bewußtsein*" or "historically effected consciousness"? What could be more retrograde to the Heideggerian turn away from metaphysics than to turn back toward Hegelian dialectic? But as we saw with their readings of the Greeks, Gadamer's philosophical departures from his teacher always remain within the same hermeneutical and phenomenological vicinity.

Aside from their mutual interest in Aristotelian *phronēsis*, Gadamer and Heidegger also have in common a profound emphasis on the question of language. But whereas in the later Heidegger's "poetical" and seemingly metaphorical way of speaking, language becomes "the house of being," Gadamer describes language more prosaically as "being that can be understood." We should not be misled, however, by the apparently epistemological bent of this Gadamerian formulation. While one of the later Heidegger's driving concerns is to address the question of language in ontological terms by way of a *Destruktion* of the history of *Seinsvergessenheit*, the forgetfulness of being, Gadamer does not concern himself with the traditionally complementary problem of "knowledge"; rather, he proceeds from a very different *Fragestellung*: a phenomenology of understanding (*Verstehen* as opposed to *Verstand*) and consciousness (or as I will refer to it, "being-conscious," *Bewußt-sein*) expressed in terms of what he calls the history of "Sprach*vergessenheit*," the "forgetfulness of *language*." While these two attitudes may appear initially divergent, I would argue that they in fact converge within the domains of language and being and even coincide insofar as they both implicitly raise the question of the historical forgetfulness of *finitude*.

It is true that Gadamer addresses this forgetfulness almost exclusively in terms of *human* finiteness, while Heidegger is ultimately concerned (at least in the later work) with the finitude of being itself. But as I will try to show, this amounts to much the same thing, since for Gadamer human finitude is profoundly ontological, and for Heidegger the finitude of being is never entirely severed from human being. In other words, even though in his later work, after the so-called turning (or on recognizing the turning in being), he moves away from thinking human being as the being for whom "in its very being, that being is an issue,"[2] Heidegger never completely abandons *Dasein*; he merely thinks it differently, reconsiders its proximity to being, now thought more *topo*logically than logically as *Ereignis* and the "fourfold." And, finally, for both philosophers the question of finitude unfolds in the realm of human language; or, as Gadamer puts it, it becomes a question of the inescapable linguisticality (*Sprachlichkeit*) of human being. Initially, however, Heidegger's project of fundamental ontology is also concerned precisely with *human* finitude. Thus, we should now turn our attention to what Heidegger refers to as the finitude of the "*Dasein* in man."[3]

The Finite Locale of Dasein *and the Language of Topology*

Fundamental ontology characterizes metaphysics as the attempt to foreground being by logical analysis, to render being intelligible, to define it. Such attempts forget, however, that human beings (thought in terms of their own being or "there-being," *Dasein*) find themselves always already thrown into a totality of involvements; they find themselves, that is, always already involved in an implicit understanding of being before such explications can even begin. Being—or even the understanding of being—is not something one can step outside of in order to objectify and analyze it. Heidegger, of course, later criticized his own early work as still too caught up in the very subjectivity it attempted to dismantle; one could perhaps see his early work as precisely an attempt to "objectify" being, to delineate a "science of Being."[4] One might even argue that he had not quite escaped (if he ever really did) from the Husserlian notion of *Philosophie als strenge Wissenschaft*. However, in his first major published works (especially from *Being and Time* in 1927 through *Kant and the Problem of Metaphysics* in 1929) Heidegger tries to think being as the condition for the possibility of the very philosophizing that attempts to objectify it, and since the only phenomena that yield to such objectification are ontic rather than ontological, such objective inquiries into the precise nature of being inevitably fall short; they become, wholly without realizing it, Heidegger asserts, inquiries into the nature of beings, entities, or that which is (*Seienden*), rather than being itself (*Sein*). Human subjectivity, in other words, finds itself unable to appropriate being as its own object, unable to totalize being through logical analysis and definition. We can see then that there is an immediate transcendental sense in which *Dasein* is finite: it is limited with respect to its ability to render being transparent as a topic of inquiry since being is the very condition for the possibility of any such objectification; but this would be, for *Dasein*, merely a manifestation of the forgetfulness of being and hence a sort of derivative, "inauthentic," finitude.

Authentic human finitude is characterized in *Being and Time* (if somewhat peripherally) as *Dasein*'s being-toward-death, that is, *Dasein*'s authentic pre-understanding of the possibility of its own utter impossibility.[5] This seems at first glance to be rather far afield from Heidegger's later move away from any subjectlike conception of human being and toward an emphasis on the essential finiteness of being itself in its withdrawal. In *Kant and the Problem of Metaphysics*, however—a pivotal text in which, though still in the throes of fundamental ontology, he begins radicalizing the notion of finitude—Heidegger directly equates the understanding of being with human finitude: "As a mode of Being," he writes,

> existence is itself finitude, and as such it is only possible on the basis of the understanding of being. There is and must be something like Being where finitude has come to exist. Thus the understanding of being which thoroughly dominates human existence, although unknown in its breadth, constancy, indeterminacy, and indisputability, manifests itself as the innermost ground of human finitude.[6]

Indeed, he even goes so far as to call human finitude the "fundament" of "[t]he unveiling of the constitution of the being of *Dasein*."[7] Hence the project of fundamental ontology concerns itself directly with "the problem of finitude in human beings, which is decisive for the purpose of making the understanding of being possible."[8]

Looking back toward *Being and Time*, then, we can see that insofar as being-toward-death is, in effect, *Dasein*'s understanding of its own authentic temporality, hence its own finite existence, it is a mode of *Dasein*'s understanding of being, and understanding (*Verstehen*) is *Dasein*'s fundamental mode of being-in-the-world. Thus we find a traditionally epistemological concept, understanding, revealed in terms of its profoundly ontological ground—the philosophical point of departure, in fact, for Gadamer's hermeneutic phenomenology.[9] But in Heidegger's later works we find him gradually dis-locating or de-centering *Dasein* and finally dropping most references to *Dasein* altogether in favor of such expressions as "future man" and "mortals," thereby attempting to distance his own thinking still further from the taint of subject-object Cartesianism. Already in the Kant book (as we noted, above) we find him speaking not so much of individual *Dasein*, but of the "*Dasein* in man." And shortly thereafter, by the time of *Beiträge zur Philosophie*, Heidegger dis-places *Dasein* altogether as an immediate characterization of human being; he now defers *Dasein* to the future, to the eventuality of an "other beginning" beyond the history of metaphysics and the technological age. "In the sense of the other beginning," he tells us in the *Beiträge*, "*Dasein* is what is still completely strange to us, something that we never come across, . . . that clearing of being [*Lichtung des Seins*] into which future man must place himself in order to hold it open."[10] *Dasein* as *Da-sein*, as "there-being," is now no longer seen as "that being for whom its own being is a question," but as the location, the "here/there," the "*Da*" of being, the *Lichtung* or clearing in being itself that human being has yet to occupy.[11] Now *Dasein* begins to reveal itself in explicitly spatial terms, as a site, a *topos, ein Ort*. Heidegger now tries to think it specifically from out of its topological essence (*Wesen*) rather than from its onto-theo-logical *essentia*, which the transcendental orientation of *Being and Time* could not quite completely overcome. From the *Beiträge* on, Heidegger's language becomes increasingly topological rather than teleological; it becomes "aletheiological" in the sense of a nonlinear revealing and concealing—the middle-voiced gathering of truth in its event-character—rather than propositional, linear, apodeictic truth.

It is important to remind ourselves once more, however, that even though Heidegger pushes *Dasein* farther and farther away from the center of his own thinking, thus dislocating it completely from the traditional place of the subject as "*die Sache des Denkens*," he never altogether abandons *Dasein*. His later thinking of *Ereignis* stills attempt to think the belonging together of man and being; only, instead of *Dasein* "needing" being, as he tells us in *Being and Time*, being now needs human being.[12] Thus even though Heidegger's discussions have shifted away from the finiteness of human *Dasein* toward the finitude of being itself—that is, the withdrawal of being, its concealment, its absencing[13]—the implication of *human* finitude remains, insofar as for Heidegger it makes no sense to think being as entirely removed from the vicinity of human being, especially (as it turns out) in terms of the fourfold. For the fourfold *is* the vicinity of human being; it is the primordial oneness of earth, sky, divinities, and *mortals*, the worlding of the world in which man dwells.[14] And in this profusion of topological metaphors we get a hint of why, for Heidegger, traditional philosophical discourse falls short in its attempt to think the truth of being.

One essential historical/epochal aspect of *Seinsvergessenheit* is, for Heidegger, the unacknowledged failure of philosophy's attempt to render being intelligible by analyzing entities from within and through what he calls the "language of metaphysics." Hence the increasingly arcane and metaphorical rhetoric of Heidegger's later works, beginning with "Origin of the Work of Art." In these later texts language or, more specifically, the search for a nonmetaphysical language which can somehow express (or better, "co-respond to," *ent-sprechen*) a nonreductive, nonobjectifying relation to being, takes a central place. And to correspond to being in this way, such a language must somehow remain sensitive not only to being as it manifests itself but to being's withdrawal, that is, to its radical finitude. This search, however, does not take the form of a "philosophy of language," if one means by this a systematic logical analysis of language, for precisely the same reason that, for Heidegger, any attempt to objectify being must ultimately fail. Linguistic analysis, in other words, must fall short of its ideal of total objectivity because all the categories that such a project would necessarily employ (meaning, expression, sign, etc.) are but artifacts of language. Language itself, in other words, is the very condition for the possibility of any analysis of language, just as being (at least from the perspective of fundamental ontology) shows itself to be the transcendental condition for the possibility of any inquiry into being. This is not to say that nothing can be said about either language or being—only that they both share this resistance to the objectifying move that is inherent in the teleological linearity of the so-called "language of metaphysics." And since Heidegger's philosophical imperative (at least after fundamental ontology) is not to engage in aggressive conceptual analysis but, as he puts it, to "heed the call of being," to respond appropriately to both its manifestation and its withdrawal, he must find a nonteleological, nonmetaphysical way of addressing this imperative.

Heidegger's awareness of the inadequacy of traditional philosophical categories and the logic that employs them is already apparent in *Being and Time*; to get some hint of this, one need only attend to such words as "*Angst*," "*Sorge*," "*Rede*," and so forth, as well as his insistence on the hermeneutic circularity of the structure of being. But, soon thereafter, he criticizes the strategy of *Being and Time* (i.e., the attempt to render being intelligible by projecting it along the transcendental horizon of temporality) and subsequently the entire project precisely because, in spite of itself, fundamental ontology tended to reduce being to the status of something ontic that could somehow be, if not objectified per se, mastered or totalized through language; almost as much as the traditional philosophy that it was criticizing, it ran the risk, as Jean Grondin puts it, of "reifying Being according to a purely metaphysical horizon of intelligibility."[15] It is primarily in order to obviate the risk of such reification that Heidegger began his sojourn into apparently "poetical," "metaphorical," and frequently "tautological" ways of addressing being. And it is no coincidence that Heidegger's overt attempt to distance himself from the conceptual language of metaphysics coincides with his gradual explication of the radical finitude of being. For it is being's essential finiteness that metaphysical language is unable to express. Thus Heidegger's attempts in the later works to think being through bizarre neologisms and arcane phrases such as "the worlding of the world," "the thinging of things," and "language speaks" are, for him, a direct response to the demand of being itself for a nonmetaphysical way of understanding and addressing its finitude.

One can hardly fail to notice many such untraditional expressions scattered liberally throughout Heidegger's abstruse prose. Some of them, however, appear at first glance to be standard terminological pairs: presencing/absencing, revealing/concealing, being/nothing, birth/death, ground/groundless, even No/Yes; and (to make matters worse) these apparent conceptual dualities are frequently associated with a certain movement that one might interpret as a kind of covert dialectic, a back-and-forth dynamic that either leads to or constitutes some particular moment in Heidegger's ontology. Heidegger himself, of course, discourages such a reading by characterizing dialectical thinking as symptomatic (perhaps even paradigmatic) of the onto-theo-logical essence of the philosophical tradition. Who, after all, are the great advocates of dialectical thought but Plato and Hegel, the quintessential bookends of the history of metaphysics?

The last thing I would wish to do is read Heidegger as a dialectician, but his proximity to the dialectic, I would argue, presents us with a hermeneutical moment that should not be overlooked. And I think one of the best places to look for such a proximity is not in his texts on Plato and Hegel[16]—which, in addressing the dialectic directly, tend to obscure Heidegger's own relation to it—but in his engagement with Hegel's friend and compatriot, Friedrich Hölderlin.[17] An exhaustive explication of these texts is beyond the scope of this book, but I would like to indicate at least one possible path along which one could venture in carrying out such a task. My intention at this point is twofold: First, I would like to illustrate how Heidegger's embrace of poetic thinking is intimately connected with the demands that the radical finitude of being places on language; and, second, I want to show how their respective nearness to and the manner in which they distance themselves from the dialectic of German Idealism (and particularly its teleological thinking of the infinite) can serve as a ground on which to further explore this constantly counter-turning relationship between Heidegger and his pupil, Gadamer.

Hölderlin's (Non)Dialectical Poetics

Heidegger would perhaps disagree with Philippe Lacoue-Labarthe's assertion that tragedy is the origin of dialectic and that Hölderlin "collaborated in the most intimate manner possible in the building of the speculative dialectic—on the model of tragedy."[18] But, if we follow Hegel's definition of the "dialectical moment" as "the self-sublation of . . . finite determinations and their transition into their opposites,"[19] I would argue that a close look at Hölderlin's theoretical writings on tragedy reveals something that approximates the movement of the Hegelian dialectic.

The "Highest Fire"

Hölderlin's enigmatic writings resist interpretation. The dense complexity—indeed, the near opacity—of Hölderlin's three "Empedokles" drafts, and particularly the "theoretical" writings associated with them, throws the very possibility of interpretation into question. And yet the philosophical, historical, and poetical significance of these works is not easily denied. These texts virtually cry out to be interpreted. I do not intend this as an *apologia*. On the contrary, this is simply an affirmative statement of the fundamental challenge that Hölderlin's work presents to the enterprise of hermeneutics—a challenge directed both at the potential interpreter of Hölderlin and at the interpretive process itself.

If, along with Gadamer, we think the interpretive process itself dialectically—that is, if we see hermeneutics manifesting itself in the maieutic interplay between the whole and the part, text and context that constitutes the occurrence of understanding[20]—and if we also engage Lacoue-Labarthe's thesis that tragedy is the origin of dialectical thought, we begin to discern an aporetic circularity in the task of interpreting the Hölderlinian *Trauerspiel*. If, that is to say, both interpretation and tragedy bear the structure of dialectical thought,[21] and if Hölderlin did indeed help to build the speculative dialectic using the model of tragedy, how is it that some of the most intense and obviously significant moments in his work can appear to be hermeneutically—that is to say, dialectically—impenetrable?

Without asserting the validity of either Gadamer's dialectical view of hermeneutics or Lacoue-Labarthe's tragic view of speculative dialectics, but rather by way of *assuming* their *potential* validity as a way of framing the problem, I want to push the irony of my formulation even further. I want to suggest that Hölderlin's work on tragedy may be but one extreme yet highly revealing example of an resistance to interpretation that is inherent (to some degree) in all texts, and, ironically, that it may only be in the face of such hermeneutic opacity that interpretation is even possible. I propose to explore this thesis by examining in detail what I take to be the central *Fragestellung* in Hölderlin's theory of tragedy: namely, the problematic nature of what Hölderlin himself calls the tragic caesura, the moment of "counter-rhythmic rupture" during which the tragic hero brings to consciousness the necessity of his own death, or, as I will refer to it (appealing to Gadamer), the *epochal moment* in the peculiarly Hölderlinian presentation of tragedy.[22]

The dauntingly complex structure of Hölderlin's dramatic and theoretical works, beginning around 1797, may well stem directly from an unattributed text,"Das älteste Systemprogramm des deutschen Idealismus," which was apparently written by Hegel, Schelling, and Hölderlin together in the early part of that same year.[23] In it we find all the elements of Hölderlin's "poetological" conflation of art, religion, politics, history, and philosophy. As characterized, for example, by the political-theological treachery of Kritias and Hermocrates in the first version of *Der Tod des Empedokles*, early on in the "Systemprogramm" the authors lambast both the dehumanizing mechanical structure of the state and the hypocrisy of the priesthood.[24] Shortly thereafter—in a passage that prefigures Hölderlin's retrieval of the mythopoetic ethos of the Greeks—we find philosophy and history sublated in the ascendancy of poetry and the aesthetic:

> For I [Hölderlin?] am convinced that the supreme act of reason, because it embraces all ideas, is an aesthetic act, and that only in *beauty* are *truth and goodness* of the same flesh.—The philosopher must possess as much aesthetic force as the poet . . . The philosophy of spirit is an aesthetic philosophy. One can in no way be inspired—one cannot even ruminate on historical matters in an inspired way—without an aesthetic sense.
>
> Poesy will thereby attain a higher dignity; in the end she will again become what she was in the beginning—*the instructress of ~~history~~ humanity*; for there will no longer be any

> philosophy, any history; the poetic art alone will survive all the other sciences and arts.[25]

A few lines later, we come across the call for a "mythology of reason," followed by an identification of the aesthetic with the mythological, and finally, an exhortation for mythology to become philosophical and philosophy to become mythological.[26]

In one form or another (as I shall try to show) each of these ideas finds some degree of expression in Hölderlin's "theory" of tragedy. I can perhaps only gesture, however, toward what I see as the necessity and yet inevitable inadequacy of interpreting these "elements" as separable dialectical constituents of Hölderlin's tragic holism. That is to say, the terminological components of Hölderlin's theoretical statements, insofar as they each appear to pass over into their opposites, would seem to compel one to read them in terms of the speculative dialectic; and yet this Hegelian reading is constantly frustrated. In this regard, Andrzej Warminski's erudite "reading" (in contradistinction to an "interpretation"[27]) of what he calls Hölderlin's "chiasmic reversal," will prove invaluable for our discussion inasmuch as it poses a formidable critique of the interpretive process itself and its problematic application to Hölderlin.

Warminski wants to deconstruct the various dialectical interpretations of Hölderlin by displacing the mediate ground whereon the confrontation between opposites and any subsequent *Aufhebung* might be seen to take place. He first attacks what he takes to be Peter Szondi's attempt at a Hegelian reading (based primarily on Hölderlin's 1801 letter to Casimir Böhlendorff), wherein the distinction between *das Fremde* (the foreign) and *das Eigene* (the proper) becomes coextensive with the distinction between the ancient (Greek) and modern (Hesperian) historical epochs. According to the Böhlendorff letter, Hesperian *culture* (that which is originally foreign to us [i.e. the Germans], that which we appropriate from the Greeks) is coincident with Greek *nature* (that which is proper or natural to the Greeks: namely, "sacred pathos" and the "fire from heaven"), and Greek *culture* (that which was originally foreign to the Greeks, that which they appropriated through Homer) coincides with Hesperian *nature* (that which is proper to us: namely, "clarity of representation" and an "occidental Junonian sobriety").

As Szondi sees it, the "mirror symmetry" of this epochal conception allows Hölderlin to overcome classicism "without turning away from the classical" by recognizing that the modern (Hesperian) poet is not, after all, condemned to imitate the ancients, in spite of the Winckelmannian imperative[28]; the Greeks, however, remain "'indispensable' for the Hesperian poet because in their art he encounters his own proper [*eignen*] origin as a foreign element [*als einem Fremden*]."[29] Warminski offers the following characterization of Szondi's reading:

> Szondi saves the Greeks (while giving them up as a model to be imitated) elegantly: Hölderlin would not have us surrender *das Eigene* at the cost of *das Fremde* or vice versa—they are of equal rank (*Gleichrangigkeit*), says Szondi—but rather would have us become ourselves, Hesperians, by recognizing ourselves in an other, the Greeks, which, because it *re*presents (in their art) that which is our own *as* foreign, allows us to gain a distance on it and thereby to appropriate it, master it, freely.[30]

In other words, by focusing on and resolving dialectically what he sees as Hölderlin's central dichotomy—the distinction between Greece and Hesperia—Szondi provides us, as Warminski puts it, with an "eminently sensible interpretation—whose conception of the negative is powerful enough ultimately to totalize Hölderlin's biography with his poetry, his poetry with his poetics, his poetics with his philosophy of history, etc."[31]

Warminski, however, remains suspicious of Szondi's elegant and apparently complete interpretation precisely because it seems to work so well. In his view, Szondi totalizes Hölderlin by (mis)reading Greece and Hesperia as symmetrical opposites, as direct and complete negations of each other, as each other's other. Such a reading presupposes a reciprocal (i.e., Hegelian[32]) identification of "self" with "*das Eigene*" and "other" with "*das Fremde*"—an identification that Warminski rejects. As he sees it, Szondi's dialectical interpretation breaks down essentially because that which is foreign to what is *already* foreign to one is not one's *own* foreign. In Greek art, the Hesperian poet may indeed, as Szondi says, encounter his own proper origin as *a* foreignness, but this is not *his* foreignness; it "belongs," as it were, to the Greeks, and for Warminski this "double remove" of otherness destroys the symmetry of the Szondian dialectic. Warminski prefers to "read"[33] this formulation of Greek and Hesperian nature and culture in linguistic rather than philosophical terms; he sees it as a parallel yet *a*symmetrical relationship—a "chiasmic reversal"—wherein there resides a radical undecidability, an insuperable difference (even *différance*) that resists dialectical negation and sublation and, hence, any semblance of "interpretation"—at least, if interpretation implies the determination of univocal meaning and necessarily entails an expectation of closure or completion.

Warminski stresses the pure textuality of language and warns against superfluously imposing a "philosophical" interpretation on any text. "The texts of Hölderlin," he writes,

> are exemplary in this respect: whether 'poetic' or 'theoretical,' the logic of these texts' self-reflection is not only rigorous enough to withstand the machinations of any dialectical [Hegelian] or ontological [Heideggerian] interpretation and its negative but also *linguistically* 'self-reflexive' enough, 'aware' enough of its own *textual* conditions, to resist these machinations and give the lie to any interpretation whose negative would reduce Hölderlin's texts to extralinguistic, extratextual, conditions, whether they be called 'self-consciousness' or 'Being.'[34]

We will (at least implicitly) challenge this reading of Heidegger's Hölderlin as we proceed. Warminski also goes on to chide Lacoue-Labarthe, whose essay "The Caesura of the Speculative" is a more "deconstructive" reading than Szondi's, but who nevertheless "takes over too readily Szondi's Hegelian dialectical interpretation of Hölderlin's theoretical, poetological, writings: to do so, he, like Szondi before him, must ignore the explicitly linguistic (indeed rhetorical) framework and categories Hölderlin employs."[35] Warminski thus throws into stark relief the challenge that Hölderlin's work presents to the hermeneutic enterprise by shifting the playing field, so to speak, by denying the validity of the dialectical strategy whereby a coherent understanding is synthetically "imposed" on the text. Whether or not we agree with his insistence on what he calls "reading" as a purely textual, linguistic, grammatical, or rhetorical activity—whether or not it thereby becomes incumbent on us to discover the undecidability of a given trope by seeing it in terms of a "chiasmic reversal"—we should at least take quite seriously Warminski's problematizing of dialectical reduction, especially in regard to its application to Hölderlin.

Even for Gadamer the formal dialectical aspect of hermeneutical inquiry contains a reductive element: namely, the process of discerning among or distinguishing between the various "parts" that constitute a possible "whole" (the Platonic-Aristotelian notion of *diairesis*[36]); and this reductive process inevitably destroys the holistic integrity of that which it purports to understand. That is to say, the 'object' of hermeneutical inquiry—the so-called "thing itself" (in this case, the texts of Hölderlin)—insofar as it must be subjected to this kind of "analytical" or "abstractive" process, and precisely because it cannot be wholly divorced from its historical situation, can never be understood "completely." Warminski's critique, however, pushes this problem to its limits. It implies not only that a dialectical interpretation (be it Gadamerian or Hegelian) is inadequate to the task of complete understanding, but that the very orientation of hermeneutics—what Gadamer refers to as the "*Vorgriff der Vollkommenheit*," the "anticipation of meaning," the "movement of understanding" toward the "harmony of all the details with the whole"[37]—is an attunement rooted in self-delusion. For Warminski it is of the essence of the text (and especially Hölderlin's texts) to resist reduction, and hence totalization, no matter how provisional or historically conscious that reduction may be. (Gadamer, by the way, would agree with this.) For even if we choose not to abandon hermeneutics entirely at this point (as Warminski would have us do), Hölderlin's tragic works themselves urgently compel us to take this critique seriously, to further scrutinize the potential efficacy of an interpretive process that finds itself confronted with a body of work that strenuously resists dialectical reduction. And perhaps it is best to begin this task by tentatively engaging in an interpretation of our own.

In spite of Warminski's admonitions, once we begin to examine the works in question—particularly the so-called "Grund zum Empedokles" and "Das Werden im Vergehen"—it becomes difficult to deny that some sort of speculative dialectical structure or mechanism seems to be operative in them, even if Hölderlin's "logic" must ultimately be seen as something *other* than what we have come to know as either Hegelian or Platonic dialectic. In the "Grund" essay, for example, Hölderlin begins the section actually entitled "Grund zum Empedokles" by describing the relationship between nature and art: "In pure life," he writes,

> nature and art are only opposed harmoniously. Art is the blossom, the perfection of nature; nature only becomes divine in conjunction with the diverse yet harmonious art; when everything is entirely what it can be, and one combines with the other, supplements the other [*ersetzt den Mangel des andern*], which that one must necessarily have in order to be entirely that which it can be as a particular, then there exists perfection, and the divine rests in between the two.[38]

In this "combination of harmonious opposites," we appear to have a patently dialectical relationship. But (and this seems to be typical of Hölderlin) rather than a clear Hegelian *Aufhebung* in which the two original terms pass over into each other in their mutual negation and are thus sublated under the third, it is only in the "synthesis" of nature and art that each term becomes "entirely that which it can be *as a particular.*" And the third term, "perfection" or "the divine," rather than subsuming the other two, seems to arise as a characteristic that somehow "rests in between" them with the unexpected effect of intensifying their particularity. And, as we shall see, this intensification is precisely what Heidegger picks up on.

It would, of course, prove extremely difficult (not to mention overly reductive) to analyze the entire Hölderlinian tragic oeuvre in these terms. But we can, perhaps, detect in this passage the trace of a pattern, a pattern marked by a dialectical interaction *of sorts* between various conceptual dualities that stand in opposition to one another or, at least, in some kind of reciprocal relation (art and nature, the organic and the aorgic, the particular and the universal, the finite and the infinite, objectivity and subjectivity, the real and the ideal, and so on). The only apparently consistent feature of these interactions, however, is that, as they come into confrontation, each term or element or aspect is affected in some way by its other—usually by means of a third element that either effects the intensification of both or is itself effectively intensified—in an overall (albeit oscillating) trajectory of greater and greater intensity. And (insofar as it can be distinguished) this "effective" third term—the term "in between" the other two—seems eventually to coincide with the end-point or *telos* of this trajectory and thus appears to be of primary importance for Hölderlin. The end, however, toward which this "dialectic of intensification" (if you will) inclines itself is the point or the moment in which all of the "elements" mentioned above seem to converge in their greatest extremes or in their highest intensity (their "highest fire," as Hölderlin puts it). Thus, insofar as they retain their extreme particularity rather than passing over into each other and moving forward developmentally, what we seem to miss in the Hölderlinian formulation of the dialectic is precisely what Hegel calls the "speculative moment" or the moment of "positive reason" that "apprehends the unity of the determinations in their opposition—the affirmative that is contained in their dissolution and transition."[39] In Holderlin's dialectic there seems to be neither a dissolution nor a real unity of these opposites.[40] And if a transition of some kind does occur here, it would seem not to be one in which the opposites pass over into each other (as they would for Hegel), but one in which they "move" only toward a higher state of intensity.[41]

Unfortunately, although one retains a strong sense of what I am calling the dialectic of intensification throughout the "Grund" essay, it becomes increasingly difficult to discern the specific terms of the dialectic and their corresponding effect. For example, in the same paragraph as the passage cited above, Hölderlin writes:

> However, this life exists only in sentiment and not for knowledge. If it is to be known, then it must present itself by *separating itself* in the excess of inwardness [*Innigkeit,* interiority, intensity, or intimacy] where the *opposed principles interchange* so that the organic, which surrenders itself too much to nature, and which forgot its essence and consciousness, transcends into the extreme of the autonomous activity and art and reflection, whereas nature, at least in its *effects* on reflective man, transcends into the extreme of the aorgic, the incomprehensible, the non-sensuous, the unlimited, until through *the progression of the opposed reciprocal effects* the two originally united [principles] meet again as in the beginning, only that nature has become more organic through the forming, cultivating man, through the form-giving drives and forces as such, whereas man has become more aorgic, universal, infinite.[42]

Terms like "universal" and "infinite" seem to evoke a Hegelian "flavor," but it would be quite difficult (if at all possible) to impose a speculative reading on this passage. In fact, it might also be possible (though perhaps even more difficult) to read these passages in terms of a Warminskian chiasmic reversal. But for the sake of our inquiry into the nature of interpretation, let us follow the path of dialectical intensification as far as we can.

At the risk of hypostatizing this rather tentative reading, I would like to focus here exclusively on the moment of intensity. But rather than developing an interpretation of it as such, I want to try to characterize the apparent aporia of Hölderlin's tragic moment in such a way as to offer a glimpse not of its susceptibility to deconstructive strategies but of its hermeneutic fecundity. In other words (to phrase the problematic as a question), how is it that even though in this moment both the "dialectic of intensification" and the possibility of interpreting dialectically seem to break down completely, it is precisely here that the potential for hermeneutic productivity manifests itself most fully?

This moment of "highest fire," the "tragic" moment, reveals itself throughout Hölderlin's writings in many different forms. In his "Remarks on Oedipus," it is a spatially described dramaturgical device: "the counter-rhythmic interruption," the "pure word," the "caesura," that breaks "the rhythmic succession of ideas" thus clearing a space for the "tragic *transport*" to emerge.[43] In the "Remarks on the Antigone," on the other hand, it becomes a profoundly temporal moment wherein "time reverses" and "the move from the Greek to the Hesperian" occurs; it becomes "[t]he boldest moment in the course of a day or in a work of art . . . where the spirit of the age and nature, the heavenly, by which man is overwhelmed, and the object, in which he is interested, come to oppose each other most violently. . . ."[44] And yet, it is also the supremely religious moment when "God in his immediacy becomes wholly One with Man," when "God, in the form of death, is present"[45]; and by the end of the "Remarks on Antigone" it has even become political and "specifically Republican," and takes the form of a revolt (broadly conceived) or a "national reversal," wherein

> the whole shape of things changes, and nature and necessity, which always remain, tend to a new shape, whether going over into a wilderness or into a new form; in a change like this, all mere necessities are biased in favour of the change, whence, in the eventuality of such a change, even a neutral man . . . is forced to be patriotic, and present in the infinite form, in the religious, political and moral form of his fatherland. (*profanethi theos.*) [Appear, oh God!][46]

Most of these characterizations are also articulated or alluded to (in one way or another) in the "Grund zum Empedokles," but only in "Das Werden im Vergehen"—the one piece devoted exclusively to the tragic moment itself—do we find it rendered in an explicitly philosophical and (at least proximally) dialectical manner. Although it is not as pronounced as in the "Grund," I think we also get a sense for the dialectic of intensification in "Das Werden im Vergehen." At any rate, we need venture no further than the first paragraph to encounter the same kind of (non)dialectical movement, only now with a particular emphasis on temporality:

> The declining fatherland, nature and man, insofar as they bear *a particular relation of reciprocity,* insofar as they constitute a special world which has become ideal and [constitute] a union of things and insofar as they dissolve, so that from the world and from the remaining ancestry and forces of nature, there emerges a new world, a new yet also particular *reciprocal relation* just as that decline emerged from a pure yet particular world. For the world of all worlds, the all in all which always is, only presents itself *in all time—or in the decline, the instant or, more genetically, in the becoming of the instant and in the beginning of time and world,* and this decline and beginning is—like language—expression, sign, presentation of a living yet particular whole which in its *effects* become like the former ones . . . In the living existence there prevails a *mode of relation* and of thematics, even though all others can be intuited within it; *the possibility of all relations* is predominant in the *transition,* yet the particular one needs to be taken, to be derived from it so that through it there emerges infinity, the finite *effect.*[47]

Even the title of this piece, "Becoming in Dissolution," would seem to prompt a Hegelian dialectical reading which, once again, the text itself seems to frustrate. However, insofar as this particular text focuses on the temporal and, more specifically, the *transitional* character of the tragic moment, the historical emphasis that we find in the Böhlendorff letter (and in the "Notes" and the "Grund" as well) seems to take on a more historicophilosophical, a more "epochal"—and slightly more Hegelian—cast.

Now, an "epoch" obviously has to do with historical or at least temporal periods, but in his essay, "Concerning Empty and Fulfilled Time," Gadamer offers an interpretation of what I am calling Hölderlin's "epochal moment," which focuses precisely on the limits of the dialectic without resorting to a purely linguistic or deconstructive reading: "An epoch-making event," he tells us,

> establishes a caesura. It establishes that which preceded as old, and everything which now comes, as new. In some circumstances the concepts of old and new have a dialectic of profound inner uncertainty. What is new rapidly becomes obsolete, and what is old proves to be new. But when it is a question of the concept of epoch, *this dialectic of old and new comes, so to speak, to a halt.* For an epoch-making event

> clearly ordains such a separation between old and new which we ourselves do not create and which we nevertheless must follow.[48]

Gadamer's "epoch-making event" is a profoundly temporal phenomenon which, as he says, "is determined by the character of *transition*," but "transition," for Gadamer, "does not mean the dialectical mediation of the old and the new . . . It has to do, rather, with the real uncertainty and the open infinity of the event itself."[49] Thus, on Gadamer's reading, we have here not necessarily a dialectic of intensification but a movement in which the dissolution and transition of the opposites, rather than perpetuating a developmental movement toward something like absolute spirit, establishes a "ceasura," a discernable break in the historical sequence, an "epochal moment."[50]

Interestingly enough, the notion of an epochal transition—a patently philosophical notion that Gadamer gleans directly from "Das Werden im Vergehen"—does precisely the same work for a hermeneutical reading that the chiasmic reversal does for the deconstructive one: it disrupts the dialectic—or, more properly, it "reads" the moment where Hölderlin's would-be dialectic disrupts itself. With this observation, what we might call a hermeneutical counter-challenge to Warminski's approach begins to show itself. As Gadamer's interpretation of the "epoch-making event" shows, an account that itself arises from a dialectical activity (at least insofar as it professes to be hermeneutical) need not commit itself to a totalizing metaphysical (i.e., in Warminski's terms, Hegelian) reading. But let us turn for a moment to Hölderlin's own attempt to implement his theories of tragedy.

In *Der Tod des Empedokles*, the moment of tragedy is at once philosophical, historical, political, religious, mythological, poetological (even autobiographical, insofar as it can be seen as the poet's self-reflection on the possibility of writing a modern tragedy); and yet it is none of these because of the overwhelming individuality of the moment—it is, ultimately, Empedocles' moment. "Thus," writes Hölderlin,

> Empedocles is a son of his heaven and his time, of his fatherland, a son of the tremendous oppositions of nature and art in which the world appeared before his eyes. A man within whom those oppositions are united *so* intimately [so intensely, *so innig*] that they become *one* within him . . .

> Thus Empedocles was supposed to become a victim [*ein Opfer*] of his time. *The problems of the destiny in which he matured were to resolve seemingly within him, and this solution was to present itself within him* . . .
>
> Thus his time is individualized in Empedocles, and the more it is individualized in him, the brighter and more real and visible the riddle appears solved within him, the more necessary becomes his ruin. . . .
>
> In his most independent situation the destiny of his epoch resolves in the first and last problem . . .[51]

Thus, all these forces (historical, religious, political, and so on) unite so intensely in Empedocles that his fate becomes one with the fate of his epoch, and he becomes aware of the inescapable necessity of his ruin, his death, his sacrifice. Empedocles, however, is not simply the vehicle or the embodiment of these various abstractions, he is (in spite of his divine aspirations) intensely human, and although his fate is preordained—ironically, *because* his fate is preordained—he is faced with perhaps the most human of all prospects: freedom. Empedocles *must* be sacrificed, any other path is rendered impossible by the overwhelming forces determining his fate. And yet he resolves to go to his death *voluntarily*.

Why, in the third draft of "The Death of Empedocles," has Manes come to Aetna? Not to deliver the verdict of the gods; not to force Empedocles to kill himself; not even to explain his destiny to him: Empedocles already understands and is resolved. Even before Manes arrives, Empedocles has told Pausanias, "Where you walk, I do not; my blossoming / Elsewhere awaits me. And that of which I speak / Not now has come about, not on this day, / But at my birth [it] was already decided."[52] But, as if to emphasize the free will and rationality of Empedocles' human soul, Manes—Empedocles' alter ego, his "evil spirit," his conscience—appears, seemingly from nowhere, and prods his humanity: "You wish it, and so be it! Yet not unthinking / As now you are, would I have you go down . . . "[53] Manes, insisting that Empedocles be acutely aware, *humanly* aware, of his situation, reiterates the gravity of Empedocles' perception of himself as "The One," "the new saviour," the *daimon* who mediates between the gods and men and who does what must be done *"by his own choice."* And, finally, testing Empedocles' resolve, he asks, "Are you that man? The same? That very man?"[54] In the end, Empedocles declares his freedom in reproof of both Manes and the gods:

That here I may cut and put an end
To the long chain of suffering, *liberated*
From other duties, in *self-chosen death*
And in accordance with god-given laws!
Forbidden fruit for you, man! Therefore leave me,
And if you cannot follow me, do not judge![55]

Thus, as Lacoue-Labarthe says (paraphrasing Schelling), "the subject *manifests* its liberty 'by the very loss of its liberty.' The negative, here, is converted into the positive: the struggle [for philosophical, religious, political, poetic, (*interpretive*?) goals] (be it ever so vain or futile) is in itself productive."[56] It is in this struggle (or perhaps this dialectic) between the fated necessity and the concomitant impossibility of one individual shouldering the burdens of an entire epoch that Empedocles finally becomes conscious of his freedom—even if it is only the very narrowly delimited freedom that he finds in choosing his own death.

The fundamental problematic—the paradox—of this dialectical reading is already contained in its original formulation. If Hölderlin's dialectic is something *other than* Hegelian or Platonic, then, strictly speaking, we probably have no grounds for saying that it *is* a dialectic per se in that the would-be moment of speculation, the moment in which the unity of the opposites is apprehended and thereby facilitates the progressive development, is frustrated. The *Aufhebung*, in other words, does not complete itself.[57] And yet, this oscillating Hölderlinian movement does exhibit a structure that is unmistakably dialectic*al*. And in its proximity, its similarity, its near identity, to the speculative dialectic of German idealism—in fact, because of this proximity—it de-constitutes, de-constructs, dis-mantles, dis-appropriates, the very logic that it employs.[58] This is why the tragic moment is so difficult to approach dialectically, so difficult to reduce to a collection of *constituent* "elements": the elements *of* the moment do not constitute the moment—if anything, they constitute themselves, in their most extreme particularity. There is no speculative moment, no resolution, no *Aufhebung*; there is only a moment of "paralysis" in which what was "natural" to the Greeks ("the fire from heaven," "sacred pathos") gives way in the inexorable progression of a logic that cannot contain itself—the logic of "Junonian sobriety" and the "clarity of representation." Thus the "tragic" moment becomes the "epochal" moment, the moment of transition, in which one historical/religious/political epoch gives way to another.

And yet, to try to isolate a specific "reason" for this transition, to try to discover the underlying structure or mechanism of epochal change, is to jeopardize the very possibility of explaining it systematically—*in specifically textual terms, that is*. To this extent, Warminski is right. To concentrate on the texts themselves is to discover in Hölderlin an inevitable undecidability; the texts *in and of themselves* resist interpretation. Nevertheless, as Lacoue-Labarthe again points out, the very indeterminacy of this moment, its dialectical paralysis, its impossibility, is precisely what animates the Hölderlinian work of tragedy, what, in some (perhaps logically undecipherable) sense "frees" the tragic hero and at the same time allows for the possibility of *interpreting* the tragedy (and not simply "reading" it) in terms of an epochal dialectic. That is to say, it is the inherent incompleteness and "incompletability" (or as Gadamer puts it, the "real uncertainty") of the Hölderlinian *Trauerspiel* that opens it up to the possibility of adopting *a* (not *the*) perspective that will be productive of understandings, of interpretations, which, paradoxically, will allow us as readers, as interpreters, to get closer to the whole that is Hölderlin, just as for Hölderlin himself the tragic poet can only get close to the truth of tragedy by distancing himself through dramatic characterizations.[59]

If we can at least agree on the necessity of reading certain texts (whether hermeneutically or deconstructively)—a necessity that itself may not be logically demonstrable—then perhaps it is only in the space between this necessity and the impossibility of "achieving" understanding in any completely coherent sense that we are ever free to interpret anything. For if it were possible to understand a given text completely, then there would be no room at all for interpretation (or discovering chiasmic reversals for that matter). Or at least what we now refer to as "hermeneutics" would be reduced to the status of a strict, almost mathematical, logic or methodology, a mere equation for deducing a single determinate and determinable meaning. Perhaps, then, part of Hölderlin's poetic greatness lies precisely in his interpretive opacity; perhaps, ironically, the necessity of interpretation can ultimately reveal itself only in and through its tragic impossibility—an impossibility that reveals itself at the same time as a profound openness. And if Gadamer's hermeneutical approach would seem to accommodate this radical openness, then I would also argue that this inherent—and productive—ambiguity is also precisely what Heidegger finds valuable in Hölderlin's work.

It is plainly *not* a strictly speculative dialectical movement being demonstrated in these texts, if for no other reasons than the lack of systematic development and the absence of any clear moment of sublation. But even if we cannot legitimately call the movement of Hölderlin's poetical theorizing "dialectical," we can at least detect a kind of family resemblance that makes us want to characterize it in terms of its proximity to the dialectic of Hegel. And, if we look closely, I believe we can detect something roughly similar in Heidegger as well—an ironic counter-turning toward the dialectic that occurs precisely within his most overt attempt to turn away from it. Moreover, in Heidegger's encounter with Hölderlin we also find the phenomenological seeds for our reading of the Heidegger-Gadamer dialogue as a hermeneutical movement away that constantly and simultaneously turns back on itself.

Heidegger's Hölderlinian Dwelling

For Heidegger, the movement of revealing and concealing, for example, cannot be dialectical, not only because it is neither logical nor teleological but also because it is not a symmetrical duality.[60] Revealing is not the "opposite" of concealing. For they are not static "concepts" that could be placed into a relation of opposition and thus negate each other (and themselves), thereby generating a dialectical movement. They are themselves movements which occur simultaneously, independent of any subjectlike construction. Self-negation, the engine of the Hegelian dialectic, can thus find no foothold in this kind of phenomenological movement. Reiner Schürmann is quite helpful on this point. He warns us against being seduced by mere "lexical matches" and draws our attention to Heidegger's use of prepositional phrases that destroy any real hope for a "bipolar mechanics":

> birth is "*toward* death"; "the clearing, *for* concealment" (GA65, 351); "the groundless is the ground's *originary way of being*" (GA65, 379); nothingness, "what is *more originary in* being" (GA65, 247); the No, "*of an even deeper essence than* the Yes" (GA65, 178).[61]

Such asymmetrical relations do not allow for a teleological Hegelian reading of these lexical pairs, but do they not remind us of the radically particularizing movement we found above in Hölderlin? And is it not, from a Heideggerian perspective, precisely logic and teleology that have historically covered over the possibility of being revealing itself *as* concealing? Hegel's dialectic, in other words, in spite of its invaluable critique of the logic of judgment, remains for Heidegger a function of subjectivity and progressive logical development and is thus incapable of thinking the essential finitude of being. As Schürmann also observes, Heidegger's topological phenomenology (and I would argue that this holds for Hölderlin's poetics of tragedy as well) is capable of "what both Aristotle and Hegel have held to be impossible . . . : [to] think the particular as particular"[62]—that is, to think the particular in its essential finitude rather than as but one moment in an inevitable trajectory toward the universal and the infinite. But I also want to argue that the sharp distinction between the respective movements of these two phenomenologies is grounded in a very real relation—a relation that we can at least partially uncover by examining Heidegger's lecture course from 1942 entitled, *Hölderlins Hymne Der Ister.*[63]

In Part One of the volume, we find Heidegger concerned with a profoundly topological, but explicitly nongeographical and nonsymbolic reading of the Ister hymn. He sees the river neither in terms of its specific historical and geographical location nor as a metaphysical (or even metaphorical) symbolic image of some universal human truth, but as a poetic enigma. The Ister unveils itself simultaneously as "journeying" (*Wanderung*) and as the "locality" of human dwelling on the earth. It thus both changes and remains constant at the same time. The question, then, could be seen as one of explicating this peculiar relationship between "change" and "constancy." For a Hegelian dialectic, these two terms would need to be seen as otherwise static concepts[64] whose opposition to each other would generate a progressive movement. Change, that is, insofar as it is the negation of constancy (and vice versa) would ultimately pass over into its opposite in such a way that both would be canceled and yet lifted up and preserved within a third term. This passing over would constitute the movement or development of the concept insofar as the two terms would thus be sublated, *aufgehoben*, in the course of their mutual self-negation. Such a reduction to the bare concepts, "change" and "constancy," however, would strip "journeying" and "locality" of their essential poetic context, and Heidegger is at great pains to keep us acutely aware of the poetic ground of these terms. The river, in other words, does not "represent" change, constancy or both, it does not for that matter, represent journeying and locality. The river Ister *is* both the journeying of locality and the locality of journeying, and the poem itself both reveals and conceals this truth. It reveals a journeying of human beings toward being at home within their essential abode (i.e., being), and their dwelling within this locality reveals itself as a journeying so long as the poem is read with an eye (or an ear) to the proximity of *Dichten* and *Denken*, poetizing and thinking. But the poem also conceals this truth in one sense by its appearance as a traditional poetical/metaphorical "work of art," as an aesthetic construct—in other words, insofar as the hymn appears to the average reader to be a typical poem, its phenomenological significance gets covered over by standard literary analyses. At a deeper level, however, the truth of the poem is covered over in its very uncovering. That is, if what is revealed in the hymn is human being journeying toward its essential dwelling place, being, then that very "homecoming" is shown to be a "coming to be at home" in journeying itself, in an essential *alienation* from being. Thus, I would argue, Heidegger leads us into an elaboration of both Hölderlin's hymn, *The Ister*, and Sophocles' *Antigone*[65] as (non)dialectical occurrences of poetizing thinking. Such a reading is made possible by, among other things, Heidegger's attention to Hölderlin's entire body of work as well as the poet's historical situation and intellectual proximity to Hegel, Schelling, and the Greeks. And it is precisely with this sensitivity to context, as I see it, that Heidegger's own hermeneutical relationship to Hölderlin begins to resemble Gadamer's relationship to Plato with its profound awareness of the dramatic and playfully serious manner in which the dialectic plays itself out in the dialogues.

Heidegger characterizes Hölderlin in this text and others[66] as engaging in a dialogue of his own—one with the Greek world and, most specifically, with Sophocles. But he also speaks of Hölderlin's relationship to Hegel and German metaphysics. Heidegger points out that because in "Bread and Wine" and elsewhere Hölderlin mentions "spirit" (*Geist*), many people have assumed that Hölderlin merely borrowed this concept from philosophy—complete with all of its metaphysical connotations—and adapted it to his poetry as he saw fit. But Heidegger points out that "even though Hölderlin maintains a relation to this metaphysical thinking in a poetic encounter with it, he maintains this relation to it in a manner of overcoming and turning away from it, which does not in turn mean a condemnation of philosophy."[67] In other words, Hölderlin's relationship to Hegelian and Schellingian metaphysics is one of *Destruktion*. But this "turning away" from philosophy is by no means a total rejection or a complete severing, as though metaphysics had never existed, but entails a specific and profound hermeneutical proximity, the structure of which is recapitulated not only in Heidegger's readings of Aristotle, Hölderlin, Nietzsche, and so on, but in Hölderlin's relationship to the Greeks and in the very phenomenological movement that Heidegger describes in the course of his own *Auseinandersetzung* with Hölderlin, namely, what Heidegger refers to as "counter-turning" (*Gegen-wendigkeit*).

For Heidegger, German Idealism sets out to harness negativity and bend it to the service of the Absolute, to render it "harmless," to turn it into something "positive."[68] In so doing, however, it merely takes up the idea of the negative dogmatically as yet another concept, thereby failing to touch upon its "essential origin." In coining the term "counter-turning," however, Heidegger hopes to rethink the negative as always already in motion, as a counter-movement that is never abstractable from the phenomena themselves for whom this counter-turning constitutes the truth.[69] He embarks on this deconstruction of negativity in Part Two of his lecture course on Hölderlin's hymn "The Ister." Here he provides us with a Hölderlinian reading of Sophocles' *Antigone* and specifically with an interpretation of the Greek word *deinon* as it occurs in the first strophe of the first choral ode.

Heidegger translates *deinon* as "*das Unheimliche*" (in English, "the uncanny") and, playing specifically on the root word "*Heim*" or "home," tries to draw out the notion of human *Da-sein* as dwelling within or being at home in being. He looks, therefore, to the etymologically equivalent though semantically different German word, "*heimisch*" (literally "homely" in the sense of "being at home") to develop a reading of *deinon* as "*un-heimisch*" or "un-homely," being not at home. This translation, in turn, sets up an oscillating dynamic in which humans are both "at home" or "homely" and un-homely at the same time—in fact, we find that human beings come to be *heimisch* precisely in their being *unheimisch*. And so, just as with the river Ister, which we saw as *both* journeying and locality simultaneously, we have another instance of what Aristotelian logic would see as a contradiction and Hegelian logic would think as opposed concepts "waiting" to be *aufgehoben*. But the precise nature of this opposition, for Heidegger, does not really emerge until the chorus elaborates on the ways in which the human being shows itself as the most uncanny of beings.

In the middle of the second strophe (1. 360), the chorus refers to the human being as:

pantoporos aporos ep ouden erchetai

which Heidegger translates as:

> Überall hinausfahrend unterwegs erfahungslos ohne Ausweg kommt er zum Nichts.[70]
> (Everywhere venturing forth underway, experienceless without any way out he comes to nothing.)

He specifically draws our attention to the phrase *pantoporos aporos*, which he renders, "everywhere underway coming to nothing."[71] In this phrase he sees not a contradiction but a kind of reversal, a *counter-turning*, which characterizes the uncanniness of the human being insofar as it is of human essence to be underway toward being homely while being fated at the same time to un-homeliness. Human beings, in other words, are uncanny in that they can only be at home insofar as they are *not* at home in being. He finds a reiteration of this counter-turning in the phrase *hupsipolis apolis*, "towering high above the site, forfeiting the site," from lines 370–371.[72]

Heidegger translates "*polis*" not with the usual "city" or "city-state" but, playing on its etymological connection to the Greek "*polos*" from which we get the English, "pole," he sees it as "*die Stätte*" ("the site"), "that realm and locale around which everything question-worthy and uncanny turns in an exceptional sense"[73]; it thus becomes "a particular realm of *poros* [the passage or passage through to something], as it were, one field in which it emphatically comes to pass."[74] The *polis*, then, the site of human being, is related intimately to the *poros*, the passage of human being. He thereby establishes a link between his two seemingly oxymoronic phrases (*pantoporos aporos* and *hupsipolis apolis*) while at he same time leading us to think once again of the relationship between the "locality" and "journeying" of the Ister from Part One. But, he says,

> The *polis* is here not some indifferent space that in turn admits of the empty possibilities of "towering high" and of downfall; rather, it is the essence of the *polis* to thrust one into excess and to tear one into downfall, and in such a way that the human being is destined and fitted into both these counterturning possibilities and thus must be these two possibilities themselves. Human beings do not "have" these possibilities in addition to and extrinsic to themselves, rather their essence consists in being those who, in ascending within

> the site of their essence, are at the same time without site. To be in such a way, however, means to be determined in essence by the unhomely, to be counterturning.[75]

Human beings, in other words, are *human* beings precisely insofar as their abode, their dwelling place, their *polis*, their *being*, is determined in and through their counter-turning relationship to being itself: their being at home in being un-homely. And in this way, human beings *are*, essentially, a counter-turning.

Heidegger gives us the supreme example of this counter-turning essence in the figure of Antigone herself. In the opening dialogue, Ismene argues with her sister over the latter's intention of burying their brother, Polyneices, directly in the face of the law decreed by their uncle, Creon (1. 93). Ismene remarks,

> archēn de thēran ou prepei tamēchana

Heidegger renders this:

> Als Anfang aber jenes zu erjagen, unschicklich bleibt's,
> wogegen auszurichten nichts.[76]
> (Yet to commence in pursuit of that, remains unfitting,
> against which nothing can avail.)

His point here is to bring the opening word of this line, *archēn*, "the all-determining commencement (origin) of all human being," into contact with the last word, *tamēchana*, "that which is of no avail."[77] On this reading, Ismene does not merely point out the futility of her sister's gesture, she offers us a specific indication of Antigone's uncanniness, her un-homeliness—Antigone commences a counter-turning movement in pursuing that against which nothing can avail. At one level, then, from Ismene's perspective, Antigone is uncanny in that "it is not fitting [*nicht schicklich*] to make that which is of no avail into the all-determining commencement (origin) of all human being"[78]; and yet this is precisely her destiny, her *Geschick*. Ismene points out that her sister's project is "unfitting," and yet Antigone "take[s] up into [her] own essence the uncanny that here and now appears" (1. 96). In other words, she appropriates for her own essence, takes up *as fitting*, that very unfittingness, thus intensifying her own *Unheimlichkeit*. Her counter-turning, therefore, is such that she becomes "utterly unhomely," "the most uncanny," "the supremely uncanny."[79] Here we begin to see that other aspect of the Hölderlinian non-dialectic at work: the back and forth movement, "the counter-rhythmic rupture," which produces not a Hegelian sublation but an *intensification of particularity*.

Heidegger characterizes Antigone's intensifying counter-turning possibilities by asking, "What if that which were most intrinsically unhomely, thus most remote from all that is homely, were that which in itself simultaneously preserved the most intimate belonging to the homely?"[80] The possibility occurs, in other words, for that which is most closely related to the homely to be preserved within its own most extreme unhomeliness, for the most intimate nearness to being to be preserved within those most incapable of being at home within it—that is, human beings. This formulation clearly resonates with Heidegger's notion of human *Dasein*'s essential *Seinsvergessenheit*. Only human beings can dwell essentially within the forgetfulness of being because only human beings have an essential relationship to being in the first place. But I am equally interested in the idea that the intensification *preserves* the extremes, for here we have yet another point of proximity to the dialectic in that *Aufhebung* also entails the preservation of the original terms. The difference, however, is that the Hölderlinian tragic moment is one of both reciprocity and singularity, an intensification of the particular in the very counter-movement that brings the two elements into contact with one another, rather than—as in the speculative dialectic—a linear development toward the universal brought about by mutual negation.

My point, therefore, is not at all that Hölderlin and Heidegger should be seen as "closet" speculative idealists or as epigones of or mere reactionaries to Hegelian metaphysics. This would be an absurdly reductionistic misunderstanding of both of the poet and the thinker. But even if the Heideggerian movement of being is patently and essentially not dialectical, I think it would nevertheless be fair to say that it does retain certain echoes of the dialectic that might be traced back through his admiration for Hölderlin. And if Hegel refers to the thinking of Absolute Spirit as "speculatively dialectical," perhaps we could refer to Hölderlin's poetizing, in apposition (if not in opposition) to Hegel's philosophizing, as "poetically *non*dialectical." Heideggerian *Denken*, then, might be seen as a kind of nondialectical counterpart to Hölderlinian *Dichten*, the point being simply to cast into relief a certain proximal relation to the dialectic of German Idealism—an implicit and ironic counter-turning relation not entirely dissimilar, as we shall see, to Gadamer's quite explicit and ironically Heideggerian turn away from Heidegger toward Hegel.

FOUR

Gadamer's Hegelian Liberation of Language and Being

Gadamer's overall project, seemingly less radical and certainly less poetical, inverts (perhaps even converts) but does not oppose Heidegger's. Gadamer does not attempt to carry out (as Heidegger does) a radical dismantling of the philosophical tradition that ultimately demands an entirely different way of thinking and speaking; he wants, rather, beginning from Heidegger's basic critique of philosophical thinking and the initial context for this critique (i.e., fundamental ontology), to offer an interpretation of what thinking, being, and language are and how they occur. He is putting forward, in other words, a hermeneutic phenomenology that permits the Heideggerian critique to carry itself out from within the very linguistic tradition in which it originally finds itself. Heidegger, of course, held that the problem with such criticism-from-within is that it tends to re-inscribe the sort of Kantian transcendental critique that it was meant to escape. This is why he explicitly tried to distance himself from philosophical critique as a methodology by recasting it in terms of phenomenological *Destruktion und Wiederholung*. Gadamer acknowledges that fundamental ontology is still very much circumscribed by the tradition it deconstructs, but it is precisely this quality that he effectively embraces. He wants to allow the language of the Western tradition, Heidegger's "language of metaphysics," to speak in such a way as to criticize *itself*, to deconstruct *itself*, thus obviating the need for an Archimedean point or a Kantian transcendental analysis—or, for that matter, a Heideggerian flight into poetizing thinking.

I would even argue that, in doing this, he is in some ways attempting to move along a path that is more Heideggerian than Heidegger's own. Heidegger, for instance, is very good at allowing the "premetaphysical" language of Heraclitus and Parmenides and the "nonmetaphysical" language of the poets to speak. Gadamer wants to do the same thing for the language of metaphysics itself by entering directly into the heart of the philosophical tradition and allowing it to give voice to the hermeneutical dialogue that he sees lying dormant within—a *dialectic*, that is, held captive within the cocoon of metaphysics by a rigid and overdetermined logic. But rather than rejecting the dialectic as anathema to postmetaphysical thinking, Gadamer attempts to recuperate it as the nonmetaphysical center of his own phenomenological project. By focusing intently on its commencement in Plato and following the example of Hegel's speculative renovation of the Platonic dialectic, Gadamer enacts his own *Destruktion* of the history of metaphysics by rethinking the monological structure of propositional logic in terms of a dialogical interpretation of the structure of language itself. Whereas Heidegger looks to Hölderlinian poetics for an implicit dismantling of Hegelian dialectic, in the third section of *Truth and Method* Gadamer attempts to liberate dialectical thinking from what he sees as its dependency on the grammar of the proposition without destroying its speculative character.[1] Rather than remaining encased in the closely circumscribed logic of the Concept, Gadamer wishes to release the dialectical movement of "*die Sache selbst*" into "the logic of question and answer" and all of the attendant contingencies and particularities of live conversation. At least two significant questions arise at this point in our discussion. The explicit question posed by Gadamer himself has to do with whether and how language can have a "speculative structure" given that he specifically rejects not only the teleological self-development of the Concept but the very vehicle of that development, the logical proposition, as the primary mode of expression for dialectical thinking. This would seem to leave very little of the dialectic intact. From the perspective of Hegel's *Logic*, in fact, Gadamer's reliance on certain "fundamental" concepts—experience, finitude, even history and language—could appear preeminently reflexive and perhaps even transcendental (i.e., Kantian). And yet Gadamer maintains that "there is something *speculative* about the hermeneutic experience," and he does not hesitate to resort to certain key Hegelian notions such as *Aufhebung* and the immanent self-movement of *die Sache selbst*.[2] But if Gadamer rejects the form of the speculative sentence as well as the development of the Concept, how can such "speculative structures" as these operate? Where does Gadamer's *Aufhebung* take place?[3] This is the question to which a short section from Part Three of *Truth and Method*, "Die Mitte der Sprache und ihre spekulative Struktur,"[4] addresses itself and one that I think is central to any attempt to clarify Gadamer's interpretation and appropriation of Hegelian dialectic. I would like to pose another, deceptively simple question, however, that lies implicit in the very title of this section and which, I think, offers a way of entering into the larger, more explicit one: namely, What does Gadamer mean by *"die Mitte" der Sprache*? But before we can occupy ourselves directly with an elaboration of these passages, we need to address Gadamer's most striking point of departure from Hegel's thinking: the hermeneutic denial of absolute knowledge.

Hegel and the Question of Finitude

The middle third of *Truth and Method* painstakingly develops the idea that as humans we find ourselves within history, and that (contra Hegel) "being historical means never being entirely exhausted in self-knowing."[5] For Gadamer all human experience is at once historically conditioned and linguistically constituted, thus "experience," as he sees it, "is experience of human finitude."[6] Obviously, from the perspective of the *Logic*, such a claim to think finitude in terms of experience would be problematic.[7] It seems to fall precisely into the hypostatizing error of the Kantian notion of understanding (*der Verstand*) or external reflection. For does not the thought of something finite, insofar as it logically entails a limit, automatically posit a beyond to that limit? And is this not precisely the Hegelian critique of Kant's "thing-in-itself"—that the very positing of a thing which cannot be made intelligible is in fact to render it intelligible? At a particular moment in the "Logic of Being," in fact, we discover that finitude contains within it the infinite and vice versa.

Having moved through the transitions from "being" to "nothing" to "becoming," the reader of the *Logic* finds him- or herself in the sphere of "determinate being" or *Dasein*. *Dasein* shows itself to be *a* determinate being or "something" insofar as its two qualities, "reality" and "negation," are reflected back into it. And yet something, as the negation of a negation, the mediation of itself with itself, is simply another form of *being* and, therefore, *in itself*, is also *becoming*, "which, however, no longer has only being and nothing for its moments."[8] This first moment, the being of something, is now a *determinate* being and its second moment "is equally a *determinate* being, but determined as a negative of the something—an *other*."[9] Both something and other, therefore, are initially determinate beings or somethings.[10] Furthermore, "the mediation through which something and other each as well *is*, as *is not*," Hegel calls "limit."[11] In other words, insofar as something *is not* its other, and the other (inasmuch as it is also something) *is not* the something that *its* other is, each is equally determined to be what it *is* in *not being* its other. And this non-being of the other (which is also the non-being of itself) is the "ceasing-to-be" or the "limit" of something in its other.[12]

But limit is itself only a preliminary moment here. For we quickly find ourselves involved in yet a further determination of "something": "Something with its immanent limit, posited as the contradiction of itself, through which it is directed and forced out of and beyond itself, is the *finite*."[13] Something, therefore, becomes determined as "finite" in that both its being and its ceasing-to-be are equally determinate and thereby come into contradiction. In the "unrest" brought about by its inability to contain the contradiction within itself *as a contradiction*, something is impelled out *beyond* itself. Hence the common notion of finitude, the conception of finitude that the understanding holds on to: A thing is finite insofar as it is limited and its very limitedness necessitates the thought of something beyond its limit. This way of thinking finitude, of course, appears to make perfect sense, and Gadamer's thinking of human finitude trades off this to a certain extent.[14]

For Hegel, however, thinking finitude in this way is not "wrong" it just remains underdetermined, incomplete. It fixes the negation of something in itself, "and it therefore stands in abrupt contrast to its affirmative."[15] The understanding, that is, while insisting on the determination of finite things as their inherent ceasing-to-be, reifies this determination, rendering it "imperishable and absolute."[16] In other words, the understanding persists in viewing that which is inherently destined to die as nonetheless eternal. However, it also places the finite in irreconcilable opposition with its other, "the infinite," and thus "[b]eing, absolute being, is ascribed to the infinite" (*Logic* 131). Thus, both the finite and the infinite are seen to be absolute. But, as we continue to think through the concept, this hypostatizing move shows itself to be untenable.

In the further development of this determination, Hegel refers to this essential limitedness of finite things as "not merely limit as such, but *limitation*," and "In order that the limit which is in something as such should be a limitation, something must at the same time in its own self transcend the limit, it must in its own self be related to the limit as something which it is not."[17] This tendency to transcend the limit, this tendency for the limit also *not* to be the limit of something, he calls "the ought." And herein lies the seed of Hegel's problem of holding on to finitude as an absolute determination: "The finite is thus inwardly self-contradictory; it sublates itself, ceases to be"; however, "in ceasing to be, the finite has not ceased to be; it has become in the first instance only *another* finite which, however, is equally a ceasing-to-be as transition into another finite, and so on to *infinity*."[18] This "and so on to infinity" is precisely the problem for Hegel, for in it the understanding shifts its false reification to the infinite. The infinite, he says, "is held [by the understanding] to be absolute without qualification for it is determined expressly as the negation of the finite, and reference is thus expressly made to limitedness in the infinite . . . and the presence of the infinite in such limitedness is denied."[19] Once again, we arrive at patently unresolved contradiction. The *in*finite wants to be *un*limited, but it is *inherently* limited insofar as it is *not* the finite. As Hegel points out, there are now "*two* determinatenesses; *there are two worlds*, one infinite and one finite, and in their relationship the infinite is only the *limit* of the finite and is thus only a determinate infinite, an *infinite which is itself finite*."[20] What the understanding forgets is that these alternating determinations of the finite and the infinite are ultimately (as indeed they have been all along) determinations of one unified something. And to view the finite and the infinite as *two* somethings (as it must inevitably do if it persists in this line of thought) is merely to reiterate, *ad infinitum*, the finitude of the infinite. The understanding overlooks the fact that "they are *inseparable*, but their *unity* is *concealed* in their *qualitative* otherness, it is the *inner* unity which only lies at their base."[21] It fails to realize that this very unity, "is itself the infinite which embraces both itself and finitude—and is therefore the infinite in a different sense from that in which the finite is regarded as separated and set apart from the infinite."[22] This second determination of the infinite, in which both the finite and the infinite sublate themselves, the infinite in which the unified finite and the unified infinite are but moments, shows itself to be the "other side," as it were, of the "spurious" and one-sided "infinite progress" of the two prior unities that is carried forth in their simple alternation.

This is not to say, however, that this new unified, "affirmative" infinite will suffice on its own either. It is only in the very process that we have been trying to elaborate here that the so-called "true" infinite emerges. After rehearsing the "double meaning" that the finite had acquired in the foregoing explication (i.e., that it is both finite and infinite at the same time), Hegel explains that

> The infinite, too, has the double meaning of being [first] *one* of these two moments—as such it is the spurious infinite—and [second] also the infinite in which both, the finite and its other, are only moments. The infinite, therefore, as now before us is, in fact, the process in which it is deposed to being only *one* of its determinations, the opposite of the finite, and so to being itself only one of the finites, and then raising this its difference from itself into the affirmation of itself and through this mediation becoming the *true* infinite.[23]

The true infinite, then, is neither the spurious infinite nor the affirmative infinite alone, but the *process* itself in which the former mediates its own transition into the latter. And, as such, the true infinite shows itself to be a further determination of *becoming*.

Even in such a brief sketch we can see that in the one-sided logic that constitutes the alternation of the finite and the infinite, back and forth "on to infinity," the understanding tries (and fails) to arrest the movement of the concept which, if allowed to unfold in terms of its own dialectical *Auslegung*, logically sublates itself in the infinite. Thus from the perspective of the "Logic of Being," Gadamer's insistence on a "simple limit" to human experience appears to be merely an artifact of the perspective of external reflection. But we must remember that, although (as with Hegel) reflexive thinking per se is problematic for Gadamer, it makes no sense to speak of it as "external." External to what? Reason? But insofar as language is at least the medium of both reflection and speculative reason, this seems to imply that language itself is "external" to reason. But reason, Gadamer would say, depends on language just as much as the understanding does. This is not to denigrate reason as such, but against the transcendental philosophy of the Enlightenment—which both Hegel and Gadamer criticize, and which claims a certain degree of independence from the words through which it is expressed—Gadamer wants to reassert the universality of language:

> For every such critique which lifts itself beyond the schematism of our statements in order to understand finds its expression once again in linguistic form. To that extent, language overtakes all challenges to its authority. Its universality *keeps pace with* the universality of reason. Hermeneutical consciousness participates here only in what constitutes the general relationship of language and reason. If all understanding stands in a necessary relation of equivalence to its possible interpretation, and if, in principle, no limits are posited for understanding, then *the linguistic inclusion* which this understanding experiences in interpretation [*Auslegung*] must also carry within itself an infinitude which surmounts all limitations. *Language is the language of reason itself.*[24]

So no thinking, for Gadamer—inasmuch as it can never escape the medium of its expression (language), and insofar as language is coextensive with reason—no thinking, reflexive or otherwise, can ever be said to occur "externally," that is to say, outside of the movement of reason. And, of course, neither can Hegel's immanent self-unfolding of reason maintain any real independence from the words (reflexive or otherwise) through which it explicates itself.

But Hegel does not simply ignore language or take it for granted; indeed, he readily acknowledges that thinking cannot occur outside of language. In the Preface to the *Logic* he tells us that "The forms of thought are, in the first instance, displayed and stored in human language."[25] More specifically, however, in the *Philosophy of Spirit* he explains that "It is in names that we think":

> Words thus attain an existence animated by thought. This existence is absolutely necessary to our thoughts. We know from our thoughts when we give them the form of *objectivity*, of *being differentiated* from our *interiority*, thus giving them the shape of *externality*, and indeed *such* an externality that bears at the same time the stamp of highest *interiority*. Only the *articulated sound*, the *word*, is something exterior that is interior in this way. Accordingly, the word gives to thoughts their highest and truest existence.[26]

And, indeed, when Hegel tells us that "*language* is exposed to the fate of serving just as much to conceal as to reveal human thought,"[27] does he not begin to sound a bit like Gadamer or even Heidegger? We should bear in mind, however, that the inverse would *not* hold true for Hegel as it would for Gadamer or Heidegger—namely, that human thought is also thus fated to concealment. For it would be "ridiculous," Hegel says, "to regard as a defect of thought and a misfortune, the fact that it is tied to the word."[28] On the other hand, neither are the words themselves at fault when one fails to comprehend something. For it is always possible (and perhaps even inevitable) that "a defective, undetermined, contentless thinking"[29] will try to express itself, and of course the only way that it can do so is through words. However, for what Hegel calls "true thinking" (and certainly speculative reason must fall under this rubric), the word is fully capable of conveying the "true thought" as the matter [*die Sache*] of thinking; thus, insofar as "intelligence fulfills itself with words," as he puts it, "it takes the nature of the matter up into itself."[30] That is to say that via the "externality" of the word—as a mere sign, as a medium—intelligence is able to "interiorize" the subject matter. Therefore, even though thought is inseparable from the word, language (as a "system of signs"[31]) does not determine the course of "true thinking" within it, but remains at the surface as its mere outward manifestation.

It is particularly in this talk of the "exteriority" of the word, however, that Hegel and Gadamer part company. For, as Gadamer says in his essay, "Die Idee der Hegelschen Logik,"

> Language is not a transitional form of thinking reason which completes itself in full transparency of the thought. It is not a vanishing and transient medium of thought or its mere "casing." And its essence does not in general limit itself to merely making plain what has been thought. Rather, the thought first gains its determinate existence in that it is composed in words.[32]

Of course, as we have pointed out, for Hegel, too, thoughts gain their existence in words; but as a system of signs, as a mere medium for thought, Hegel construes language instrumentally, as a means (*das Mittel*) that reason deploys for its own ends as it sees fit. In the *Aesthetics*, in fact, on declaring that poetry "can be translated into other languages without significant detriment to its value,"[33] Hegel emphasizes this instrumentality in no uncertain terms:

> Spirit thus becomes objective to itself on its own ground and has the linguistic element only as a *means* [*nur als Mittel*], partly as communication and partly as the immediate externality from which, as from out of a *mere sign* [*als aus einem bloßen Zeichen*], from the very beginning [*von Hause aus*] it has withdrawn back into itself.[34]

For Gadamer, however, "spirit" could never sufficiently divorce itself from its ontological rootedness in language such that it could "withdraw into itself"—as if its "self" were something entirely other than language. Language, for Gadamer as for Heidegger, is indeed "the house of being." Hence Gadamer's basic problem with the Hegelian dialectic as it is played out in the *Logic*: It takes its own linguisticality, its imbeddedness in language to be essentially transparent and ultimately inconsequential. For, as Hegel says in the *Philosophy of Spirit*, "Language here comes under discussion only in the particular determinateness of a product of intelligence for manifesting its representations in an external medium."[35]

All of this, however (as Gadamer himself tries to show), does not invalidate the dialectical movement of reason; but neither does it obviate the problem of thinking finitude. For would not "reason"—even if we admitted to its rootedness in language, and particularly if it has pretensions to being "speculative"—would not reason still insist on the self-sublation of the finite? In fact, does not Gadamer's own thinking of a "linguistic inclusion which . . . carries within itself *an infinitude which surmounts all limitations*" necessarily and logically collapse of its own speculative weight? This would certainly hold true if for Gadamer the speculative movement of reason restricted itself necessarily to the dialectic of the concept, to the totalizing system of the *Logic*. But in his insistence on this fundamental finitude that relates itself dialectically to an equally fundamental infinite, Gadamer is not pretending to identify Hegel's critique of finitude and the so-called spurious or bad infinite as a point where the "Logic of Being" breaks down. Indeed, one of the things that Gadamer appreciates most about both the *Logic* and the *Phenomenology* is that in their own terms they are quite successful in demonstrating the collapse of the subject-object distinction that undergirds the tradition of reflexive thinking. Gadamer's preference for the bad infinite indicates rather his own Heideggerian orientation toward the inescapable historicity and the radical finitude of human *Dasein*[36]—an orientation that precludes Gadamer from following the "letter" of his own view of

Hegel's dialectic (i.e., the derivation of the categories according to a logic based on the speculative sentence), but perhaps not its "spirit" (i.e., the structure and movement of speculation in general). Thus we have Gadamer reading Hegel against himself in much the same way that Heidegger reads Aristotle against himself. That is, they both dismantle the metaphysical aspects of these traditionary texts and extract from them what they find phenomenologically and hermeneutically valuable. The irony, of course, is that Gadamer is able to read Hegel in a nonmetaphysical way precisely because he listens so closely to Heidegger. The full extent of this counter-turning reading of Hegel, however, will only become really clear to us once we have engaged Gadamer's at once Platonic, Hegelian, and Heideggerian notion of "*die Mitte der Sprache.*"

Gadamer and the "Spirit" of Hegel

The first occurrence of "*die Mitte*" comes at the very end of the second division of *Truth and Method* as Gadamer makes the transition from "historicity" (*Geschichtlichkeit*) to "linguisticality" (*Sprachlichkeit*). "Every conversation," he writes, "presupposes a common language, or better: it develops a common language from within. This is because something is laid down in the middle [*in die Mitte niedergelegt*] . . . in which both conversation partners participate and about which they exchange with one another."[37] We see here a striking difference from Hegel's usual employment, in the *Logic*, of "*die Mitte*" as the logical "middle term" between two polar "extremes" that allows for the sublation of these opposites. Of course, as we have already pointed out, Gadamer is speaking here of what he will call "dialectic" as it occurs in living dialogue between two people (or between a person and a text) rather than of a strictly logical dialectic based on the grammar of the speculative proposition. But this is precisely the sharp divergence that will allow Gadamer to maintain a certain connection to Hegel. (And we should by no means assume that Hegel's formal use of the "middle term" will go unexploited by Gadamer.)

At this point in the text we do not yet have a direct identity between language and this "middle" between interlocutors. In the next subsection, however, in fact on the very next page, we find that "Language is the middle [*die Mitte*] in which the coming-to-an-understanding of the partners [*die Verständigung der Partner*] and agreement about the subject matter [*die Sache*] carry themselves out [*sich . . . vollzieht*]."[38] I have deliberately employed a more literal translation of the reflexive verb, "*sich . . . vollzieht*" (usually rendered with the passive, "is carried out" or "is accomplished") because it focuses our attention on an important aspect of something Gadamer has been developing for several hundred pages and will continue to develop throughout the text—that the play of conversation and the movement of *die Sache* (much like—but also essentially different from—the movement of the Concept for Hegel) is an immanent process that is not dependent on the external impositions or reflections of an acting subject, but quite literally "carries itself out."[39] And if (at least at this point) language as *die Mitte* is the locus of this self-movement or the medium in which it occurs, we can already begin to discern "something speculative" about what Gadamer calls the "occurring of the hermeneutic experience."[40]

The actual phrase in question ("*die Mitte der Sprache*") makes its appearance directly on the heels of a discussion of medieval Christian theology. Here Gadamer further develops the relationship of reason and language in terms of what he sees as the primary advance of Scholastic philosophy over the Greeks: To think "the unity of thinking and speaking"—the unity, that is, of the Greek conception of *logos*, insofar as it designates something like "reason" [*Vernunft*], and the Latin *Verbum*, the "Word" of the Incarnation. Indeed, it is from out of this particular historical horizon that the unity of reason and language establishes itself as point of continuity, a consistent and significant moment in the movement of the philosophical tradition that Gadamer follows.[41] But the real impact of this moment is not developed explicitly by Augustine or Aquinas. Gadamer himself points out that "The inner unity of thinking and speaking to oneself which corresponds to the Trinitarian mystery of the Incarnation implies that the interior word of the mind *is not formed through a reflexive act*. . . . For the word does not express the mind, but rather the subject matter intended [*die gemeinte Sache*]."[42] He thus draws an inference for hermeneutics that begins to look toward (and perhaps even beyond) his appropriation of Hegel insofar as what Plato referred to as "the dialogue of the soul with itself" shows itself to be *inherently* and *generally* nonreflexive.[43]

As a consequence of thinking through this Scholastic encounter with the Greeks, Gadamer introduces us to "*die Mitte der Sprache*" as a fundamental way of conceiving language, albeit only in its preliminary historical and philosophical determination, according to its mediating role in the Incarnation event as interpreted by medieval theology:

> *In the middle of the penetration of Christian theology by the Greek conception of logic, something new begins to show itself: The middle of language in which the Mediation* [das Mittlertum] *of the occurrence of the Incarnation first brings itself to its full truth.* Christology turns out to be the pioneer of a new anthropology which mediates in a new way the spirit of humanity in its finitude with the divine infinite. Here, what we have called the hermeneutic experience will find its proper ground.[44]

The hermeneutic experience, then, will "find its proper ground" in the "middle of language," which is not something separable from reason. Language, in other words, "is the language of reason itself." But we find another important foreshadowing of speculation here in that language (as the "Word") performs a sort of nascent ontological mediation between the divine infinite and finite mortality, between the "One" of God and the "many" of creation. Thus, even though Hegel's speculative dialectic has yet to make an appearance in the text, we see here a crucial move for Gadamer in that his insistence on the primacy of language and what he calls the "dialectic of the question"[45] will leave neither reason nor being behind.

In the opening paragraphs of "The Middle of Language and its Speculative Structure," Gadamer reiterates two primary moments in the development of philosophical hermeneutics: namely, that "the all-determining ground [of the hermeneutic phenomenon] is the *finitude of our historical experience*" and that "language is the mark of human finitude."[46] But here we can begin to discern more clearly the speculative path along which Gadamer's thinking is moving. He tells us here explicitly that "It is *the middle of language* from out of which our entire world-experience and, in particular, the hermeneutic experience unfolds itself."[47] And even more emphatically, "It is the middle of language *alone*," he declares, "which, related to the whole of that-which-is [*das Ganze des Seienden*], mediates the finite-historical essence of humanity with itself and with the world."[48] The posing of the question concerning the speculative structure of hermeneutic occurrence, then, is preceded by and grounded in "*die Mitte der Sprache.*" More important, however, language begins to show itself here not just as the medial ground of the unity of thinking and speaking, but as actively carrying out a dialectical mediation between human finitude and "*das Ganze des Seienden*" which allows this unfolding to occur. But precisely how does Gadamer conceive of "the speculative" and to what extent does it approximate Hegelian speculative dialectic?

Although critical of what he takes to be the strict systematic methodology of Hegel's *Logic*, Gadamer by no means dismisses the speculative proposition as wrong or somehow irrelevant. Quite to the contrary, in this very subsection of *Truth and Method* he quotes Hegel extensively in this regard. In the Preface to the *Phenomenology*, Hegel criticizes the understanding for two different "habits" of thought to which it falls prey and the respective failure of these two habits to take on "the strenuous effort of the Concept."[49] On the one hand, the problem with the habit of "*Vorstellungen*" (or "picture-thinking," as Miller translates it) which, he says, "should be called material thinking, a contingent consciousness that is absorbed only in material stuff" is that it "finds it hard work to lift the self clear of such matter, and to be with itself alone."[50] On the other hand (at what he calls the "opposite extreme"), purely formal argumentation, which "adopts a negative attitude toward the content it apprehends" and sees itself as "freedom from all content,"[51] falls prey to its own negativity. For, as Hegel points out, "That something is not the case, is a merely negative insight, a dead end which does not lead to a new content beyond itself."[52] What is lacking here is the realization that "the negative belongs to the content itself, and is the *positive*, both as the immanent movement and determination of the content, and as the whole of this process."[53] Neither of these modes of reflection allows the inherent logic of rational thought to take its own course. The first, "picture-thinking," attempts to impose certain external constraints on thinking that it either inherits as given or draws from its seemingly apparent surroundings, whereas the second, formalistic ratiocination, shuts thinking down just as effectively by holding fast to the apparent freedom of arbitrary refutation.

The essential limitation of all such modes of thought is that they cling to a particular structure in which a subject term is posited as a base to which a variety of accidents or predicates is attached, and from which the movement of thinking runs back and forth. In so doing, it either abstracts from or disregards the original subject, the knowing 'I' itself. Speculative thinking, however, does not take the concept to be "a passive Subject inertly supporting the Accidents."[54] What was conceived as the subject term actually passes over into its predicate: "[I]t enters into the differences and the content and constitutes the determinateness, i.e. the differentiated content and its movement instead of remaining inertly over against it."[55] Thus the subject is no longer anchored in opposition to its predicate, but the entire sentence becomes a proposition of identity between the two according to the speculative function of the copula. The predicate is no longer merely an attribute of the subject but expresses its essence. However, as Hegel quickly points out, "the identification of the Subject and Predicate is not meant to destroy the difference between them, which the form of the proposition expresses; their unity, rather, is meant to emerge as a harmony."[56] Consequently, the radical difference posited between the two terms in predication is destroyed in the speculative movement of the content while the formal difference is preserved, at least insofar as it is still expressed as a proposition.

Gadamer recognizes the importance of this rethinking of the logical proposition and draws on it heavily for his hermeneutical project. He follows Hegel's distinction between representational thinking (*Vorstellungen*) and conceptual thinking and even quotes from the Preface at length in order to pinpoint what he calls "the speculative essence of all philosophy."[57] He explains that, for Hegel, "the philosophical proposition is a judgment only with respect to its external form," and, rather than being a simple act of predication, it "expresses the truth of the subject in the form of the predicate" (GW1, 470). Instead of moving out beyond the subject to its various predicates at will (and here Gadamer quotes Hegel directly), thinking

> suffers, as we might put it, a counter-thrust [*Gegenstoß*]. Starting from the subject as though this were a permanent ground, it finds that, since the Predicate is really the Substance, the Subject has passed over into the Predicate, and, by this very fact, has been sublated; and, since in this way what seems to be the Predicate has become the whole and independent mass, *thinking cannot roam at will, but is impeded by this weight*.[58]

For Gadamer, this "counter-thrust," this moment of sublation that holds thinking in check to the extent that it allows the subject matter (*die Sache*) to move according to its own consequences, is precisely what is common to all dialectical speculation, both ancient and modern. (For that matter, can we not hear an echo of the Hegelian *Gegen-stoß* in Heidegger's Hölderlinian *Gegen-wendung*?)

The problem for Gadamer (and we will explore this more fully as we proceed) is that, in its emphasis on derivation and strict logical deduction, this propositional logic remains just as one-sided, in its own way, as the predicative logic of the judgment that it implicitly criticizes and subsumes. Gadamer wants, in a certain sense, to bring the Hegelian critique of reflexive thinking to bear on Hegel's own speculative dialectic—not that it is somehow wrong or inherently untrue, just that it remains one-sided and ultimately incomplete as long as it fails to take account of its own linguisticality. This, of course, would be an entirely unsatisfactory objection to raise for the Hegelian, who would point out that Gadamer employs a series of categories in his critique (including "linguisticality" and "finitude") that he does not account for logically, thereby simply reviving the necessity of the critical project. But from the perspective of philosophical hermeneutics the critical project itself would seem to rest on the (unwarranted) assumption that its own language is simply a transparent medium, a tool, that it can employ quite unproblematically and unequivocally.[59] Far from denying the immanent self-movement of reason, however, by emphasizing the linguisticality of all human experience, Gadamer wishes simply to release it into the less formal yet no less powerful self-movement (or play) of the dialogue (*das Gespräch*)—release it, that is, from the logic of the proposition into what he refers to as "the logic of question and answer."

"The intimate relation that displays itself between question and answer," writes Gadamer, "gives the hermeneutic experience its true dimension."[60] There is a moment in the happening of understanding when the actual meaning of whatever is meant (be it stated or written) has yet to be determined. This is not to say that what is intended is meaningless, simply that its "truth-possibility" remains, for the moment, suspended—that is, it is placed *in question*. And "such bringing-into-suspension," says Gadamer, "is the proper and original essence of questioning. Questioning always allows the possibilities of a situation to be seen in suspension."[61] Questioning, in other words, does for the hermeneutical process of understanding what the speculative proposition does for Hegelian logic. For Hegel, as a series of propositions is allowed to develop, the immanent self-movement of the Concept is allowed to unfold. Similarly, for Gadamer, the questioning which occurs in any genuine dialogue, by suspending all merely arbitrary impositions—external impositions, that is, which are intended specifically to disrupt the possibility of understanding, such as, perhaps, certain dogmatic displays or demagoguery in which an interlocutor refuses to put his or her own agenda at risk—such questioning allows the subject matter to unfold according to its own consequences. What determines the course of this self-movement is the matter's own historical situatedness as it fuses with the historical horizon of the interlocutors. Thus, for Gadamer, "all understanding is always more than merely an after-effect of an unfamiliar intention. Insofar as it questions, it lays open possibilities of meaning, and what is meaningful passes over with it into one's own meaning."[62] And in this "passing over" of meaning from one side to the other in the play of the conversation, we have our first indication of a hermeneutical *Aufhebung*. Gadamer's *Aufhebung*, then, is essentially the happening of understanding itself that occurs only in the course of dialogue—whether it be between two people or between a person and a text—in the logic of question and answer. That such a "logic" could be considered "dialectical" in the Socratic or Platonic sense (at least insofar as it occurs in and through dialogical engagement) is not too difficult to see, but the extent to which it corresponds to Hegel's refinement of Greek dialectic and precisely to what extent it therein becomes "speculative," is a question that we still need to explore in more detail.

We have already alluded to the fact that Gadamer's dialectic looks back beyond Hegel toward their mutual source of inspiration in the so-called negative dialectic of the Platonic dialogues and beyond and through these to the thinking of Parmenides. This, for Gadamer, is precisely the origin and locus of his own proximity to Hegel. "The Greeks have something over us," he writes, for

> [t]hey did not seek to establish the objectivity of knowledge from out of subjectivity and for it. Their thinking saw itself from the beginning as a moment of being itself. Parmenides glimpsed in it the most important signpost on the way to the truth of being. Dialectic, this transpiring of the *logos*, was not for the Greeks, as we have emphasized, a movement which thinking carries out, but rather a movement of the matter itself [*Bewegung der Sache selbst*] which thinking is able to experience. That such a turn of phrase sounds like Hegel bespeaks no false modernization but bears witness, rather, to an historical context. In the situation of modern thinking that we have characterized, Hegel has consciously taken up the model of Greek dialectic. . . . His dialectic of thought-determinations as well as his dialectic of the forms of knowledge

> repeat in explicit fulfillment the total mediation of thinking and being that was formerly the natural element of Greek thought.[63]

As Gadamer sees it, Hegel detected something in ancient Greek dialectic that was absent in the reflexive methodology of the Enlightenment, namely, "[a] subject matter unfolding according to its own consequences," to which belongs "the holding at bay of ideas 'that tend to insert themselves' and the persevering of the consequences of the thought."[64] Hegel, of course, goes beyond the traditional view of Platonic and Eleatic dialectic in which a "mere opinion" or an idea of some kind contradicts itself in the course of the reasoning and thereby collapses. But what is significant for Gadamer is that this dialectical movement occurs dialogically, according to the logic of the question, rather than monologically, according to the logic of the proposition. And yet this dialogical dialectic is nevertheless "speculative," at least to the extent that it relies "entirely on the force of thinking and does not allow the self-evidence of appearances to obtain."[65] But at first glance this explanation does not seem very satisfactory. Insofar as the dialogical movement of *die Sache selbst* is not oriented toward a logically determinable future, then philosophical hermeneutics would not seem to be all that speculative. Gadamer, however, retains the term "speculative"—a term, by the way, which Heidegger would find far too metaphysically laden—because it also refers to the self-movement of the Concept, and Gadamer wishes to retrieve precisely this self-moving aspect of thinking, albeit into a phenomenologically different context.

But the dialogical movement of the Platonic dialectic also represents the point at which Gadamer differentiates himself from both Hegel and Plato. No matter how "speculative" Gadamer's rethinking of the conversational dialectic may show itself to be, it still proceeds, in much the same way as Hegel's logic, according to a methodology that divorces itself from the general linguisticality of human world-experience. It still suffers, as Gadamer puts from "the subordination of language to the 'statement.' "[66] For Gadamer, that is, neither the Platonic nor the Hegelian dialectic unfold themselves explicitly from out of "*die Mitte der Sprache.*" Their speculative movement is restricted to a series of written statements and does not occur in the context of what he calls "*die lebendige Virtualität des Sprechens*" wherein the activity of *die Sache selbst* becomes manifest as "the accomplishing of meaning, as the occurring of discourse, of intelligibility, of understanding."[67] In this dialogical dialectic, language *qua* language sublates itself as it allows what is finitely spoken to resonate "with an infinitude of what is unsaid in the unity of one meaning and allows it thus to become understood."[68] Thus, following Heidegger, Gadamer appeals to the unsaid, to the resonance of the entire field of meaning behind what is spoken, that is, to human linguisticality.[69]

But perhaps a more difficult and fundamental divergence from Hegel happens with respect to the question of a beginning. As we have seen, Gadamer's hermeneutical approach insists that human experience is always already linguistically determined and historically situated. Therefore, any philosophizing is essentially an interpreting that cannot separate itself from both the present moment *and* the tradition that the interpretation puts into question. Furthermore, as Gadamer tells us, "This is not a regrettable distortion that detracts from the purity of understanding, but the condition of its [i.e., understanding's] possibility, which we characterize as the hermeneutic situation."[70] From Hegel's perspective, such a statement would appear patently transcendental. But for Gadamer it accounts for the very possibility of any rational discourse, Hegelian or otherwise, and has the added virtue of never encountering the problem of a beginning such as occurs for Hegel at the start of the *Logic*.[71] This is not to say that Hegel does not adequately deal with the question of a beginning. His claim to a "presuppositionless" start for the *Logic* might be accounted for by, among other things, simply appealing to the utter indeterminacy of the concept of being, or perhaps by seeing the collapse of the distinction between being and thought at the end of the *Phenomenology* as an "enabling condition" for the *Logic* rather than a logical presupposition. My point is just that, insofar as Gadamer is not attempting to lay out an airtight logical system, the question of beginning never really arises—unless, that is, one insists on raising what I take to be the pseudoproblem of relativism, which itself assumes the validity and necessity of logical categories.[72]

These difficulties notwithstanding, however, Gadamer's appropriation of Hegelian dialectic shows itself in the mediating ontological role that language plays in the happening of understanding. Just as the *Phenomenology of Spirit* allows the *Science of Logic* to work by first demonstrating the original unity of thinking and being, Gadamer argues that language shows itself to be "a middle in which I and world join themselves together, or better: present themselves in their original belonging-together."[73] And this "middle of language" exhibits itself in the logic of the question, the essence of which is to allow for the activity of *die Sache selbst* such that the actual act of interpretation sublates itself as the "coming into language of meaning."[74] The ontological effect of this movement is such that "[w]hoever speaks is comporting himself speculatively insofar as his words do not portray beings, but rather express and allow a relation to the whole of being [*zum Ganzen des Seins*] to come to language."[75] Thus we can see not only the Heideggerian aspect of the hermeneutic experience here (i.e., that it shows itself ontologically rather than ontically), but the Hegelian aspect also, in that the speculative structure of interpretation consists precisely in this coming-to-language. More than simply allowing for this ontological activity of the matter itself, however, insofar as it allows for the presentation of this "relation to the whole of being,"

> Coming-to-language does not mean that a second existence is acquired. What something presents itself as [*Als was sich etwas darstellt*] belongs to its own being [*Sein*]. It is thus a question, with all that is language, of a speculative unity, a distinction in itself between being [*sein*] and presenting itself, a distinction which is also precisely not a distinction.[76]

Thus we seem to come full-circle back to the dialectical function of the speculative proposition—the sublating of differences such that the difference is preserved in a new identity. The dual role of the middle of language in this speculative movement is to be at once the *medium* in which the "objectivity" of *die Sache selbst* and the "subjectivity" of historical consciousness occur as well as *the middle term* between the extremes of I and world that, in the act of sublating itself, allows the difference between them to be maintained in the identity that is the hermeneutic experience. Ultimately, however, Gadamer does not view even Hegel's propositional logic as being entirely at odds with his own logic of the question. Rather, his view of the speculative sentence comes across as a sort of logical condensation of the consequences of thinking from out of *die Mitte der Sprache*. For even though Gadamer's hermeneutical project is essentially a critique of the philosophical truth-claims of systematic methodologies, he nevertheless recognizes that

> the primordiality of the conversation, as of the relatedness of question and answer, shows itself even in such an extreme case as when it presents itself as a philosophical method in

> Hegelian dialectic. To unfold the totality of thought-determinations as it was the concern of Hegel's logic, is, as it were, the attempt to come to terms in the great monologue of modern "method" with the continuum of meaning, each particular instance of which produces what is articulated in conversation. When Hegel poses for himself the task of making abstract thought-determinations fluid and infusing them with spirit, this means that logic, by virtue of the meaning of words, fuses the concept back into the accomplished form of language—a magnificent reminder, even in failure, of what dialectic authentically was and is. Hegel's dialectic is a monologue of thinking that wants to carry out in advance what ripens little by little in each genuine dialogue.[77]

Even if one attends closely to its Hegelian dimensions, however, Gadamer's dialogical hermeneutics might still look rather one-sided. His insistence on retaining such heavily laden words as "speculation" and "consciousness" could make his project look like an attempt to find a complementary epistemology for Heideggerian ontology—a project that Heidegger would obviously reject as being too subject-bound and therefore still inescapably metaphysical. But this appearance fades quickly when one realizes that Gadamer's temporal/historical way of conceiving human consciousness (or as I refer to it, "being-conscious" *Bewußt-sein*) arises directly from the profoundly ontological conception of understanding (*Verstehen*) that Heidegger provides in *Being and Time*. For Gadamer as for Heidegger, understanding, rather than being some mechanical activity of the mind, is *Dasein*'s mode of being-in-the-world. Aside from their diverging paths—one moving evasively away from the metaphysical tradition, the other moving directly back into dialogue with it—the real difference between them is one of emphasis: Gadamer focuses not on being itself or human being per se, but on human being-*conscious* as an event, a process, a temporal and historical phenomenon that occurs in and through the "middle of language." That is to say that, for Gadamer, language is a "middle" in a sense roughly analogous to the middle term in a logical syllogism or in a Hegelian dialectical transition. On the one hand, this sense of middle—the middle that language is ("*die Mitte der Sprache*," objective genitive)—thinks language in its role as that which mediates the ontological movement of revealing and concealing that constitutes the happening of understanding in the course of human dialogical encounters. *Da-sein* and *Bewußt-sein*, in other words, are both essentially linguistic and temporal and, therefore, finite. On the other hand, being and understanding always occur within a linguistic milieu, from within or out of the middle of language ("*die Mitte der Sprache,*" subjective genitive) thought as the phenomenological location, the playing field, as it were, upon which understanding and being reveal themselves in the play of conversation. Hence—precisely at this moment of the most extreme distanciation from his famous mentor—Gadamer, too, thinks the *Wesen* of both being and language in essentially topological terms. But since his project is more implicitly than explicitly ontological, Gadamer refrains from overt pronouncements about the character of being itself other than to say that "being that can be understood is language." Let us, however, allow Heidegger's more poetic equivalent, "language is the house of being," to lead us briefly back once more into the topological middle of both language and being.

The Middle of Language : The Middle of Being

As we have already glimpsed with the "Ister" lectures discussed above, throughout Heidegger's *Gesamtausgabe,* but most evidently in the works on language and poetry, one finds repeated invocations that, were it not for their Heideggerian context, one would naturally take to be metaphors functioning as surrogates for underlying philosophical concepts. A number of these discussions are centered around particular words and phrases (such as "path," "clearing," "dwelling," "the house of being," and even "the regions" of the fourfold) which evoke images of places, locations, sites. These "topological" words and phrases, however, are not to be construed as metaphorical constructs, but as various ways in which being reveals (and conceals) itself in language. They indicate, in other words, not the dialectical movement of concepts but various places in which we might discern the movement or the turning (*die Kehre*)—one might even say the *counter*-turning (*die Gegen-wendung*)—in being itself. Heidegger recognizes that thinking need not remain locked into its traditional role as the proper object and mode of epistemology (hence metaphysics). Taking its cue from a nonphilosophical mode of addressing being, that is, poetizing (*Dichten*), thinking (*Denken*) can perhaps rethink its own relation to being. *Dichten,* in other words (and, most particularly, Hölderlin's poetizing), allows Heidegger to release *Denken* from the two-dimensional straitjacket of logical exposition into the multidimensional openness of a topological phenomenology.

Let us return for a moment to Section 19 of Heidegger's lectures on Hölderlin's hymn "The Ister," to a place in the text where he specifically thematizes the relationship between thinking and poetizing. In this particular section we find Heidegger referring poetically and topologically not, as Gadamer does, to *language* but to *being* as *die Mitte.* Upon asserting the intrinsic equivocality of the ancient Greek poetic work ("The Greeks had a 'natural' ear for the unsaid in what is said, and they thought and spoke from out of the unsaid"[78]), Heidegger invokes Fragment 7 of the Pythagorean, Philolaos:

> That which essentially unfolds [*das Wesende*] as originary harmony, the unifying One, in the middle of the sphere, is called "hearth."

Heidegger's commentary on this fragment thus brings him (and us) back into the general vicinity of the Gadamerian middle:

> Accordingly, the hearth is the middle of that which is [*die Mitte des Seienden*], to which all of what is, precisely because and insofar as it is what is, remains originarily related. This hearth-ly middle of that which is is being. Being is the hearth. For the essence of being for the Greeks is *phusis*—that lighting [*Leuchten*] that proceeds from out of itself, that is mediated by nothing else, but is itself the middle. This middle is that which originarily remains and gathers everything around itself—that wherein all of what is has its place and, as that which is, is at home [*als das Seiende heimisch ist*].[79]

For Heidegger, then, being, as *phusis* and the hearth, is *die Mitte*—at least in this particular context (the continuation of his reading of the choral ode in *Antigone*). Heidegger even refers to the choral ode itself as the "innermost middle" or the "essential middle" of the "poetic work of tragedy as poetic work."[80] And the poetic work, as middle, is (to put it in Gadamerian terms) essentially linguistic. The chorus, he tells us, is "that which is to be poetized" [*das zu Dichtende*],[81] and "That which is poetically to be said is the poetic truth. The poetically true word is that word that poetically names that which is."[82] Having thus brought the poetic middle of tragedy (i.e., "that which is to be poetized") directly into the realm of language—or at least into the realm of what is said (*das Sagende*), "that word which poetically names that which is"—Heidegger completes the circle of *die Mitte* with one last pronouncement: "What essentially unfolds [*west*] as that-which-is-to-be-poetized [*das Zu-Dichtende*]," he tells us, "cannot be a being [*ein Seiendes*]. That-which-is-to-be-poetized, that which essentially unfolds in the poetic work, is never that which is, but being [*Sein*]."[83] For Heidegger, therefore, the middle shows itself poetically (as the hearth) to be both ontologically and linguistically constituted—effectively the same constitution as Gadamer's *Mitte*, but with a special emphasis on being (*Sein*). We should recall, however, that Gadamer's *Mitte der Sprache* names a phenomenological occurrence, a dynamic happening. Lest we complacently allow ourselves, then, to see Heidegger's *Mitte des Seins* as a mere metaphor that simply represents or refers to the essence of being in a way that makes it into a calcified concept, we would do well to look briefly at another Heideggerian reference to *die Mitte* from earlier in the same text.

In section 6, as cited above, Heidegger begins to draw out the notion of the counter-turning relationship of humans to being itself in terms of Hölderlin's poetic rivers as both journeying and locality. This time Heidegger invokes the opening strophes of another poem, "Voice of the People":

> Um unsre Weisheit unbekümmert
> Rauschen die Ströme doch auch, and dennoch
>
> Wer liebt sie nicht? und immer bewegen sie
> Das Herz mir, hör ich ferne die Schwindenden
> Die Ahnungsvollen, meine Bahn nicht
> Aber gewisser ins Meer hin eilen.
>
> Unconcerned with our wisdom
> The rivers still rush on, and yet
>
> Who loves them not? And always do they move
> My heart, when afar I hear them vanishing
> Full of intimation, hastening along not
> My path, yet more surely seaward.[84]

Here Heidegger interprets the simultaneous journeying and locality which the rivers are as a concurrent locating and dislocating of the middle of human life. "[T]here is," he writes,

> indeed a belonging to the rivers, a going along with them. It is precisely that which tears onward more surely in the rivers' own path that tears human beings out of the habitual middle [*der gewöhnlichen Mitte*] of their lives, so that they may be in a center [*einem Zentrum*] outside of themselves, that is, be excentric. The prelude to inhering in the ex-centric middle of human existence [*der exzentrischen Mitte des menschlichen Seins*], this "centric" and "central" abode in the ex-centric, is love. The sphere proper to standing in the ex-centric middle of life is death.[85]

Die Mitte, in other words, is not seen simply as a the static location of being or of human being, but as itself a counter-turning movement. For Heidegger, the river is at once "love" in that it draws human beings out of the "habitual middle of their lives" (presumably the mode of existence of "*das Man*" within the oblivion of being) into "the sphere proper to standing in the ex-centric middle of life," that is, into a genuine relation to being (human "being toward death") that is nevertheless still not a dwelling directly within the sphere of being itself. The river is at once the centrality and ex-centricity of human being, the ex-centric middle of—a counter-turning within—human existence. If we therefore see this dwelling that is not a dwelling in terms of an "un-homely" being at home, then we can connect this earlier discussion to the later interpretation (in Sophocles' choral ode) of *das Unheimliche* as the hearth, as "the innermost middle of the poetic work of tragedy." The hearth, then, the topological "middle of being," can also be seen as a counter-turning movement rather than a static location.

And so, with Heidegger we find a convergence of poetizing and thinking in a dynamic topological middle, the phenomenological and poetological domain of both language and being. Thinking, for Heidegger, no longer remains tied to the philosophical concept, but releases itself into the nondialectical movement of what is both spoken and remains unspoken in the tragic choral ode. This, of course, is not an explicitly dialogical phenomenon; the song of the chorus in Greek tragedy, in fact, often seems to be a monologue almost entirely unrelated to the dialogue of the actors. We should remind ourselves, however, that Heidegger's places his entire interpretation within and effectively recapitulates Hölderlin's dialogue with the Greeks, the dialogue between "the foreign" and "one's own." But, if we wish to find a more direct convergence of Heidegger's poetic thinking with Gadamer's ontological notion of dialogue, we need not look far for a specific reference by Heidegger to the dialogical character of human being.

In section 7 of Heidegger's lecture course, *Hölderlin's Hymns "Germania" and "The Rhine"*,[86] we find a subsection entitled "The Being of Humans as Dialogue." The immediate focus of Heidegger's interest here is the following fragment of an untitled poem by Hölderlin:

> Viel hat erfahren der Mensch.
> Der Himmlischen viele genannt,
> Seit ein Gespräch wir sind
> Und hören können voneinander.
>
> Much has humanity experienced.
> And named many of the divine,
> Since we are a dialogue
> And can listen to one another.[87]

Heidegger's attention is drawn to the third line: "*We are a dialogue.* What should this mean? That language constitutes, determines, our being."[88] A little later, he elaborates:

> We are—a linguistic occurrence [*ein Sprachgeschehnis*], and this occurrence is temporal, but not only in the external sense that it flows away into the time according to which beginning, duration, and cessation in each case are measurable, but rather the linguistic occurrence is the commencement and ground of the authentic historical time of human beings. This dialogue does not commence some time or other within a flowing away of 'historical' events, but rather: since such dialogue occurs, it *is,* generally speaking, time and history. But this commencing dialogue is poetizing, and "poetically dwells / man upon this earth" ("In the lovely blue . . . ," VI, 25, V, 32 f.) His *Da-sein* has its standing ground as historical in the dialogue of poetizing.[89]

Poetizing, in other words, is inherently dialogical, and human *Dasein* occurs linguistically within this dialogue. Except for saying that "man dwells poetically," such a formulation comes extremely close to Gadamer's notion of the linguisticality (*Sprachlichkeit*) of the hermeneutic situation. But here, too, Heidegger takes pains to complicate this dialogical interpretation of human *Dasein*—it, too, takes on the character of a counter-turning. We are a dialogue but, at the same time, "not yet *the dialogue itself*."[90] In the first instance, we are genuinely dialogical in the sense of poetic dwelling:

> Our being [*Seyn*] occurs as dialogue, in the occurrence of the fact that the gods address us, place us under their claim [*Anspruch*], *bring us to language*, whether and how we are, how we answer, accept or deny [*zu-sagen oder versagen*] to them our being. Our being occurs, consequently, as dialogue insofar as we, thus eloquently addressed/claimed, bring to language beings [*das Seiende*] as such, open up beings in what and how they are, but also at the same time veil and conceal them. Only where language occurs do being and not-being open themselves. We ourselves are this opening and veiling.[91]

And this implies that we are "equiprimordially" a dialogue not only when we are speaking to one another, but also when we are not actively engaged in speech, insofar as we are "a keeping silent." But we also occur dialogically in terms of mere conversation, idle talk (*Gerede*). This Heidegger refers to as "the essence of dialogue to which non-essence necessarily belongs."[92] We could perhaps say, then, that we find ourselves dwelling as a dialogical counter-turning: insofar as we can never entirely escape idle talk, we are at home in *not* being at home within language as poetic dialogue. Heidegger thereby defeats the reader's reductionistic impulses. We must, he says, "exhaust the entire riskiness [*Gefährlichkeit*] of language in order to experience what the linguistic occurrence, the dialogue, is *as what we are*. We are an historically initiated and thus historically concluded dialogue as the most violent word, as poetizing, as remaining silent,—as idle chatter."[93] We dwell dialogically, in other words, not just in deep philosophical discussions, but in all kinds of vocalizing—even in remaining silent.

But neither does the dialogical and dialectical character of language occur, for Gadamer, only within the context of some pristinely deferential conversation. At the heart (or "hearth"?) of philosophical hermeneutics lies the notion of the "living virtuality of language" (*die lebendige Virtualität des Sprechens*) in which the whole of what is unsaid in living speech of any kind reverberates in the essential multivocity of what is actually spoken. In other words, Gadamer's interpretation of the fundamental linguisticality of human being-conscious is constituted by the same phenomenological structure or movement of revealing and concealing, the same ontological *Wesen* as Heidegger's poetizing thinking. Both attempt to liberate being, thinking, and language from the fetters of logical analysis by indicating the movement and multidimensionality of what has traditionally been examined through a static, two-dimensional lens.

One should not say, of course (and I am not saying), that Heidegger's various gestures toward (or formal indications of) the counter-turning movement of being (as *Dasein*, as *die Mitte*, as *Ereignis*, as *Geviert*, etc.) are reducible to Gadamer's dialogical dialectic or to his notion of the essential linguisticality of human being. Far from it. Also, it does not make sense to see Gadamerian hermeneutics as a mere complement or even a corrective to the Heideggerian project. The two projects are not compatible in this sense—but neither are they incompatible. Any such attempts to "make sense" of the two or to "figure them out" as "doing the same thing" simply reinscribe the very mode of two-dimensional logical analysis that they both eschew. Nevertheless, I would argue that the phenomenological resonances that reverberate between *Gegenstoß* and *Gegenwendung*, between *die Mitte des Seins* and *die Mitte der Sprache*, between *Sprachgeschehnis* and *Sprachlichkeit*, between Hölderlinian tragedy and Hegelian dialectic, offer a few points, a few locations or sites, within which and from out of which a hermeneutical encounter, a counter-turning dialogue between Heidegger and Gadamer might reveal itself.

Conclusion: The Counter-turning Dialogue

As I have tried to show throughout this inquiry, the Heideggerian and Gadamerian projects, while taking leave of one another as soon as they begin, seem to come nearest each other in their most disparate moments. Gadamer, for example, embraces Heidegger's deconstruction of Aristotelian *phronēsis* only to appropriate it as a way of simultaneously undermining and reclaiming for his hermeneutics the notion of *Anwendung* or application operative in most metaphysical conceptions of truth. On finding the inception of this very notion of truth lurking within the work of Plato, however, Heidegger chooses not to engage Aristotle's teacher, but instead seeks Aristotle himself and a range of traditionally problematic thinkers, including Hölderlin and the poets, as his preferred dialogue partners. But Gadamer not only embraces Plato but takes up the thought of *methexis* (Plato's traditional "Achilles' heel") as phenomenological rather than metaphysical participation in an attempt to undermine all "doctrinal" readings of the theory of ideas—even Heidegger's. And the Platonic dialectic of question and answer becomes Gadamer's model for how all human beings participate in the hermeneutical situation in which they find themselves.

As we have seen, Heidegger's efforts to avoid metaphysics lead him into the realm of poetic thinking—a realm in which his topological deconstruction of traditional logic (a task already begun in *Being and Time*) finds its most forceful expression. His dialogue with Hölderlin provides him a new venue in which to explore the phenomenological possibilities of nonlinear, nonconceptual thinking. Ironically, however, in the very midst of his most strenuous endeavors at undialectical, unmetaphysical interpretation, his poetic interlocutor's own nearness to German Idealism lures Heidegger into close proximity to the speculative dialectic. Gadamer, meanwhile, chooses the path of greatest resistance, as it were. Rather than staking out his territory in an inherently nonphilosophical domain, as Heidegger did, Gadamer deliberately maintains a dialogue with German idealism in his attempt to show how Hegel's dialectic can deconstruct itself when released from the strictures of propositional logic into the openness of living dialogue.

The attendant irony revealed by our examination of Heidegger's and Gadamer's nineteenth-century connections—an irony not so evident in their interpretations of the Greeks—is that the points of proximity occur precisely at the most dramatic fork in their respective philosophical paths. Heidegger's impetus carries him directly away from the so-called language of metaphysics, while Gadamer's own Heideggerian sensibilities carry him straight back into the teeth of the metaphysical tradition. What looks from one interpretive framework like a philosophical confrontation, a mutual critique, an *Auseinandersetzung* in the sense of a sharp disagreement, appears in another framework like a harmonious relationship, complementary elaborations of the same project, an *Auseinandersetzung* in the sense of mutual explication. I am trying to suggest that viewing the complex relationship between these two thinkers from either one of these two perspectives exclusively does a disservice to both of them. We must see Gadamer as neither simply carrying on his teacher's work nor merely taking from it what he likes and discarding the rest. Thus Jürgen Habermas' famous pronouncement that Gadamer has "urbanized the Heideggerian province"[1] only makes sense if we see this "urbanizing" as a twofold movement of carrying on Heidegger's project, while simultaneously putting it at risk by leading it back into the realm of academic philosophizing. We might even go so far as to see Gadamer commencing his own tragic counter-turning (in the manner of Antigone) toward "that which is of no avail." But the tragic, as we have seen, is no mere catastrophe, no mere failing, but a dialogue, a movement of dismantling and retrieval, a dialectic of question and answer that characterizes human being in the world.

If, however, both Gadamer and Heidegger can be seen as "tragic" thinkers, then does this not make them *ironic* thinkers as well? All throughout this book we have spoken of the irony of this famous student-teacher relationship, but does this term imply no more than a juxtaposition of apparently opposed intellectual circumstances? Perhaps the word "irony" really helps us here only if we see it as a Hölderlinian counter-turning or a Hegelian counter-thrust, a dynamic phenomenon of both being and being-conscious that can reveal for us not only the philosophical distance but the interpretive proximity that obtains between Gadamer's dialectical hermeneutics of being-conscious and Heidegger's nondialectical topology of being. But if irony thus becomes more than merely circumstantial, more than a rather self-congratulatory postmodern attitude, then perhaps we can begin to glimpse the longer and wider path that Gadamer's brand of deconstructive interpretation opens up for us. If, by means of this counter-turning dialogue, irony reveals itself to us as not just a rhetorical trope but a thoroughly ontological phenomenon, then perhaps Gadamer's ambiguous and refractory relationship with Heidegger can show us that in its efforts to avoid the traps of metaphysical naïveté thinking need not dwell indefinitely in the realm of deferral and undecidability. For if hermeneutics sees itself as not just a mode of questioning but an ontological mode of being in question, a mode of human being-at-home in *not* being at home in our own questioning, then the radical openness of the hermeneutic "logic" of question and answer becomes a logic of deep phenomenological ambiguity. But insofar as it embraces this ambiguity rather than constantly evading it, and insofar as it sees the inherent irony of being not as the death knell of philosophy but as the very condition for the possibility of philosophizing, Gadamer's hermeneutics may well open up for us the radical and intoxicating possibility of salvaging a renewed and dynamically productive mode of philosophical comportment from the very wreckage of the metaphysical tradition. Gadamer, in other words, may well be exhorting us to engage the history of Western thought in a philosophical dialogue of our own, a counter-turning dialogue that we might be surprised to learn is always already underway—if only we have ears to hear.

Notes

Introduction

1. Theodore Kisiel, *The Genesis of Heidegger's "Being and Time."* Berkeley: University of California Press, 1993. 277.

2. See Gadamer's "Die Sprache der Metaphysik (1968)," GW3, 229–238.

3. See Schürmann's *Heidegger on Being and Acting: From Principles to Anarchy*, trans. Christine-Marie Gros (Bloomington: Indiana University Press, 1990); also, Theodore Kisiel, "Towards the Topology of Dasein," *Heidegger: The Man and the Thinker*, ed. Sheehan, Thomas (Chicago: Precedent, 1981), 95–106; and Otto Pöggeler, "Metaphysics and the Topology of Being in Heidegger," trans. Parvis Emad, *Heidegger: The Man and the Thinker*, 173–186.

4. These include such jibes as, "*Wirkungsgeschichtliches*, perhaps, but *Bewußtsein*, nevertheless," which was related to me by Parvis Emad in 1991 (original source uncertain), presumably indicating that Gadamer was still too wrapped up in an epistemological framework for Heidegger's tastes. Gadamer himself, however, indicated to me in July of 1993 that Heideger actually recommended *Wahrheit und Methode* personally to Jacques Lacan. And the fact that Gadamer was asked to write the introduction to the 1960 edition of "Ursprung des Kunstwerks," would seem to suggest that Heidegger's attitude toward his student's work was anything but hostile.

5. Winter Semester 1922–1923 at Freiburg.

6. GW1, 320 (Gadamer's italics); TM, 315.

7. Robert Bernasconi, "Heidegger's Destruction of *Phronēsis*," *The Southern Journal of Philosophy*, vol. 28, supplement (1989): 127–147. The following will deal primarily with this particular essay because it lays bare the specific issue at hand. For another view of Bernasconi's essay, see Walter Brogan, "A Response to Robert Bernasconi's 'Heideggers Destruction of *Phronēsis*,' " *The Southern Journal of Philosophy*, vol. XXVIII, supplement (1989): 149–153. For further discussions of the importance of Aristotle for *Being and Time*, see R. Bernasconi, "The Fate of the Distinction Between *Praxis* and *Poiēsis*," *Heidegger Studies* 2 (1986): 111–139; Jacques Taminiaux, "Phenomenology and the Problem of Action," *Philosophy and Social Criticism* 11(1986): 207–219; J. Taminiaux, "*Poiēsis* et *Praxis* dans l'articulation de l'ontologie fondamentale," *Heidegger et l'idée de la phénoménologie* (Dordrecht: Kluwer, 1988), 107–125; Franco Volpi, "*Being and Time*: A Translation of the *Nicomachean Ethics*?," trans. John Protevi, *Reading Heidegger from the Start: Essays in His Earliest Thought*, eds. T. Kisiel and J. van Buren (Abany: State University of New York Press, 1994), 195–212; Thomas Sheehan, "Heidegger's Philosophy of Mind," *Contemporary Philosophy: A New Survey*, vol. 4, ed. G. Floistad (The Hague: Nijhoff, 1983), 287–318; T. Sheehan, "Heidegger, Aristotle and Phenomenology," *Philosophy Today* (Summer 1975): 87–94; Walter Brogan, "Heidegger and Aristotle: Dasein and the Question of Practical Life," *Crises in Continental Philosophy*, eds. Arleen Dallery and Charles Scott (Albany: State University of New York Press, 1990), 137–146; W. Brogan, "The Place of Aristotle in the Development of Heidegger's Phenomenology," *Reading Heidegger from the Start: Essays in His Earliest Thought*, eds. T. Kisiel and J. van Buren (Abany: State University of New York Press, 1994), 212–229; Dennis Schmidt, "Economics of Production: Heidegger and Aristotle on Poiesis," *Crises in Continental Philosophy*, eds. Arleen Dallery and Charles Scott (Albany: State University of New York Press, 1990); John van Buren, *The Young Heidegger: Rumor of the Hidden King* (Bloomington: Indiana University Press, 1994), esp. 220 ff.; and William McNeill, *The Glance of the Eye: Heidegger, Aristotle, and the Ends of Theory*, (Albany: State University of New York Press, forthcoming), esp. Chapter 3.

Chapter One

1. PhA.

2. Bernasconi 130.

3. GA19, 56.

4. Bernasconi 132.

5. Kisiel 321. Cf. *Der Begriff der Zeit* (Tübingen: Max Niemeyer, 1989); English-German edition, *The Concept of Time*, trans. William McNeill (Oxford: Blackwell, 1992).

6. GA19, 22.

7. Bernasconi 130.

8. Kisiel 9.

9. Kisiel 250.

10. PhA: German 256; English 378.

11. PhA: German, 255; English, 377.

12. GA19, 53 ff.

13. Bernasconi 137.

14. Bernasconi 138.

15. Bernasconi, 141. He does, however, reject the idea of associating the distinction explicitly with the two published divisions of *Being and Time* if that association is linked to the distinction between authenticity and inauthenticity (a view which he attributes to Taminiaux). He concludes that this would make *Being and Time* more about ethics rather than an ontologizing of *phronēsis* (142).

16. Although Kant seems to recognize this alternate Aristotelian thought-path as he distinguishes between pure and practical reason, even *The Critique of Practical Reason*—when viewed from a Heideggerian perspective—would remain enclosed within the general framework of the epistemological tradition (as would, I suspect, the work of the American pragmatists). Among modern philosophers, only Hegel, as he attempts to collapse such distinctions altogether, might be seen to offer yet another possible road to travel in this regard (see Part Two, below).

17. PhA: German 259; English 381–382.

18. See, for example, Kisiel 17.

19. PA 47. Paul Natorp gave Gadamer a manuscript copy of the Aristotle *Einleitung* in 1923.

20. GW1, 319; TM, 314 (my emphasis).

21. GW1, 320; TM, 314. For commentary on Gadamer's appropriation of *phronēsis*, see the following: Francis J. Ambrosio, "Gadamer and Aristotle: Hermeneutics as Participation in Tradition," *Proceedings of the American Catholic Philosophical Association* 62 (1988): 174–182; Joseph Dunne, "Aristotle after Gadamer: An Analysis of the Distinction Between the Concepts of Phronesis and Techne," *Irish Philosophical Journal* 2 (1985): 105–123; J. Dunne, *Back to the Rough Ground: 'Phronesis' and 'Techne' in Modern Philosophy and in Aristotle* (Notre Dame: University of Notre Dame Press, 1993); John Ibbet, "Gadamer, Application and the History of Ideas," *History of Political Thought* VIII, no. 3 (1987): 545–555; Schuchman, Paul, "Aristotle's *Phronesis* and Gadamer's Hermeneutics," *Philosophy*

Today (Spring 1979): 41–50; and Matthew Foster, *Gadamer and Practical Philosophy: The Hermeneutics of Moral Confidence* (Atlanta: Scholar's Press, 1991).

22. GW1, 320; TM, 315.

23. PHC, 107.

24. GW1, 322; TM, 317.

25. *Nicomachean Ethics*. II, i, 1103a, 14.

26. Unfortunately, the problem cannot be satisfactorily addressed without a good deal of exegetical and hermeneutical work in the original Greek, which lies outside the scope of this book.

27. VI, viii, 1142a, 12 ff.

28. PHC, 136–137. Except for a few emendations and the fact that it was originally written in French, the argument presented by Gadamer in this paper is virtually identical to the relevant section in *Truth and Method* (312–324) where the corresponding term for "ethical sciences" is translated into English as "philosophical ethics" and "ethical consciousness" is rendered as "moral consciousness."

29. GW1, 325; TM, 320.

30. Cf. NE II, ii, 1103b, 32.

31. GW1, 326; TM, 320.

32. GW1, 326, n259; TM, 321, n259. Though not specifically warranted in the passages from NE that he cites (VI, 10 [*sic*], 1142 b 33, 1140 b 13, 1141 b 15.), his interpretation of *phronēsis* as an "ethical *hexis*" is not hermeneutically implausible. Although Aristotle classifies *phronēsis* initially as an intellectual virtue and frequently refers to it as a *dunamis*—a faculty or a capacity—its intimate role in the attainment of the moral virtues (which, along with the vices, are examples of *hexis*) makes hard and fast distinctions difficult. Heidegger, of course, reads *phronēsis* as an *alētheuein*, a mode of being true, and points out as one of the basic difficulties in understanding these distinctions is precisely that for Aristotle neither *sophia* nor *phronēsis* is a *hexis* (GA19, 168).

33. GW1, 328; TM, 322. By an "alienation" or a "denaturing," Gadamer presumably means that other ways of construing experience philosophically tend to see it as either a derivative epistemological state or (as with Hegel) a subordinate stage on the way to a higher form of knowledge (cf. GW1, 363 ff., TM, 357 ff.).

34. GW1, 363; TM, 357.

35. GW1, 363; TM, 357.

36. Although, on Heidegger's reading, *phronēsis* only qualifies as a intellectual virtue insofar as it is already informed by *sophia.*

37. GW1, 319; TM, 314.

38. His thinking about Plato goes as least as far back as his 1922 doctoral dissertation written under Paul Natorp at Marburg (PA, x).

39. Originally published as Gadamer's first monograph in 1931, it appears in GW5, 3–164. English translation: *Plato's Dialectical Ethics: Philosophical Interpretations Relating to the Philebus,* trans. Robert M. Wallace (New Haven: Yale University Press, 1991).

40. See, in particular, "Platos dialektische Ethik—beim Wort genommen" in *Plato im Dialog,* GW7.

Chapter Two

1. "Das Wesen der Lust in den platonischen Dialogen," University of Marburg (unpublished).

2. PA, 23.

3. PA, 23.

4. PA, 23 (my translation).

5. *Political Hermeneutics: The Early Thinking of Hans-Georg Gadamer* (University Park: Pennsylvania State University Press, 1989), 18.

6. PA, 44.

7. *Plato,* Bollingen Series vol. 59, trans. Hans Meyerhoff (Princeton: Princeton University Press, 1973), 123.

8. Friedländer, 120.

9. PA, 43.

10. Although he does acknowledge a certain degree of direct influence from the Georgians, and he did deliver a paper in 1983 on "The Influence of Stefan George on Scholarship" (Sullivan, 48), judging from certain of his written remarks, I would say that George's effect on Gadamer had to do rather with a kind of general milieu of ideas propagated by the academic philologists who followed George. I would certainly tend to disagree with Sullivan's heavily Georgian reading of Gadamer in *Philosophical Hermeneutics*—particularly with his assessment that "the failure to write a [Georgian] *Gestalt*-biography of the Platonic state is the single most significant failing of the early period of Gadamer's career. Indeed, it is this failing that puts an end to Gadamer's early period, and it is probably

the main reason why so little attention has been paid to his early writings" (139). In fact, I find it a little odd that when Sullivan quotes from Gadamer's letter to Richard Bernstein, where Gadamer makes the claim that, "As important as Heidegger and his 1923 *phronēsis* interpretations were for me, I was already prepared for it on my own, above all by my earlier readings of Kierkegaard, by the Platonic Socrates, and by the powerful effect of the poet Stefan George on my generation" (Sullivan, 26), he leaves off the very next sentence, a parenthetical caveat which apparently qualifies the extent of George's influence on him: "(But I did not have any real sympathy with the esoteric atmosphere surrounding this poet)." (Bernstein, *Beyond Objectivism*, 265).

11. IG, 2.

12. IG, 5.

13. Gadamer views Plato, for example, as engaging in a dialectic with Athenian culture. Thus the question behind the dialogues becomes the question of Sophism—the question of a culture besieged by a moral relativism precipitated by the corruption and abuse of language by the Sophists. As Gadamer sees it, Plato wants (among other things) to establish a new and more philosophical form of poetry and myth that is impervious to the Sophistic techniques of linguistic "deconstruction," and thus reinstate them as the traditional tools of Greek moral education.

14. He also found limited what he saw as the "concealed, unacknowledged Hegelianism" behind the work of Cohen, Natorp and their successors (IG, 2). Gadamer's own Hegelianism, as we shall see, becomes quite explicit.

15. IG, 3.

16. IG, 3.

17. IG, 3–4.

18. "Plato and Heidegger," *The Question of Being*, ed. and trans. Mervyn Sprung (University Park: Pennsylvania University Press, 1978), 49.

19. Although not, as we shall see, Heidegger's notion of an inflexible "language of metaphysics" endemic to the first twenty-five hundred years of this history.

20. "Plato and Heidegger," 49.

21. "Plato and Heidegger," 49–50.

22. "H.-G. Gadamer's Heideggerian Interpretation of Plato," *JBSP*, vol. 12, no. 3 (October 1981): 215.

23. See Jaeger's *Aristotle: Fundamental of the History of His Development*, 2nd. ed. trans. Richard Robinson (London: Oxford, 1948).

24. IG, 7.

25. IG, 9.

26. IG, 22.

27. Gadamer's primary writings of this period include his *Habilitationsschrift*, entitled "Der aristotelische Protreptikos und die entwicklunsgeschichtliche Betrachtung der aristotelischen Ethik (1927)" (GW5, 164–186), "Praktisches Wissen (1930)" (GW5, 230–248), Platos dialektische Ethik (1931)" (GW5, 3–163; English translation: *Platos' Dialectical Ethics: Philosophical Interpretations Relating to the 'Philebus,'* trans. Robert M. Wallace, New Haven: Yale University Press, 1991), "Die neue Platoforschung (1933)" (GW5, 212–219), "Plato und die Dichter (1934)" (GW5, 187–211; English translation: "Plato and the Poets," *Dialogue and Dialectic: Eight Hermeneutical Studies on Plato*, trans. P. Christopher Smith, New Haven: Yale, 1980, 39–72), "Antike Atomtheorie (1935)" (GW5, 263–281), and "Platos Staat der Erziehung (1942)" (GW5, 249–262; English translation: "Plato's Educational State," *Dialogue and Dialectic*, 73–92). He also reviewed (among other works) Werner Jaeger's *Aristoteles* in 1928, and W. D. Ross' *Aristotle's Metaphysics* in 1929 (GW5, 283 ff.).

28. In fact, a new volume of the *Gesammelte Werke* has recently been published, bringing the number of volumes devoted exclusively to Greek philosophy to three (out of a total of ten).

29. On the other hand, when scholars do attempt to take more than just *Truth and Method* into account, there is a tendency among them to fall ironically into the very pattern of constructing developmental chronologies for which Werner Jaeger is criticized by Gadamer himself. This is, unfortunately the very temptation that Robert Sullivan succumbs to in his recent (and in many ways valuable) book on Gadamer's early work entitled *Political Hermeneutics* (see above).

30. Although this is understandable given that Gadamer's writings on Aristotle are less extensive and that he rarely discusses Aristotle independently of Plato.

31. "Gadamer and the Ontology of Language: What Remains Unsaid," *JBSP* 17, 2 (May 1986): 139. In this same essay Ambrosio makes some very appropriate remarks on this topic by way of discussing P. C. Smith's interpretation of Gadamer:

> First, whatever else it may seek to do, *Wahrheit und Methode* constitutes primarily a kind of apologia for Gadamer's actual hermeneutical practice as exemplified in his interpretation of major elements in the *Wirkungsgeschichte* of the philosophical tradition. As such, *Wahrheit und Methode* operates chiefly at the level of a reflective formulation, and offers a generalized theory of understanding as

> universal hermeneutics. Thus, to approach Gadamer's thought as a whole solely, or even principally, through *Wahrheit und Methode* is in an important sense to put the cart before the horse. Such a move proceeds too quickly to press hard-won philosophical insights into service in such areas of application as aesthetics, history, or literary criticism before they have first been fully appropriated on their own philosophical terms. Second, not only is it true to say that Gadamer's hermeneutical essays on the philosophical tradition illustrate and warrant the reflective position taken in *Wahrheit und Methode*, but more importantly the philosophical foundations on which that position ultimately rests cannot be adequately understood apart from an explicit recognition of how deeply Gadamer's thought has been permeated and affected by the insights he reaches in the context of his interpretive encounters with Plato, Hegel, and Heidegger (132).

32. Jean Grondin, in fact, makes a very persuasive argument that *Wahrheit und Methode* is not simply what we, as English speakers, have come to know as *Truth and Method*, but rather comprises the entire first two volumes of the *Gesammelte Werke*, which explains why both volumes bear the title, *Wahrheit und Methode*. (See his article, "Zur Komposition von Wahrheit und Methode," *Dilthey Jahrbuch*, vol. 8 [1992–1993]: 57–74.)

33. PHC, 105. This essay is essentially a statement of certain prominent themes of *Truth and Method*.

34. Michael Ermarth, "The Transformation of Hermeneutics," *Monist* (April 1981): 178.

35. Ermarth 179.

36. Ermarth 179.

37. Ermarth 179.

38. Ermarth 183 (my italics).

39. *Radical Hermeneutics: Repetition, Deconstruction and the Hermeneutic Project* (Bloomington: Indiana University Press, 1987). See especially 1–11. Caputo, however, tends to see very little in Gadamer that is "radical."

40. See especially section 20 of Heidegger's *Die Grundprobleme der Phänomenologie* (Frankfurt am Main: Klostermann, 1975), 389 ff.; English translation: *Basic Problems of Phenomenology*, trans. Albert Hofstadter (Bloomington: Indiana University Press, 1988), 275 ff.

41. PHC 106.

42. GA19, 189.

43. GA19, 11.

44. See pages 52ff.. For Gadamer's readings of Heidegger on Plato, see "Heidegger und die Griechen," *Alexander von Humbolt Stiftung: Mitteilungen* 55 (August 1990): 29–38; and "Plato (1976)," GW3, 238–248; English translation by John W. Stanley: "Plato," *Heidegger's Ways* (Albany: State University of New York Press, 1994).

45. For further commentary on Heidegger's reading of Plato, see the following: Robert J. Dostal, "Beyond Being: Heidegger's Plato," *Journal of the History of Philosophy,* vol. 23, no. 1 (Jan. 1985): 71–98; Michael Gelven, "Eros and Projection: Plato and Heidegger,". *Thinking About Being: Aspects of Heidegger's Thought,* eds Robert W. Shahan and J. N. Mohanty (Norman: University of Oklahoma Press, 1984), 125–136; Michael Hudac, "The Ontological Difference and the Pre-Metaphysical status of the Being of Beings in Plato," *Man and World* 23 (1990): 191–203; Douglas R. McGaughey, "Husserl and Heidegger on Plato's Cave Allegory: A study of Philosophical Influence," *International Philosophical Quarterly* 16 (1976): 331–348; Michael Murray, "Husserl and Heidegger: Constructing and Deconstructing Greek Philosophy," *Review of Metaphysics* 41, no. 3 (March 1988): 501–518; Paul Friedländer, "Aletheia," *Plato,* Bollingen Series, vol. 59, trans. Hans Meyerhoff (Princeton: Princeton University, 1973), 221–229; Christopher Nwodo, "Friedländer Versus Heidegger: *A-letheia* Controversy," *JBSP,* vol. 10, no. 2 (May 1979): 84–93; and Adriaan T. Peperzak, "Heidegger and Plato's Idea of the Good," *Reading Heidegger: Commemorations,* ed. John Sallis (Bloomington: Indiana University Press, 1992), 258–285.

46. PLW, 130; English, 261.

47. PLW, 130; English, 261.

48. PLW, 135–136; English, 265.

49. PLW, 136; English, 265.

50. For Heidegger, of course, the word "doctrine" (at least in this essay) carries a quite different connotation from the traditional sense. Rather than the literal meaning of a series of propositions, "The 'doctrine' of a thinker is the unsaid in his saying, to which man is exposed such that he expends himself upon it" (PLW, 108; English, 251). This hermeneutical rather than metaphysical employment accounts for his constant use of the word in quotation marks.

51. NI.

52. NI, 236; English, 204.

53. NI, 199; English, 171; emphasis added.

54. NI, 221; English, 191.

55. NI, 221; English, 190.

56. *JBSP*, vol. 12, no. 3 (Oct. 1981): 211–230. For further commentary on Gadamer and Plato, see the following: P. C. Smith, "Plato as Impulse and Obstacle in Gadamer's Development of a Hermeneutical Theory," *Gadamer and Hermeneutics*, ed. Hugh J. Silverman. (New York: Routledge, 1991), 23–41; Francis J. Ambrosio, "The Figure of Socrates in Gadamer's Philosophical Hermeneutics," *The Philosophy of Hans-Georg Gadamer, Library of Living Philosophers*, vol. 24 (Chicago: Open Court, 1997), 259–273, and "Gadamer, Plato, and the Discipline of Dialogue," *International Philosophical Quarterly* 27 (1987): 17–32; and Donald G. Marshall, "Deconstruction, Sophistic and Hermeneutics: Gadamer, Gorgias, Plato and Derrida," *Journal of Contemporary Literature and Aesthetics*, vol. 9, nos. 1–2 (1986): 83–108.

57. *The Republic*, trans. Richard W. Sterling and William C. Scott (New York: Norton, 1985), 200.

58. Sterling and Scott, 200.

59. Sterling and Scott, 201.

60. I would suggest, however, that this very "in-betweenness" is ironically what *makes* the divided line philosophical—not because it itself *is* Plato's philosophy, but because consideration of it helps to illuminate the path that the philosopher must travel.

61. Insofar as both *dia-lexis* and *dia-logos* can be translated literally as "through speech" or "through language."

62. In the course of our discussion, however, we will also attend to the ways in which Gadamer's deconstruction of the traditional methodological definitions of Platonic dialectic both informs and is informed by his reading of the dialectic in German idealism. (See Part Two, below.)

63. *The Seventh Letter* 341c–d; *Phaedrus and Letters VII and VIII*, trans. Walter Hamilton. (London: Penguin, 1973), 136. (My italics.)

64. E. A. Havelock, *The Literate Revolution and its Cultural Consequences*. Princeton: Princeton University Press, 1982. 122–125. See also, H. I. Marrou, *A History of Education in Antiquity*, trans. George Lamb (New York: Mentor, 1964), 31 ff.; Arthur Adkins, "Orality and Philosophy," *Language and Thought in Early Greek Philosophy*, ed. Kevin Robb (LaSalle: Hegeler Institute 1983), 207–227; and Joseph Margolis, "The Emergence of Philosophy," *Language and Thought in Early Greek Philosophy*, 228–242.

65. PP, 47.

66. Havelock 8.

67. Havelock 8 (my italics).

68. Havelock sees the propositional possibilities of written language and the concomitant advent of conceptual discourse as an opportunity for breaking out of limitations imposed by nonliterate speech rather than the covering over of more originary modes of discourse. For yet another view of the problem of writing in Plato, see Jacques Derrida; especially, "Plato's Pharmacy," *Dissemination*, trans. Barbara Johnson (Chicago: The University of Chicago Press, 1981), 61–172.

69. Havelock 11.

70. William Harris, *Ancient Literacy* (Cambridge: Harvard, 1989), 89 ff.

71. Harris 90–91.

72. Rudolf Pfeiffer, *History of Classical Scholarship* (Oxford: Clarendon, 1968), 32.

73. PP, 47.

74. PP, 43.

75. PP, 44.

76. PP, 50.

77. PP, 50.

78. PP, 50.

79. PP, 63.

80. PP, 63.

81. Paul Friedländer, *Plato*, trans. Hans Meyerhoff, (Princeton: Princeton University Press, 1973), 122.

82. PP, 65.

83. Friedländer, 122–123.

84. PP, 71.

85. Just exactly what Gadamer means by "dialectical" and why hermeneutics is inherently dialectical will, I hope, become clearer as we proceed.

86. GW1, 367; TM, 361.

87. GW1, 369; TM, 363.

88. One is reminded here of the movement of Heideggerian *Destruktion* and *Wiederholung*. But, perhaps more important, we have here a foreshadowing of Gadamer's appreciation for Hegel's dialectic. If Socrates' initial dialectical encounters with sophistic resistance amount to examples of allowing something to become its opposite (i.e., the sophist's

opinion becoming its opposite, and thereby disintegrating), then there is certainly an element of the speculative dialectic here. But the more genuine Hegelian movement begins as the dialogue carries itself beyond its essentially destructive commencement under the impetus of *die Sache selbst*. See Part Two, below, for a detailed explication of Gadamer's reading of Hegel.

89. "Gadamer's Heideggerian Interpretation of Plato," 218.

90. "Gadamer's Heideggerian Interpretation of Plato," 218.

91. One thinks, of course, of the discussions in the *Phaedrus* and elsewhere of the techniques of collection and division (*sunesis* and *diairesis*) but even these are not so much skills to be learned, but general hermeneutical principles which stand in direct contrast with the cut-and-dried sophistic rhetorical techniques (see *Phaedrus* 265d ff.).

92. PP, 70.

93. PA, 185.

94. "Gadamer's Heideggerian Interpretation of Plato," 218.

95. GW1, 396; TM, 393 (cf. Plato, *Seventh Letter* 341c, 344c, and *Phaedrus* 275).

96. "Plato's Unwritten Dialectic," *Dialogue and Dialectic: Eight Hermeneutical Studies on Plato*, trans. P. C. Smith, (New Haven: Yale University Press, 1980), 127. German text: "Platos ungeschriebene Dialektik (1968)." GW6, 131.

97. GW1, 374; TM, 368 (my italics).

98. Plato himself, of course, finds (as does Gadamer) a great deal of seriousness in play. See, in particular, the elaborate word "play" on *paidia* (play) and *paideia* (education) throughout the *Phaedrus* (esp. 276d ff.)

99. For alternative views of *methexis* in Plato, see Charles P. Bigger, *Participation: A Platonic Inquiry* (Baton Rouge: LSU Press, 1968); and Leo Sweeney, S. J., "Participation in Plato's Dialogues: *Phaedo, Parmenides, Sophist* and *Timaeus*," *New Scholasticism* 62 (1988): 125–149.

100. IG, xxii (translator's introduction).

101. Aristotle's own point, of course, is that, except in thought, the forms have no existence independent of the things in which they inhere. Thus on this reading they would not be far apart at all—and this critique of Aristotle's critique constitutes the core of what Gadamer calls the "unitary effect [*Wirkungseinheit*] connecting Plato's and Aristotle's logos philosophy" (IG, 1). See especially, "Aristotle's Critique of the Idea of the Good," IG, 126–158.

102. John Sallis, *Being and Logos: The Way of Platonic Dialogue*, 2nd ed., (Atlantic Highlands: Humanities, 1986), 414. For a complementary reading of Plato, see: Herman L. Sinaiko, *Love, Knowledge, and Discourse in Plato: Dialogue and Dialectic in Phaedrus, Republic, Parmenides* (Chicago: University of Chicago Press, 1965).

103. Sallis, 417.

104. IG, 20.

105. See Chapter 4 below.

Part Two (Introduction)

1. One is tempted to use the word "authentic" here (as opposed to "fallen"), but the existentialist overtones of this term from *Being and Time* tend to be misleading.

Chapter Three

1. See the Introduction, above.

2. SZ, 12; BT, 32.

3. KPM, 159.

4. Albeit a "science" which attempts to dismantle the traditional notions of the so-called scientific method. Cf., for example, SZ 4.

5. SZ, 330; BT, 387.

6. KPM, 156.

7. KPM, 158.

8. KPM, 159.

9. Cf. GA24; esp. section 9. The lecture course contained therein was being conducted at the University of Marburg in the summer of 1927, the same year that *Being and Time* first appeared in print.

10. GA65, 297.

11. Although *die Lichtung* appears already in *Being and Time, Dasein* is now no longer describe as an *entity* which is itself the clearing (cf. SZ 133; BT 171).

12. Cf. GA65, 488, *Vier Seminare* (Frankfurt am Main: Klostermann, 1986), 108–109, and *An Introduction to Metaphysics*, trans. Ralph Mannheim (New Haven: Yale University Press, 1959), 163 ff.

13. Obviously, a more traditional (a more "logical") mode of philosophizing would have difficulty with Heidegger's way of thinking the finitude of being. For a Hegelian, for instance, to be finite is to be limited, bounded, and consigned to an end; and such a notion would seem to turn being into a (limited) being, which, of course, would be to objectify being and thus collapse the ontological difference. But for Heidegger, being is not finite in the sense that it is limited, but rather in the sense that it withdraws, it conceals itself as it reveals itself, or, more properly speaking, it *is* this very withdrawing, concealing, and revealing—being is occurrence, phenomenality itself. Indeed to say that being *is* "finite" is somewhat misleading. A better way of putting it would be to say that being occurs as finitude. When one speaks of the "finitude *of* being" in this Heideggerian sense, therefore, one should try to hear in this phrase the finiteness that being is or that being occurs as finitude rather than hearing finitude as a attribute, or a quality, or a accident of a substance called being. But even this way of referring to being is susceptible to reification, which is precisely while Heidegger moves gradually away from conceptual language altogether.

14. See especially, *Unterwegs zur Sprache* (Pfullingen: Neske, 1959), "Bauen Wohnen Denken," and "Das Ding," (both from *Vorträge und Aufsätze,* Pfullingen: Neske, 1954).

15. Jean Grondin, "Prolegomena to an Understanding of Heidegger's Turn," *Graduate Faculty Philosophy Journal,* vol. 14, no. 2 through vol. 15, no. 1 (1991): 102–103.

16. Heidegger's main texts on Hegel include *Hegel,* GA68 (Frankfurt am Main: Klostermann, 1993); *Hegels Phänomenologie des Geistes,* GA32 (Frankfurt: Klostermann, 1980); English translation by Parvis Emad and Kenneth Maly: *Hegel's Phenomenology of Spirit* (Bloomington: Indiana University Press, 1988); and "Hegels Begriff der Erfahrung," *Holzwege* (Frankfurt am Main: Klostermann, 1950), 105–192; English translation by Kenley Royce Dove: *Hegel's Concept of Experience* (New York: Harper & Row, 1970). For commentaries on these texts and Heidegger's general relationship to Hegel, see the following: Walter Biemel, "Heidegger im Gespräch mit Hegel: Zur Negativität bei Hegel," *Man and World* 25 (1992): 271–280; David Couzens Hoy, "The Owl and the Poet: Heidegger's Critique of Hegel," *Martin Heidegger and the Question of Literature,* ed. William V. Spanos (Bloomington: Indiana University Press, 1979), 53–70; David Kolb, *The Critique of Pure Modernity: Hegel, Heidegger, and After* (Chicago: University of Chicago Press, 1986); D. Kolb, "Hegel and Heidegger as Critics," *Monist* 64 (Oct. 1981): 481–499; Jan van der Meulen, *Heidegger und Hegel oder Widerstreit und Widerspruch,* 3rd ed. (Meisenheim: Hain, 1959); Adriaan T. Peperzak, "Einige Fragen zum Thema 'Hegel und Heidegger,' " *Heideggers These vom Ende der Philosophie,* eds. Marcel F. Fresco, et al. (Bonn: Bouvier, 1989), 49–74; Dennis Schmidt, *The Ubiquity*

of the Finite: Hegel, Heidegger, and the Entitlements of Philosophy (Cambridge: MIT, 1988); Gerhard Schmitt, *The Concept of Being in Hegel and Heidegger* (Bonn: Bouvier, 1977); Herbert W. Schneider, "Hegel, Heidegger, and 'Experience'—A Study in Translation," *Journal of the History of Philosophy* 10 (July 1972): 347–350; P. Christopher Smith, "Heidegger, Hegel, and the Problem of 'das Nichts,' " *International Philosophical Quarterly* 8 (1968): 397–405; P. C. Smith, "Heidegger's Critique of Absolute Knowledge," *New Scholasticism* 45 (Winter 1971): 56–86; Jon D. Stratton, "Identity and Difference as *Austrag*: Hegel and Heidegger," *Kinesis* 3 (Spring 1971): 81–92; Jacques Taminiaux, "Finitude and Absolute: Remarks on Hegel and Heidegger," *Heidegger: The Man and the Thinker*, ed. Thomas Sheehan (Chicago: Precedent, 1981), 187–208; Walsh, Robert D. "When Love of Knowing Becomes Actual Knowing: Heidegger and Gadamer on Hegel's *die Sache Selbst*," *The Owl of Minerva* 17, 2 (Spring 1986): 153–164; Robert R. Williams, "Hegel and Heidegger," *Hegel and His Critics*, ed. William Desmond (Albany: State University of New York Press, 1989), 135–162; and Edith Wyschograd, *Spirit in Ashes: Hegel, Heidegger and Man-Made Mass Death* (New Haven: Yale, 1985).

17. See below. For further commentary on Heidegger's readings of Hölderlin, see the following: Véronique M. Fóti, *Heidegger and the Poets: Poēisis, Sophia, Technē* (New Jersey: Humanities, 1992); V. Fóti, "Mortals within the Fourfold and the Hölderlinian Figure of Man," *Philosophy Today* (Winter 1993): 392–401; Annemarie Gethmann-Siefert, "Heidegger und Hölderlin. Die Überforderung des Dichters in dürftiger Zeit," *Heidegger und die praktische Philosophie*, eds. A. Gethmann-Siefert and O. Pögeller (Frankfurt am Main: Suhrkamp, 1988), 191–229; Karsten Harries, "Heidegger and Hölderlin: The Limits of Language," *The Personalist* (Winter 1963): 5–23; Friedrich-Wilhelm von Herrmann, "'The Flower of the Mouth': Hölderlin's Hint for Heidegger's Thinking of the Essence of Language," *Research in Phenomenology* XIX (1989): 27–41; Irmgard Hobson, "Hölderlin Our Contemporary: 'Empedocles' and German Intellectuals of the 1970s," *Journal of European Studies* viii (1978): 258–273; Dominique Janicaud, "The 'Overcoming' of Metaphysics in the Hölderlin Lectures," *Reading Heidegger: Commemorations* (Bloomington: Indiana University Press, 1992), 383–391; Otto Pöggeler, "Philosophy in the Wake of Hölderlin," *Man and World* 7 (May 1974): 158–176; Kathleen Wright, "Heidegger and the Authorization of Hölderlin's Poetry," *Martin Heidegger: Politics, Art, and Technology*, eds. Karsten Harries and Christoph Jamme (New York: Holmes & Meier, 1994), 164–174; K. Wright, "Heidegger's Hölderlin and the Mo(u)rning of History," *Philosophy Today* (Winter 1993): 423–435; and Susanne Ziegler, *Heidegger, Hölderlin und die: Martin Heideggers Geschichts-denken in seinen Vorlesungen 1934/35 bis 1944*, (Berlin: Dunker & Humblot, 1991).

18. "The Caesura of the Speculative," *Typography: Mimesis, Philosophy, Politics*, edited by Christopher Fynsk (Cambridge: Harvard University Press, 1989), 209. Reiner Schürmann, in fact, offers a provocative

counter-thesis in his essay, "Ultimate Double Binds" (*Graduate Faculty Philosophy Journal*, vol. 14, no. 2 through vol. 15, no.1, 1991), to the effect that it is precisely its dissymmetry rather than any resemblance to the dialectic that makes tragedy what it is (224 ff.).

19. EPW, 172 (section 81). See also the Introduction to WL, 49 ff.; English, 52 ff.

20. Insofar as the interpreter is engaged in a dialogue with the text just as, for Gadamer, the interlocutors in Platonic dialogue are engaged in a dialectical interaction (see Chapter 2, above).

21. Just what that structure entails is precisely the issue here.

22. See below (page 93f.).

23. Although written in the hand of Hegel, the "Systemprogramm" seems to be a collaborative effort of the three young scholars, Hegel, Schelling, and Hölderlin. For a provocative discussion of the philology and authorship of this text, see David Farrell Krell's translation and commentary, "The Oldest Program Towards a System in German Idealism," *The Owl of Minerva*, 17, 1 (Fall 1985): 5–19. All subsequent references to the text are from this translation.

24. Krell, 9–10 ("Systemprogramm," recto, lines 16–31).

25. Krell, 11 ("Systemprogramm," recto, line 36 and verso, lines 1–11).

26. Krell, 12 ("Systemprogramm," verso, lines 20–24).

27. For Warminski, as we shall see, "interpretation," in that it calls for decisions on the part of the reader, remains trapped within the realm of metaphysics. Insofar as any such decision must be imposed on the text from the outside, therefore, it cannot help but do violence to the text. A deconstructive "reading," however, allows for the undecidability inherent in all textuality to reveal itself.

28. "The only way for us to become great or, if this be possible, inimitable, is to imitate the ancients." Johann Joachim Winckelmann, *Reflections on the Imitation of Greek Works in Painting and Sculpture,* translated by Elfriede Heyer and Roger C. Norton. from the original German essay, "Gedanken ueber die Nachahmung der griechischen Werke in der Malerei und Bildhauerkunst" (1755), (La Salle: Open Court, 1987) 5.

29. Peter Szondi, "Hölderlin's Overcoming of Classicism," trans. Timothy Bahti, *Comparative Criticism*, 5 (1983): 262.

30. Andrej Warminski, *Readings in Interpretation: Hölderlin, Hegel, Heidegger* (Minneapolis: University of Minnesota Press, 1987), 31.

31. Warminski, 32.

32. Assuming, of course, that Hegelian dialectic has to do with symmetry, reciprocity, and resolution—a question that we will address more explicitly as we proceed (see section 2, below).

33. See note 27 above.

34. Warminski, xxxii.

35. Warminski, 40.

36. See Chapter 2, above.

37. GW1, 296 ff.; TM, 291 ff.

38. ELT, 53. (Translation slightly modified.)

39. EPW, 176 (section 82).

40. As we shall see below, however, in certain texts Hölderlin does concern himself explicitly with a notion of dissolution—especially in his essay, "Das Werden im Vergehen" or "Becoming in Dissolution." (Although Hegel generally employs the word "*Auflösung*" rather than "*Vergehen.*")

41. For a somewhat more Hegelian sense of transition in the Hölderlinian dialectic, however, see the treatment of Gadamer's conception of the epochal, below.

42. ELT, 53 (my italics).

43. OT, 231.

44. OT, 238.

45. OT, 240.

46. OT, 242.

47. ELT, 96 (I have suppressed Hölderlin's italics in this passage so as to provide my own emphasis).

48. Trans. R. Philip O'Hara, *Southern Journal of Philosophy* (Winter, 1970): 350 (my italics). For Gadamer's more extended treatments of Hölderlin, see "Denken und Dichten bei Heidegger und Hölderlin (1988)," GW10, 76–86; "Dichten und Denken im Spiegel von Hölderlins Andenken (1987)," GW8, 42–54; "Die Gegenwärtigkeit Hölderlins (1983)," GW9, 39–41; "Hölderlin und die Antike (1943)," GW9, 1–19; English translation by Robert H. Paslick: "Hölderlin and Antiquity," *Literature and Philosophy in Dialogue: Essays in German Literary Theory* (Albany: State University of New York Press, 1994), 67–86; "Hölderlin und das Zukünftige (1947)," GW9, 23–38; English translation by Robert H. Paslick: "Hölderlin and the Future," *Literature and Philosophy in Dialogue*, 87–108; and "Hölderlin und George (1971)," GW9, 229–244; English translation by Robert H. Paslick: "Hölderlin and George," *Literature and Philosophy in Dialogue*, 93–110.

49. "Concerning Empty and Fulfilled Time," trans. R. Philip O'Hara, 350.

50. Invoking "Das Werden im Vergehen," he continues: "Thus with a view to tragedy, Hölderlin speaks of the ideality which the dissolution of the old requires. That means that what departed, the past world, precisely in its being over and done, is affirmed at the same time by the insight into the necessity of its dissolution" (351).

51. "The Ground for 'Empedocles,' " ELT, 54–59.

52. DE, scene two, 337.

53. DE, scene three, 353.

54. DE, scene three, 355.

55. DE, scene three, 368.

56. Lacoue-Labarthe 216. This notion of freedom, of course, is itself not un-Hegelian. Human beings, for Hegel, are only truly free in the context of necessity. For a concise and roughly compatible (albeit politically oriented) discussion of individual human freedom see Hegel's *Reason in History*, trans. Robert S. Hartman (New York: MacMillan, 1953), 22 ff.

57. Seeing the speculative moment in terms of "resolution," Lacoue-Labarthe drives home the point: "For even if Hölderlin, using all the means available to him, and to the point of exhausting his dialectical resources . . . strives to think the dramatical figure as a means or a mediation for the paradoxically adequate expression of the author or the subject, this dialectical starting device, constantly reengaged, always lacks a principle of resolution. Everything happens, therefore, as though we were dealing with (and with nothing more than) a kind of immobilized attenuation of a dialectical process that marks time in an interminable oscillation between the two poles of an opposition, always infinitely distant from each other. The act of suspension is this: quite simply, the incessant repetition of the engaging of the dialectical process in the—never changing—form of *the closer it is, the more distant it is; the more dissimilar it is, the more adequate it is; the more interior it is, the more exterior it is.*" ("The Caesura of the Speculative," 230.)

58. Lacoue-Labarthe, 212.

59. "[I]t is no longer the poet and his own experience which appear—even though every poem, thus also the tragic one must have emerged from the poetic life and reality, from the poet's own world and soul—because otherwise the veritable truth will be missing; and nothing whatsoever can be understood and animated, if we cannot translate our own mood and experience into a foreign analogical subject matter." ("The Ground for 'Empedocles,' " ELT, 51.)

60. Assuming, of course, that Hegelian opposites are symmetrical—at least to the extent that they must negate each other (and, by implication, themselves) equally.

61. "Ultimate Double Binds," 229 (my italics).

62. Reiner Schürmann, *Heidegger On Being and Acting: From Principles to Anarchy* (Bloomington: Indiana University Press, 1987), 213.

63. GA53.

64. At least when viewed from the perspective of *Verstand* or reflexive thinking as opposed to *Verstehen* or speculative thinking.

65. Part Two of GA53 is entitled "The Greek Interpretation of Human Beings in Sophocles' Antigone."

66. Cf. GA39, GA52, and *An Introduction to Metaphysics*, 115 ff.

67. GA53, 147.

68. GA53, 93.

69. The Hegelian, of course, would respond that abstraction is merely an artifact of the understanding as it tries to isolate the elements of the development of the Concept—which is itself always already underway—and that Heidegger is just as guilty of abstraction when he thematizes *Gegenwendigkeit*. But the more important distinction, I think, will be seen below in terms of the effect of this critique of Hegel and the context within which it is carried out rather than its validity.

70. GA53, 73.

71. Literally, "every-place and no-place"; most texts separate these two words, leaving *pantoporos* at the end of one line and beginning the next with *aporos*. This part of the ode is usually seen as indicating that man is all-resourceful [*pantoporos*] and is never without resources [*aporos*].

72. GA53, 95 ff. Literally, "above the city," *hupsipolis* typically connotes something like "citizen of a proud city"; *apolis* is literally "without city" and usually refers to a citizen who has been exiled or one who is no true citizen. Heidegger also seems to be playing on the etymologically related word, *hupsipolos*, which means "soaring on high," literally, "above the pole."

73. GA53, 97.

74. GA53, 95.

75. GA53, 103.

76. GA53, 116.

77. GA53, 118.

78. GA53, 118.

79. GA53, 122.

80. GA53, 123.

Chapter Four

1. Gadamer's published works on Hegel include the following: "Hegel und Heidegger (1971)," GW3, 87–104; "Die Dialektik des Selbstbewußtseins (1973)," GW3, 47–64; "Hegel und die antike Dialektik (1961)," GW3, 3–29; "Die verkehrte Welt (1966)," GW3 29–46; and "Die Idee der Hegelschen Logik (1971)," 65–86; these five essays have been translated into English by P. Christopher Smith and collected in (New Haven: Yale University Press, 1976) as (respectively): *Hegel's Dialectic: Five Hermeneutical Studies*, "Hegel and Heidegger," 100–116; "Hegel's Dialectic of Self-consciousness," 54–74; "Hegel and the Dialectic of the Ancient Philosophers," 5–34; "Hegel's 'Inverted World,' " 35–54; and "The Idea of Hegel's Logic," 75–99. For commentary on theses texts and various aspects of Gadamer's reading of Hegel, see the following: Francis J. Ambrosio, "Gadamer: On Making Oneself at Home with Hegel," *The Owl of Minerva* 19, 1 (Fall 1987): 23–40; Moltke S. Gram, "Gadamer on Hegel's Dialectic: A Review Article," *Thomist* 43, 2 (April 1979): 322–330; Jeff Mitscherling, "Hegelian Elements in Gadamer's Notions of Application and Play," *Man and World* 25 (Jan. 1992): 61–67; P. Christopher Smith, "Gadamer on Language and Method in Hegel's Dialectic," *Graduate Faculty Journal* 5 (Fall 1975): 53–72; Robert D. Walsh, "When Love of Knowing Becomes Actual Knowing: Heidegger and Gadamer on Hegel's *die Sache Selbst*," *The Owl of Minerva* 17, 2 (Spring 1986): 153–164; Merold Westphal, "Hegel and Gadamer," *Hermeneutics and Modern Philosophy*, ed. Brice R. Wachterhauser (Albany: State University of New York Press, 1986), 65–86; Kathleen Wright, "Gadamer: The Speculative Structure of Language," *Hermeneutics and Modern Philosophy*, 193–218.

2. Although, significantly, the Gadamerian movement of "the matter or issue itself" is not to be confused with the self-development of the Hegelian Concept.

3. Gadamer's reading of Hegelian dialectic as being dependent on and limited to the speculative proposition is debatable. Spirit, of course, develops though history via not just philosophy, but art and religion as well. A broader view of Hegel's thinking, then, can be seen as both problematic for Gadamer's deconstruction of the dialectic (for the speculative proposition, for instance, might be read as a "formal indication" of sorts or perhaps merely one way of viewing this larger historical movement) and amenable to it (in that Gadamer's hermeneutics is profoundly historical as

well). But Gadamer is not necessarily attempting a rigid critique, but only to explore what he calls "the tension-filled proximity that the development of philosophical hermeneutics manifests in relation to the magnificent thought project of Hegel" (*Reason the Age of Science*, trans. Frederick G. Lawrence, Cambridge: MIT Press, 1989, 53).

4. GW1, 460–477; TM, 456–473. "The Middle of Language and its Speculative Structure." The English text translates the title of this section quite misleadingly as "Language as medium and its speculative structure."

5. GW1, 307; TM, 301.

6. GW1, 363; TM, 358.

7. "Authentic experience," Gadamer argues, "is that in which a human becomes conscious of his own finitude. In it, the machinations and self-consciousness of his planning reason find their limit . . . Authentic experience is thus experience of one's own historicity" (GW1, 363; TM, 357). Obviously, to speak of "experience" as something which limits reason will also be problematic for Hegel. Unfortunately, a further elaboration of this crucial problem would take more space than is available here. It will have to suffice for the moment to indicate Gadamer's agreement with Heidegger on this point. Gadamer refers to Heidegger's analysis (in *Hegel's Concept of Experience*) which suggests that when he explains (in the Introduction to the *Phenomenology*) that "The dialectical movement that consciousness carries out in itself [*an ihm selbst*] . . . is that which is properly called experience," Hegel "does not interpret experience here dialectically but, on the contrary, thinks what is dialectical from out of the essence of experience" (GW1, 360; TM, 354). For more on this, see Gadamer: "Der Begriff der Erfahrung und das Wesen der hermeneutische Erfahrung" (GW1, 352–368; TM, 346–362) and Heidegger: "Hegels Begriff der Erfahrung" (*Holzwege*, 105–192).

8. SL, 116.

9. SL, 116.

10. This explication, given the scope of the present inquiry, must be to some extent abridged, and therefore, given the nature of the *Logic* itself, will exhibit certain unavoidable lacunae. At least one of these, however (the movement through determination and constitution), is worth some degree of elaboration here as it illustrates how Hegel typically employs term "*die Mitte.*"

Insofar as something is determined *in itself* over against its own "being-for-other," this determinateness belongs to its in-itself as its *determination*, which "implies that what something is *in itself*, is also *present in* it [an ihm]" (SL, 123). And, insofar as something is also determined from the "external" perspective of its other, the determinateness, which is nonetheless also its determinate being, does *not* belong to the something's in-itself. Something is therefore said to be *constituted* by this external relation, and the "*being-in-the-something*" thus shows itself as "falling apart into these two extremes" of determination and constitution, and Hegel refers to determinateness as such as "the simple middle term" [*die einfache Mitte*] to whose identity these extremes equally belong (SL, 124).

11. SL, 127.

12. Once again, of illustrative interest for our discussion, though not essential to it, limit is elaborated further here as *die Mitte*:

> Something has its determinate being *outside* (or, as it is also put, on the *inside*) of its limit; similarly, the other, too, because it is a something, is outside [its limit]. Limit is the *middle term* [*die Mitte*] between the two of them in which they cease. They have their determinate being *beyond* each other and *beyond* their limit; the limit as *the non-being of each* is the *other of both* (SL, 127).

13. SL, 129.

14. In fact, at one point Hegel seems to come rather close to Heidegger's thinking of Dasein's finitude in *Being and Time* as "being-toward-death." "Finite things are not merely limited," he writes,

> on the contrary, *non-being* constitutes their nature and being. Finite things *are*, but their relation to themselves is that they are *negatively* self-related, and in this very self-relation send themselves away beyond themselves, beyond their being. They *are*, but the truth of this being is their *end*. The finite not only alters, like something in general, but it *ceases to be*, and its ceasing to be is not merely a possibility, so that it could be without ceasing be, but the being as such of finite things is to have the germ of decease as their being-within-self: the hour of their birth is the hour of their death (SL, 129)

And indeed there is a good deal that remains to be explored in this tragic view of finitude with respect to both Heidegger and Gadamer (cf. GW1, 362 f.). But, for the moment, we should remain alert to Hegel's admonition that "Finitude is the most stubborn category of the understanding" (SL, 129).

15. SL, 130.

16. SL, 130.

17. SL, 132.

18. SL, 136.

19. SL, 137.

20. SL, 139–140.

21. SL, 141.

22. SL, 144.

23. SL, 148.

24. GW1, 405; TM, 401 (italics added).

25. SL, 31.

26. PdG, 278.

27. PdG, 197.

28. PdG, 280.

29. PdG, 280.

30. PdG, 280.

31. Michael Rosen, *Hegel's Dialectic and Its Criticisms* (New York: Cambridge University Press, 1982), 125 ff.

32. GW3, 82.

33. This is not an insignificant moment for Gadamer inasmuch as he takes precisely the opposite view—that poetry is essentially untranslatable (see GW1, 387 ff.; TM, 383 ff.).

34. VuA, 229 (italics added).

35. VuA, 271.

36. For Gadamer, Hegel's notion of the infinite fails to adequately deal with the open-endedness of historicity. "Hegel's *Philosophy of World History*," he says, "remained caught in the insoluble contradiction of an open progress of history and a conclusive apprehension of its meaning, and it [the contradiction] could not be repeated if one were intent on taking historicity seriously" ("The Heritage of Hegel," *Reason in the Age of Science*, Cambridge: MIT Press, 1989, 40).

37. GW1, 384; TM, 378.

38. GW1, 388; TM, 384.

39. See Gadamer's discussion of the original mediality of the play of conversation (GW1, 107 ff.; TM, 101 ff.).

40. Although this section of the text is entitled "Sprache als Medium der hermeneutischen Erfahrung," we should be careful about reducing "*die Mitte*" to a synonym for "medium," as the English translators have done. Gadamer does tell us that "language is the universal medium [*das universale Medium*] in which understanding accomplishes itself," and, moreover, that "All understanding is interpretation and all interpretation

unfolds itself in the medium of a language [*im Medium einer Sprache*] . . . " (GW1, 392; TM, 388). Insofar as he seems to use "*die Mitte*" and "*das Medium*" interchangeably in this section, one might understandably opt to render them both as "medium" without doing much violence to the text at this particular point. However, I think it best to take this as one preliminary though significant mode of explicating "*die Mitte*" rather than an exhaustive determination. Note that we do not yet see the precise genitive formulation, "*die Mitte der Sprache*," which he employs extensively later on in his discussion of the speculative structure of language.

41. More or less from the Greeks through Scholasticism, from German Idealism and the development of secular hermeneutics and historicism in Humboldt, Herder, Schleiermacher, and Dilthey, on through to the twentieth-century phenomenology of Husserl and Heidegger.

42. GW1, 430; TM, 426.

43. For a more thoroughgoing and extremely insightful discussion of Gadamer's appropriation of the *verbum interius*, see Jean Grondin, "Gadamer und Augustin: Zum Ursprung des hermeneutischen Universalitätsanspruch" in *Der Sinn für Hermeneutik* (Darmstadt: Wissenschaftliche Buchgesellschaft, 1994, 24–39).

44. GW1, 432; TM, 428 (Gadamer's italics).

45. See chapter 2 above.

46. GW1, 461; TM, 457.

47. GW1, 461; TM, 457.

48. GW1, 461; TM, 457.

49. PhS, 35.

50. PhS, 35.

51. PhS, 35–36.

52. PhS, 36.

53. PhS, 36.

54. PhS, 37.

55. PhS, 37.

56. PhS, 38.

57. GW1, 471; TM, 467.

58. PhS, 37 (quoted in GW1, 470–471; my italics).

59. The present study does not pretend to resolve this tension. I only wish to explore and raise as questions certain points of contention such as this one so as to further illustrate the hermeneutical proximity of the thinkers involved.

60. GW1, 380; TM, 374.

61. GW1, 380; TM, 374.

62. GW1, 381; TM, 375.

63. GW1, 464; TM, 460.

64. GW1, 468; TM, 464.

65. GW1, 468; TM, 464.

66. GW1, 472; TM, 468.

67. GW1, 473; TM, 469.

68. GW1, 473; TM, 469.

69. Heidegger, however, would not speak of the unsaid as a phenomenon of human linguisticality per se, but rather in terms of what is revealed in both the apparent concealment of not saying and in the equivocality of what is actually spoken or written. For instance, in the "Ister" lectures he speaks of equivocality of poetry and the Greeks' "'natural' ear for the unsaid in what is said" (GA53, 133; see the next section below). See also, for example, section 34 of *Being and Time* where he says that "only in genuine discourse [Rede] is authentic remaining silent [*eigentliches Schweigen*] possible" (SZ, 165).

70. GW1, 476; TM, 472. The "hermeneutic situation," of course, is a phrase which Gadamer originally borrows from section 45 of *Being and Time.*

71. Cf. GW1, 476; TM, 472.

72. This is not the appropriate place for an extended treatment of this topic, but for an excellent discussion, see J. Grondin, "Hermeneutics and Relativism," *Festivals of Interpretation*, ed. Kathleen Wright (Albany: State University of New York Press, 1990), 42–62.

73. GW1, 478; TM, 474.

74. GW1, 478; TM, 474.

75. GW1, 473; TM, 469.

76. GW1, 479; TM, 475.

77. GW1, 375; TM, 371.

78. GA53, 133.

79. GA53, 140.

80. GA53, 148.

81. GA53, 148.

82. GA53, 149.

83. GA53, 150.

84. GW53, 32; English, 27–28.

85. GW53, 32–33; English, 28 (translation slightly modified).

86. GA39, 68 ff.

87. GA39, 68.

88. GA39, 68.

89. GA39, 69–70.

90. GA39, 70.

91. GA39, 70.

92. GA39, 71.

93. GA39, 71.

Conclusion

1. *Philosophical-Political Profiles*, trans. Frederick G. Lawrence (Cambridge: MIT, 1983), 191 ff.

Bibliography

Primary Sources

Aristotle. "Ethica Nicomachea." Trans. W. D. Ross. *The Works of Aristotle*, vol. IX. Ed. W. D. Ross. London: Oxford, 1966.

———. *Ethics*. Trans. J. A. K. Thomson. Revised by Hugh Tredennick. London: Penguin Books, 1976.

———. *Eudemian Ethics*. Trans. H. Rackham. *Aristotle XX*. Loeb Classical Library. Cambridge: Harvard, 1981.

———. *Magna Moralia*. Trans. G. Cyril Armstrong. *Aristotle XVIII*. Loeb Classical Library. Cambridge: Harvard, 1980.

———. *Metaphysics I–IX*. Trans. Hugh Tredennick. *Aristotle XVII*. Loeb Classical Library. Cambridge: Harvard, 1980.

———. *Metaphysics X–XIV*. Trans. Hugh Tredennick. *Aristotle XVIII*. Loeb Classical Library. Cambridge: Harvard, 1980.

———. *A New Aristotle Reader*. Ed. and trans. J. L. Akrill. Princeton: Princeton University Press, 1987.

———. *The Nicomachean Ethics*. Trans. by H. Rackam. *Aristotle XIX*. Loeb Classical Library. Cambridge: Harvard, 1982.

———. *Nicomachean Ethics*. Trans. Martin Ostwald. Indianapolis: Liberal Arts Press, 1962.

———. *The Nicomachean Ethics*. Trans. David Ross, rev. J. L. Akrill and J. O. Urmson. New York: Oxford, 1980.

Gadamer, Hans-Georg. *Die Actualität des Schönen: Kunst als Spiel, Symbol und Fest.* Stuttgart: Reclam, 1977.

———. "Vom Anfang des Denkens (1986)." *Neuere Philosophie I,* 375–393.

———. "Are the Poets Falling Silent?" *On Education, Poetry, and History,* 73–82.

———. "Der aristotelische »Protreptikos« und die entwicklunsgeschichtliche Betrachtung der aristotelischen Ethik (1927)." *Griechische Philosophie I,* 164–186.

———. "Aristoteles und die imperativische Ethik." *Griechische Philosophie III,* 381–395.

———. "Aristotle's Critique of the Idea of the Good." *The Idea of the Good,* 126–158.

———. *Ästhetik und Poetik I: Kunst als Aussage. Gesammelte Werke,* vol. 8. Tübingen: J. C. B. Mohr, 1993.

———. *Ästhetik und Poetik II: Hermeneutik im Vollzug. Gesammelte Werke,* vol. 9. Tübingen: J. C. B. Mohr, 1993.

———. "Being Spirit God." *Heidegger's Ways,* 181–195.

———. "Concerning Empty and Ful-filled Time," trans. R. Philip O'Hara, *Southern Journal of Philosophy* (Winter, 1970): 341–353.

———. "On the Contribution of Poetry to the Search for Truth." *The Relevance of the Beautiful,* 105–114.

———. "Denken und Dichten bei Heidegger und Hölderlin (1988)." *Hermeneutik im Rückblick,* 76–86.

———. "Destruktion und Dekonstrucktion (1985)." *Hermeneutik II,* 361–374.

———. "The Dialectic of the Good in the *Philebus.*" *The Idea of the Good,* 104–125.

———. "Die Dialektik des Selbstbewußtseins (1973)." *Neuere Philosophie I,* 47–64.

———. "Dialektik ist nicht Sophistik. Theätet lernt das im »Sophistes.«" *Griechische Philosophie III,* 338–372.

———. "Dialektik und Sophistik im siebenten Platonischen Brief (1964)." *Griechische Philosophie II,* 90–115.

———. *Dialogue and Dialectic: Eight Hermeneutical Studies on Plato.* Trans. P. Christopher Smith. New Haven: Yale, 1980.

———. "Dichten und Denken im Spiegel von Hölderlins ›Andenken‹ (1987)." *Ästhetik und Poetik II,* 42–54.

———. "Dichten und Deuten (1961)." *Ästhetik und Poetik I*, 18–24.

———. "Dichtung und Mimesis." *Ästhetik und Poetik I*, 80–85.

———. *On Education, Poetry, and History: Applied Hermeneutics.* Eds. Dieter Misgeld and Graeme Nicholson, trans. Lawrence Schmidt and Monica Reuss. Albany: State University of New York Press, 1992.

———. "Der eine Weg Martin Heideggers (1986)." *Neuere Philosophie I*, 417–430.

———. "Das Erbe Hegels (1980)." *Neuere Philosophie II*, 463–483.

———. "Erinnerungen an Heideggers Anfänge (1986)." *Hermeneutik im Rückblick*, 3–13.

———. "Gadamer on Gadamer." Silverman, ed. *Gadamer and Hermeneutics*, 13–21.

———. "Die Gegenwärtigkeit Hölderlins (1983)." *Ästhetik und Poetik II*, 39–41.

———. "Grenzen der Sprache (1985)." *Ästhetik und Poetik I*, 350–361.

———. "Die Griechen (1979)." *Neuere Philosophie I*, 285–296.

———. *Griechische Philosophie I. Gesammelte Werke*, vol. 5. Tübingen: J. C. B. Mohr, 1985.

———. *Griechische Philosophie II. Gesammelte Werke*, vol. 6. Tübingen: J. C. B. Mohr, 1985.

———. *Griechische Philosophie III: Plato im Dialog. Gesammelte Werke*, vol. 7. Tübingen: J. C. B. Mohr, 1985.

———. "Die griechische Philosophie und das moderne Denken (1978)." *Griechische Philosophie II*, 3–8.

———. "Hegel and Heidegger." *Hegel's Dialectic*, 100–116.

———. "Hegel and the Dialectic of the Ancient Philosophers." *Hegel's Dialectic*, 5–34.

———. *Hegel's Dialectic: Five Hermeneutical Studies.* Trans. P. Christopher Smith. New Haven: Yale University Press, 1976.

———. "Hegel's Dialectic of Self-consciousness." *Hegel's Dialectic*, 54–74.

———. "Hegel's 'Inverted World.' " *Hegel's Dialectic*, 35–54.

———. "Hegel und der geschichtliche Geist (1939)." *Neuere Philosophie II*, 384–394.

———. "Hegel und die antike Dialektik (1961)." *Neuere Philosophie I*, 3–29.

———. "Hegel und die Heidelberger Romantik (1961)." *Neuere Philosophie II*, 395–405.

———. "Hegel und Heidegger (1971)." *Neuere Philosophie I,* 87–104.

———. "Hegel und Heraklit." *Griechische Philosophie III,* 32–42.

———. "Heidegger and the History of Philosophy," *Monist* 64, 4 (1981): 434–444.

———. "*Heidegger on Being and Acting: From Principles to Anarchy,* by Reiner Schürmann." (Review article). *Graduate Faculty Philosophy Journal* 13, 1 (1990): 155–158.

———. *Heidegger's Ways.* Trans. John W. Stanley. Albany: State University of New York Press, 1994.

———. "Heidegger und die Geschichte der Philosophie," *Monist* 64, 4 (1981): 423–433.

———. "Heidegger und die Griechen," *Alexander von Humbolt Stiftung: Mitteilungen* No. 55 (August 1990): 29–38.

———. "Heidegger und die Sprache (1990)." *Hermeneutik im Rückblick,* 14–30.

———. "The Hermeneutics of Suspicion." *Hermeneutics: Questions and Prospects* 54–65. Ed. Gary Shapiro and Alan Sica. Amherst: University of Massachusetts Press, 1984.

———. *Hermeneutik I: Wahrheit und Methode: Grundzüge einer philosophischen Hermeneutik. Gesammelte Werke,* vol. 1. Tübingen: J. C. B. Mohr, 1990.

———. *Hermeneutik II: Wahrheit und Methode: Ergänzungen, Register. Gesammelte Werke,* vol. 2. Tübingen: J. C. B. Mohr, 1990.

———. "Hermeneutik als theoretische und praktische Aufgabe (1978)." *Hermeneutik II,* 301–318.

———. *Hermeneutik im Rückblick. Gesammelte Werke,* vol. 10. Tübingen: J. C. B. Mohr, 1995.

———. "Hermeneutik und ontologische Differenz (1989)." *Hermeneutik im Rückblick,* 58–70.

———. "Hölderlin and Antiquity." *Literature and Philosophy in Dialogue,* 67–86.

———. "Hölderlin and George." *Literature and Philosophy in Dialogue,* 93–110.

———. "Hölderlin and the Future." *Literature and Philosophy in Dialogue,* 87–108.

———. "Hölderlin und das Zukünftige (1947)." *Ästhetik und Poetik II,* 23–38.

———. "Hölderlin und die Antike (1943)." *Ästhetik und Poetik II,* 1–19.

———. "Hölderlin und George (1971)." *Ästhetik und Poetik II,* 229–244.

———. "The Idea of Hegel's Logic." *Hegel's Dialectic,* 75–99.

———. "The Idea of Practical Philosophy." *The Idea of the Good,* 159–178.

———. "Die Idee der Hegelschen Logik (1971)." *Neuere Philosophie I,* 65–86.

———. "Die Idee der Praktischen Philosophie (1986)." *Hermeneutik im Rückblick,* 259–266.

———. "Die Idee des Guten zwischen Plato und Aristoteles." *Griechische Philosophie III,* 128–227.

———. *The Idea of the Good in Platonic-Aristotelian Philosophy.* Trans. P. Christopher Smith. New Haven: Yale, 1986.

———. "The Inverted World," trans. John F. Donovan, *Review of Metaphysics,* vol. 28, no. 3, issue no. 111 (March 1975): 401–422.

———. "Die Kehre des Weges (1985)." *Hermeneutik im Rückblick,* 71–75.

———. "Klassische und philosophische Hermeneutik (1968)." *Hermeneutik II,* 92–120.

———. "The Language of Metaphysics." *Heidegger's Ways,* 69–80.

———. "Über leere und erfüllte Zeit (1969)." *Neuere Philosophie II,* 137–153.

———. *Literature and Philosophy in Dialogue: Essays in German Literary Theory.* Trans. Robert H. Paslick. Albany: State University of New York Press, 1994.

———. "The Marburg Theology." *Heidegger's Ways,* 29–44.

———. "Die Marburger Theologie (1964)." *Neuere Philosophie I,* 197–208.

———. "Martin Heidegger's One Path." Trans. P. Christopher Smith. Kisiel and van Buren, 19–34.

———. "Mathematik und Dialektik bei Plato." *Griechische Philosophie III,* 290–313.

———. "Natural Science and Hermeneutics: The Concept of Nature in Ancient Philosophy." Trans. Kathleen Wright. *Proceedings of the Boston Area Colloquium on Ancient Philosophy,* vol. 1. Ed. John Cleary (1986).

———. *Neuere Philosophie I: Hegel Husserl Heidegger. Gesammelte Werke,* vol. 3. Tübingen: J. C. B. Mohr, 1990.

———. *Neuere Philosophie II. Gesammelte Werke,* vol. 4. Tübingen: J. C. B. Mohr, 1990.

———. "Die neue Platoforschung (1933)." *Griechische Philosophie I,* 212–229.

———. "On the Circle of Understanding." Connolly and Keutner, 68–78.

———. "Zwischen Phänomenologie und Dialektik—Versuch einer Selbstkritik." *Hermeneutik II*, 3–26.

———. "Phenomenology, Hermeneutics, Metaphysics," *JBSP*, vol. 25, no. 2 (May 1994): 104–110.

———. *Philosophical Apprenticeships*. Trans. Robert R. Sullivan. Cambridge: MIT Press, 1985.

———. *Philosophical Hermeneutics*. Trans. and ed. David E. Linge. Berkeley: University of California Press, 1976.

———. "Philosophie und Literatur (1981)." *Ästhetik und Poetik I*, 240–257.

———. "Philosophie und Poesie (1977)." *Ästhetik und Poetik I*, 232–239.

———. *Philosophische Lehrjahre*. Frankfurt am Main: Klostermann, 1977.

———. "Zur Platonischen »Erkenntnistheorie.«" *Griechische Philosophie III*, 328–337.

———. "Plato (1976)." *Neuere Philosophie I*, 238–248.

———. "Plato and Heidegger." Sprung, 45–53.

———. "Philosophy and Literature," trans. Anthony Steinbock, *Man and World* 18 (1985): 241- 259.

———. "Plato." *Heidegger's Ways*, 139–152.

———. "Plato and the Poets." *Dialogue and Dialectic*, 39–72.

———. "Platon und die Vorsokratiker (1964)." *Griechische Philosophie II*, 58–70.

———. *Plato's Dialectical Ethics: Philosophical Interpretations Relating to the 'Philebus.'* Trans. Robert M. Wallace, New Haven: Yale University Press, 1991.

———. "Platos dialektische Ethik (1931)." *Griechische Philosophie I*, 3–163.

———. "»Platos dialektische Ethik«—beim Wort genommen." *Griechische Philosophie III*, 121–126.

———. "Platos Staat der Erziehung (1942)." *Griechische Philosophie I*, 249–262.

———. "Platos ungeschriebene Dialektik (1968)." *Griechische Philosophie II*, 129–153.

———. "Plato und die Dichter (1934)." *Griechische Philosophie I*, 187–211.

———. "Practical Philosophy as a Model of the Human Sciences." *Research in Phenomenology*, vol. IX (1979): 74–85.

———. "Praktisches Wissen (1930)." *Griechische Philosophie I,* 230–248.

———. "The Problem of Historical Consciousness." Trans. Jeff L. Close. *Interpretive Social Sciences: A Reader.* Eds. Paul Rabinow and W. M. Sullivan. Berkeley: University of California, 1979, 103–160.

———. "The Question at Issue." *The Idea of the Good,* 7–32.

———. *Reason in the Age of Science.* Trans. Frederick G. Lawrence. Cambridge: MIT Press, 1981.

———. *The Relevance of the Beautiful and Other Essays.* Ed. Robert Bernasconi, trans. Nicholas Walker. Cambridge: Cambridge University Press, 1988.

———. "Auf dem Rückgang zum Anfang (1986)." *Neuere Philosophie I,* 394–416.

———. "Sein Geist Gott (1977)." *Neuere Philosophie I,* 320–332.

———. "Selbstdarstellung Hans-Georg Gadamer (1973)." *Hermeneutik II,* 479–493.

———. "Socratic Knowing and Not-Knowing." *The Idea of the Good,* 33–62.

———. "Die sokratische Frage und Aristoteles." *Griechische Philosophie III,* 373–380.

———. "Das Spiel der Kunst (1977)." *Ästhetik und Poetik I,* 869–893.

———. "Die Sprache der Metaphysik (1968)." *Neuere Philosophie I,* 229–238.

———. "Sprache und Verstehen (1970)." *Hermeneutik II,* 184–198.

———. "Die Stellung der Poesie im System der Hegelschen Ästhetik und die Frage des Vergangenheitscharakter der Kunst (1986)." *Ästhetik und Poetik I,* 221–231.

———. "Text und Interpretation (1983)." *Hermeneutik II,* 330–360.

———. "The Thinker Martin Heidegger." *Heidegger's Ways,* 61–68.

———. *Truth and Method,* 2nd rev. ed. Trans. revised by Joel Weinsheimer and Donald G. Marshall. New York: Crossroad, 1989.

———. "Die Universalität des hermeneutischen Problems (1966)." *Hermeneutik II,* 219–231.

———. "The Universality of the Hermeneutical Problem." *Lectures on Philosophical Hermeneutics* 2–10. Pretoria: University van Pretoria, 1982.

———. "Unterwegs zur Schrift?" *Griechische Philosophie III,* 258–269.

———. "The Verse and the Whole." *On Education, Poetry, and History,* 83–92.

———. "Der Vers und das Ganze (1979)." *Ästhetik und Poetik II*, 249–257.

———. "Zur Vorgeschichte der Metaphysik (1950)." *Griechische Philosophie II*, 9–29.

———. "Wahrheit in den Geisteswissenschaften (1953)." *Hermeneutik II*, 37–43.

———. "Wahrheit und Methode. Der Anfang der Urfassung (ca. 1956)," eds. Jean Grondin and H.-U. Lessing, *Dilthey-Jahrbuch*, vol. 8 (1992–1993): 131–140.

———. "Was ist Wahrheit? (1957)." *Hermeneutik II*, 44–56.

———. "The Way in the Turn." *Heidegger's Ways*, 121–138.

———. "Der Weg in die Kehre (1979)." *Neuere Philosophie I*, 271–284.

———. "Das Wesen der Lust in den platonischen Dialogen." Unpublished doctoral dissertation. Marburg: 1922.

———. "Die verkehrte Welt (1966)." *Neuere Philosophie I*, 29–46.

———. "Vom Zirkel des Verstehens (1959)." *Hermeneutik II*. 57–65.

Gadamer, Hans-Georg, Roman Jakobson, and Elmar Holenstein. *Das Erbe Hegels II*, Frankfurt am Main: Suhrkamp, 1984.

Hegel, G. W. F. *The Difference Between Fichte's and Schelling's System of Philosophy*. Trans. and ed. H. S. Harris and Walter Cerf. Albany: State University of New York Press, 1977.

———. *Enzyklopädie der philosophischen Wissenschaften im Grundrisse—Erster Teil: Die Objektive Logik*. Frankfurt am Main: Suhrkamp Verlag, 1970.

———. *Enzyklopädie der philosophischen Wissenschaften im Grundrisse: 1830—Dritter Teil: Die Philosophie des Geistes*. Frankfurt am Main: Suhrkamp Verlag, 1970.

———. *Faith and Knowledge*. Trans. Walter Cerf and H. S. Harris. Albany: State University of New York Press, 1977.

———. *Phänomenologie des Geistes*. Frankfurt am Main: Suhrkamp Verlag, 1970.

———. *Phenomenology of Spirit*. Trans. A. V. Miller. Oxford: Oxford University Press, 1977.

———. *Hegel's Science of Logic*. Trans. A. V. Miller. Atlantic Highlands: Humanities Press, 1969.

———. *Jenaer Kritische Schriften*. 3 vols. Hamburg: Felix Meiner Verlag, 1979.

———. *Vorlesungen über die Ästhetik III*. Frankfurt am Main: Suhrkamp Verlag, 1970.

———. *Wissenschaft der Logik I*. Frankfurt am Main: Suhrkamp Verlag, 1970.

———. *Wissenschaft der Logik II*. Frankfurt am Main: Suhrkamp Verlag, 1970.

Heidegger, Martin. *The Basic Problems of Phenomenology*. Rev. ed. Trans. Albert Hofstadter. Bloomington: Indiana University Press, 1982.

———. *Basic Writings from 'Being and Time' (1927) to 'The Task of Thinking' (1964)*. Ed. David F. Krell. New York: Harper & Row, 1977.

———. *Being and Time*. Trans. John MacQuarrie and Edward Robinson. New York: Harper, 1962.

———. *Being and Time*. Trans. Joan Stambaugh. Albany: State University of New York Press, 1996.

———. *Beiträge zur Philosophie (vom Ereignis)*. *Gesamtausgabe*, vol. 65. Frankfurt: Klostermann, 1989.

———. *Early Greek Thinking: The Dawn of Western Philosophy*. Trans. David Farrel Krell and Frank A Capuzzi. San Francisco: Harper & Row, 1984.

———. *The End of Philosophy*. Trans. Joan Stambaugh. New York: Harper & Row, 1973.

———. *Einführung in die Metaphysik*. Tübingen: Max Niemeyer Verlag.

———. *Die Grundbegriffe der Metaphysik*. *Gesamtausgabe*, vol. 29/30. Frankfurt am Main: Klostermann, 1983.

———. *Die Grundprobleme der Phänomenologie*. *Gesamtausgabe*, vol. 24. Frankfurt am Main: Klostermann, 1975.

———. *Hegel*. *Gesamtausgabe*, vol. 68. Frankfurt am Main: Klostermann, 1993.

———. "Hegels Begriff der Erfahrung." *Holzwege*, 105–192.

———. *Hegel's Concept of Experience*. Trans. Kenley Royce Dove. New York: Harper & Row, 1970.

———. *Hegels Phänomenologie des Geistes*. *Gesamtausgabe*, vol. 32. Frankfurt: Klostermann, 1980.

———. *Hegel's Phenomenology of Spirit*. Trans. Parvis Emad and Kenneth Maly. Bloomington: Indiana University Press, 1988.

———. "A Heidegger Seminar on Hegel's '*Differenzschrift*,'" *Southwest Journal of Philosophy* 11 (Fall 1980): 9–45.

———. *History of the Concept of Time: Prolegomena.* Trans. Theodore Kisiel. Bloomington: Indiana University Press, 1985.

———. *Hölderlins Hymne »Andenken.«* *Gesamtausgabe,* vol. 52. Frankfurt: Klostermann, 1982.

———. *Hölderlins Hymne »Der Ister.«* *Gesamtausgabe,* vol. 53. Frankfurt: Klostermann, 1984.

———. *Hölderlin's Hymn "The Ister."* Trans. William McNeill and Julia Davis. Bloomington: Indiana University Press, 1996.

———. *Holzwege.* Frankfurt am Main: Klostermann, 1950.

———. *Identität und Differenz.* Pfullingen: Verlag Günter Neske, 1957.

———. *Identity and Difference.* Trans. Joan Stambaugh, ed. J. Glenn Gray. New York: Harper & Row, 1969.

———. *An Introduction to Metaphysics.* Trans. Ralph Manheim. New Haven: Yale University Press, 1987.

———. *Kant and the Problem of Metaphysics.* 4th ed., enlarged. Trans. Richard Taft. Bloomington: Indiana University Press, 1990.

———. *Kant und das Problem der Metaphysik.* *Gesamtausgabe,* vol. 3. Frankfurt am Main: Klostermann, 1991.

———. *Logik: Die Frage nach der Wahrheit.* *Gesamtausgabe,* vol. 21. Frankfurt am Main: Klostermann, 1976.

———. *Metaphysische Anfangsgrunde der Logik.* *Gesamtausgabe,* vol. 26. Frankfurt am Main: Klostermann, 1978.

———. *Nietzsche: Der Wille zur Macht als Kunst.* *Gesamtausgabe,* vol. 43. Frankfurt am Main: Klostermann, 1985.

———. *Nietzsche I.* Pfullingen: Verlag Günther Neske, 1961.

———. *Nietzsche: Volume One: The Will to Power as Art.* Trans. David Farrell Krell. San Francisco: HarperSanFrancisco, 1991.

———. *On the Way to Language.* Trans. Peter D. Hertz. New York: Harper & Row, 1971.

———. "Phänomenologische Interpretationen zu Aristoteles (Anzeige der hermeneutischen Situation)," ed. Hans-Ulrich Lessing, *Dilthey Jahrbuch,* vol. 6 (1989): 236–269.

———. "Phenomenological Interpretations with Respect to Aristotle: Indications of the Hermeneutical Situation." Trans. Michael Bauer. *Man and World* 25 (1992): 355–393.

———. *Platon: Sophistes.* *Gesamtausgabe,* vol. 19. Frankfurt am Main: Klostermann, 1992.

———. *Plato's Sophist.* Trans. Richard Rojcewicz and André Schuwer. Bloomington: Indiana University Press, 1997.

———. "Platons Lehre von der Wahrheit." *Wegmarken,* 109–144.

———. "Plato's Doctrine of Truth." *Philosophy in the Twentieth Century: An Anthology,* vol. 3. Eds. William Barret and Henry Aiken. New York: Random House, 1962, 251–270.

———. *Poetry, Language, Thought.* Trans. Albert Hofstadter. New York: Harper & Row, 1971.

———. *Sein und Zeit.* Tübingen: Max Niemeyer Verlag, 1986. (GA 2. Originally published in 1927.)

———. *Seminare.* Frankfurt am Main: Klostermann, 1986.

———. *Unterwegs zur Sprache,* 8th ed. Pfüllingen: Neske, 1959.

———. *Vorträge und Aufsätze.* Pfüllingen: Neske, 1954.

———. *Wegmarken.* Frankfurt am Main: Klostermann, 1978.

Hölderlin, Friedrich. *Einhundert Gedichte.* Ed. D. E. Sattler. Frankfurt am Main: Luchterhand, 1989.

———. *Friedrich Hölderlin: Essays and Letters on Theory.* Trans. Thomas Pfau. Albany: State University of New York Press, 1988.

———. *Gedichte.* Stuttgart: Reclam, 1968.

———. *Gedichte Hyperion.* Munich: Wilhelm Goldmann, 1981.

———. *Hölderlin: Selected Verse.* Trans. Michael Hamburger. Hammondsworth: Penguin Books, 1961.

———. *Hymns and Fragments.* Trans. Richard Sieburth. Princeton: Princeton University Press, 1984.

———(?). "The Oldest Program Towards a System in German Idealism," *The Owl of Minerva,* 17, 1 (Fall 1985): 5–19.

———. *Poems and Fragments.* Trans. Michael Hamburger. Ann Arbor: The University of Michigan Press, 1966.

———. *Der Tod des Empedocles.* Ed. Friedrich Beissner. Stuttgart: Reclam, 1973.

———. "On Tragedy: 'Notes on the Oedipus' and 'Notes on the Antigone,' " trans. Jeremy Adler, *Comparative Criticism,* 5 (1983): 205–244.

———. *Werke und Briefe.* Ed. Friedrich Beissner and Jochen Schmidt. Franfurt am Main: Insel, 1969.

Plato. *The Dialogues of Plato.* 2 vols. Trans. R. E. Allen. New Haven: Yale, 1984.

———. *Epistles.* Trans. R. G. Bury. *Plato IX.* Loeb Classical Library. Cambridge: Harvard University Press, 1989.

———. *Phaedrus.* Trans. H. N. Fowler. *Plato I.* Loeb Classical Library. Cambridge: Harvard University Press, 1982.

———. *Phaedrus and Letters VII and VIII.* Trans. Walter Hamilton. New York: Penguin, 1973.

———. *Philebus.* Trans. H. N. Fowler. *Plato VIII.* Loeb Classsical Library. Cambridge: Harvard University Press, 1981.

———. *Plato: The Collected Dialogues.* Ed. Edith Hamilton and Huntington Cairns. Bollingen Series LXXI. Princeton: Princeton, 1963.

———. *Plato's Republic.* Trans. G. M. A. Grube. Indianapolis: Hackett, 1974.

———. *The Republic.* Trans. Richard W. Sterling and William C. Scott. New York: W. W. Norton, 1985.

———. *The Republic I.* Trans. Paul Shorey. *Plato V.* Loeb Classical Library. Cambridge: Harvard University Press, 1987.

———. *The Republic II.* Trans. Paul Shorey. *Plato VI.* Loeb Classical Library. Cambridge: Harvard University Press, 1987.

Winckelmann, Johann Joachim. *Reflections on the Imitation of Greek Works in Painting and Sculpture.* Trans. Elfriede Heyer and Roger C. Norton. La Salle: Open Court, 1987.

Secondary Works

Adkins, Arthur. "Orality and Philosophy." Robb, 207–227.

Agamben, Giorgio. *Language and Death: The Place of Negativity.* Trans. Karen E. Pinkus. Minneapolis: University of Minnesota Press, 1991.

Ambrosio, Francis J. "Dawn and Dusk: Gadamer and Heidegger on Truth," *Man and World* 19 (1986): 21–53.

———. "The Figure of Socrates in Gadamer's Philosophical Hermeneutics." *The Philosophy of Hans-Georg Gadamer Library of Living Philosophers,* vol. XXIV. Ed. Lewis Edwin Hahn. Chicago: Open Court, 1997. 259–273.

———. "Gadamer and Aristotle: Hermeneutics as Participation in Tradition." *Proceedings of the American Catholic Philosophical Association* 62 (1988): 174–182.

———. "Gadamer and the Ontology of Language: What Remains Unsaid," *JBSP* 17, 2 (May 1986): 124–142.

———. "Gadamer: On Making Oneself at Home with Hegel," *The Owl of Minerva* 19, 1 (Fall 1987): 23–40.

———. "Gadamer, Plato, and the Discipline of Dialogue," *International Philosophical Quarterly* 27 (1987): 17–32.

Anz, Heinrich and Hendrik Birus. *Hermeneutische Positionen: Schleiermacher-Dilthey-Heidegger-Gadamer.* Göttingen: Vandenhoek und Ruprecht, 1982.

Beissner, Friedrich. *Hölderlins Übersetzungen aus dem Griechischen,* 2nd ed. Stuttgart: Metzlersche Verlagsbuchhandlung, 1961.

Benjamin, Andrew. *The Plural Event: Descartes, Hegel, Heidegger.* New York: Routledge, 1993.

Bernasconi, Robert. "Bridging the Abyss: Heidegger and Gadamer," *Research in Phenomenology* XVI (1986): 1–21.

———. "The Fate of the Distinction Between *Praxis* and *Poiēsis,*" *Heidegger Studies* 2 (1986): 111–139.

———. "Heidegger's Destruction of *Phronēsis.*" *The Southern Journal of Philosophy,* vol. 28, supplement (1989): 127–147.

———. *The Question of Language in Heidegger's History of Being.* Atlantic Highlands, NJ: Humanities Press, 1985.

Bernstein, Richard J. *Beyond Objectivism and Relativism: Science, Hermeneutics, and Praxis.* Philadelphia: University of Pennsylvania, 1985.

———. "From Hermeneutics to Praxis," *Review of Metaphysics* 35 (June 1982): 823–845.

Bettendorf, Thomas. *Hermeneutik und Dialog: eine Auseinandersetzung mit dem Denken Hans-Georg Gadamers.* Frankfurt am Main: Haag & Herschen, 1984.

Biemel, Walter. "Heidegger im Gespräch mit Hegel: Zur Negativität bei Hegel," *Man and World* 25 (1992): 271–280.

———. "Poetry and Language in Heidegger." Kockelmans, ed., *Heidegger and Language,* 65–106.

Bigger, Charles P. *Participation: A Platonic Inquiry.* Baton Rouge: Louisiana State University Press, 1968.

Birault, Henri. "Thinking and Poetizing in Heidegger." Kockelmans, ed., *Heidegger and Language,* 147–168.

Bleicher, Josef. *Contemporary Hermeneutics: Hermeneutics as Method, Philosophy and Critique.* New York: Routeledge, 1980.

Boelen, Bernard J. "The Question of Ethics." *Heidegger and the Quest for Truth.* Ed. Manfred Frings. Chicago: Quadrangle, 1968.

Bröcker, Walter. "Heidegger und die Logik." *Heidegger: Perpektiven zur Deutung seines Werks.* Ed. Otto Pöggeler. Athenäum, 1984.

Brogan, Walter. "Heidegger and Aristotle: Dasein and the Question of Practical Life," *Crises in Continental Philosophy.* Eds. Arleen Dallery and Charles Scott. Albany: State University of New York Press, 1990, 137–146.

———. "The Place of Aristotle in the Development of Heidegger's Phenomenology." Kisiel and van Buren. 213–229.

———. "A Response to Robert Bernasconi's 'Heidegger's Destruction of *Phronēsis*,' " *The Southern Journal of Philosophy,* vol. XXVIII, supplement (1989): 149–153.

Bruns, Gerald L. *Heidegger's Estrangements: Language, Truth, and Poetry in the Later Writings.* New Haven: Yale University Press, 1989.

———. *Hermeneutics Ancient and Modern.* New Haven: Yale, 1992.

Bruzina, Ronald, and Bruce Wilshire, eds. *Phenomenology: Dialogues and Bridges.* Albany, State University of New York Press, 1982.

Caputo, John D. *Radical Hermeneutics: Repetition, Deconstruction, and the Hermeneutic Project.* Bloomington: Indiana University Press, 1987.

Chroust, Anton-Hermann. *Aristotle: Protrepticus—A Reconstruction.* Notre Dame: University of Notre Dame, 1964.

Connerton, Paul. "Gadamer's Hermeneutics." *Comparative Criticism* 5 (1983): 107–128.

Connolly, John M., and Thomas Keutner, eds. *Hermeneutics Versus Science?: Three German Views.* Notre Dame: University of Notre Dame Press, 1988.

Constantine, David. *Hölderlin.* Oxford: Clarendon, 1988.

———. *The Significance of Locality in the Poetry of Friedrich Hölderlin.* London: The Modern Humanities Research Association, 1979.

Cook, Daniel J. *Language in the Philosophy of Hegel.* The Hague: Mouton, 1973.

Corngold, Stanley. "Hölderlin and the Interpretation of the Self." *Comparative Criticism 5.* Ed. E. S. Shaffer. Cambridge: Cambridge University Press, 1983.

———. "*Sein und Zeit*: Implications for Poetics." Spanos, ed. 99–114.

Coutine, Jean-François. "Phenomenology and/or Tautology." Trans. Jeffrey S. Librett. Sallis, ed. *Reading Heidegger,* 241–257.

Dastur, Françoise. "Language and *Ereignis.*" Sallis, ed. *Reading Heidegger,* 355–369.

———. "Logic and Ontology: Heidegger's 'Destruction' of Logic," *Research in Phenomenology* XVII (1987): 55–74.

Davey, R. Nicholas. "A Response to P. Christopher Smith." *Gadamer and Hermeneutics.* Ed. Hugh J. Silverman. New York: Routledge, 1991.

Derrida, Jacques. *Of Spirit: Heidegger and the Question.* Trans. Geoffrey Bennington and Rachel Bowlby. Chicago: University of Chicago Press, 1989.

Desmond, William, ed. *Hegel and His Critics: Philosophy in the Aftermath of Hegel.* Albany: State University of New York Press, 1989.

deVries, Hent. "Theotopographies: Nancy, Hölderlin, Heidegger," *MLN,* vol. 109, no. 3 (April 1994): 445–477.

Dostal, Robert J. "Beyond Being: Heidegger's Plato," *Journal of the History of Philosophy,* vol. 23, no. 1 (Jan. 1985): 71–98.

Dunne, Joseph. "Aristotle after Gadamer: An Analysis of the Distinction Between the Concepts of Phronēsis and Techne." *Irish Philosophical Journal* 2 (1985): 105–123.

———. *Back to the Rough Ground: 'Phronēsis' and 'Techne' in Modern Philosophy and in Aristotle.* Notre Dame: University of Notre Dame Press, 1993.

Emad, Parvis. "The Place of Hegel in Heidegger's *Being and Time,*" *Research in Phenomenology* XIII (1983): 159–173.

Ermarth, Michael. "The Transformation of Hermeneutics," *Monist* (April 1981): 175–194.

Fay, Thomas. *Heidegger: The Critique of Logic.* The Hague: Nijhoff, 1977.

Figal, Gunter. "Phronēsis als Verstehen: eine Erörterung der philosophischen Hermeneutik." Unpublished essay.

Foster, Matthew. *Gadamer and Practical Philosophy: The Hermeneutics of Moral Confidence.* Atlanta: Scholar's Press, 1991.

Fóti, Véronique M. *Heidegger and the Poets: Poiēsis, Sophia, Technē.* New Jersey: Humanities, 1992.

———. "Mortals within the Fourfold and the Hölderlinian Figure of Man." *Philosophy Today* (Winter 1993): 392–401.

Friedländer, Paul. *Plato.* Bollingen Series vol. 59. Trans. Hans Meyerhoff. Princeton: Princeton University Press, 1973.

Fynsk, Christopher. *Heidegger: Thought and Historicity.* Ithaca: Cornell University Press, 1986.

———, ed. *Typography: Mimesis, Philosophy, Politics.* Cambridge: Harvard University Press, 1989.

Gasché, Rodolphe. "'Like the Rose—Without Why': Postmodern Transcendentalism and Practical Philosophy" (review of Reiner Schürmann's *Heidegger on Being and Acting*), *Diacritics* 19.3–4 (Fall-Winter, 1989): 101–113.

———. *The Tain of the Mirror: Derrida and the Philosophy of Reflection.* Cambridge: Harvard University Press, 1986.

Gelven, Michael. "Eros and Projection: Plato and Heidegger." Shahan and Mohanty. 125–136.

Gethmann-Siefert, Annemarie. "Heidegger und Hölderlin. Die Überforderung des »Dichters in dürftiger Zeit.«" Gethmann-Siefert and Pöggeler, eds. 191–229.

Gethmann-Siefert, Annemarie and Otto Pöggeler, eds. *Heidegger und die praktische Philosophie.* Frankfurt am Main: Suhrkamp, 1988.

Gillespie, Michael Allen. *Hegel, Heidegger, and the Ground of History.* Chicago: University of Chicago Press, 1984.

Gram, Moltke S. "Gadamer on Hegel's Dialectic: A Review Article," *Thomist* 43, 2 (April 1979): 322–330.

Griswold, Charles L. Jr., ed. *Platonic Writings/Platonic Readings.* New York: Routledge, 1988.

Grondin, Jean. "Zur Komposition von *Wahrheit und Methode,*" *Dilthey Jahrbuch* 8 (1993): 57–74.

———. *Einführung in die philosophische Hermeneutik.* Darmstadt: Wissenschaftliche Buchgesellschaft, 1991.

———. "The Ethical and Young-Hegelian Motives in Heidegger's Hermeneutics of Facticity." Kisiel and van Buren, 345–359.

———. *Hermeneutische Wahrheit?: zum Wahrheitsbegriff Hans-Georg Gadamers.* Königstein: Forum Akademicum in der Verlagsgruppe Athenäum, Hain, Scriptor, Hanstein, 1982.

———. "Die Hermeneutik der Faktizität als ontologische Destruktion und Ideologiekritik." *Zur philosophischen Aktualität Heideggers,* vol. 2. Frankfurt am Main: Klostermann, 1990. 163–178.

———. *Introduction to Philosophical Hermeneutics.* Trans. Joel Weinsheimer. New Haven: Yale University Press, 1994.

———. "Jenseits der Wirkungsgeschichte: Gadamers sokratische Destruktion der griechischen Philosophy," *Internationale Zeitschrift für Philosophie* (1992): 38–49.

———. "Der junghegelianische und ethische Motiv in Heideggers Hermeneutik der Faktizität." *Wege und Irrwege des neueren Umgangs mit Heideggers Werk.* Berlin: Duncker & Humboldt, 1991, 141–150.

———. "Prolegomena to an Understanding of Heidegger's Turn," *Graduate Faculty Journal* 14, 2–15, 1 (1991): 85–108.

———. *Der Sinn für Hermeneutik.* Darmstadt: Wissenschaftliche Buchgesellschaft, 1994.

———. *Sources of Hermeneutics.* Albany: State University of New York Press, 1995.

Haase, Ulrich. "The Providence of Language in Gadamer's *Truth and Method,*" *JBSP,* vol. 22, no. 3 (Oct 1991): 170–184.

Haar, Michel. *Heidegger and the Essence of Man.* Trans. William McNeill. Albany: State University of New York Press, 1993.

———. *The Song of the Earth: Heidegger and the Grounds of the History of Being.* Trans. Reg Lilly. Bloomington: Indiana University Press, 1993.

Habermas, Jürgen. *Philosophical-Political Profiles.* Trans. Frederick G. Lawrence. Cambridge: MIT, 1983.

Harries, Karsten. "Heidegger and Hölderlin: The Limits of Language," *The Personalist* (Winter 1963): 5–23.

Harries, Karsten, and Christoph Jamme, eds. *Martin Heidegger: Politics, Art, and Technology.* New York: Holmes & Meier, 1994.

Harvey, Irene. "The Linguistic Basis of Truth for Hegel," *Man and World* 15 (1982): 285–297.

Harris, William V. *Ancient Literacy.* Cambridge: Harvard University Press, 1989.

Harrison, R. B. *Hölderlin and Greek Literature.* Oxford: Clarendon, 1975.

Havelock, E. A. *The Literate Revolution in Greece and Its Cultural Consequences.* Princeton: Princeton, 1982.

———. *Preface to Plato.* Cambridge: Belknap, 1987.

Heede, Reinhard and Joachim Ritter, eds. *Hegel-Bilanz: zur Aktualität und Inaktualität der Philosophie Hegels.* Frankfurt am Main: Vittorio Klostermann, 1973.

Henrich, Dieter. *Die Gegenwart der Griechen im neueren Denken.* Tübingen: J. C. B. Mohr, 1960.

———. *Hegel im Kontext.* 4th, rev. ed. Frankfurt am Main: Suhrkamp Verlag, 1971.

———, ed. *Die Wissenschaft der Logik und die Logik der Reflexion: Heel-Tage, Chantilly 1971.* Bonn: Bouvier, 1978.

Herrmann, Friedrich-Wilhelm von. "'The Flower of the Mouth': Hölderlin's Hint for Heidegger's Thinking of the Essence of Language," *Research in Phenomenology* XIX (1989): 27–41.

Hobson, Irmgard. "Hölderlin Our Contemporary: `Empedocles' and German Intellectuals of the 1970s," *Journal of European Studies* viii (1978): 258–273.

Hoffmeister, Johannes. *Hölderlin's Empedokles.* Ed. Richard Müller. Bonn: Bouvier Verlag, 1963.

Hollinger, Robert, ed. *Hermeneutics and Praxis.* Notre Dame: Notre Dame University Press, 1985.

Houlgate, Stephen. *Hegel, Nietzsche and the Criticism of Metaphysics.* New York: Cambridge University Press, 1986.

———. *Freedom, Truth and History: An Introduction to Hegel's Philosophy.* London: Routledge, 1991.

———. "Thought and Being in Kant and Hegel," *The Owl of Minerva,* vol. 22, 2 (Spring 1991): 131–140.

Hoy, David Couzens. *The Critical Circle: Literature, History and Philosophical Hermeneutics.* Berkeley: University of California Press, 1982.

———. "The Owl and the Poet: Heidegger's Critique of Hegel." Spanos, ed. 53–70.

Hoy, Terry. "The Hermeneutics of Hans-Georg Gadamer: Towards the Renewal of Aristotelian Praxis." *Praxis, Truth, and Liberation.* 1–18.

———. *Praxis, Truth, and Liberation: Essays on Gadamer, Taylor, Polanyi, Habermas, Gutierrez, and Ricoeur.* New York: University Press of America, 1988.

Hudac, Michael. "The Ontological Difference and the Pre-Metaphysical status of the Being of Beings in Plato," *Man and World* 23 (1990): 191–203.

Hyppolite, Jean. "The Structure of Philosophic Language According to the `Preface' to Hegel's *Phenomenology of Mind,*" *The Structuralist Controversy: The Language of Criticism and the Sciences of Man.* Ed. Richard Macksey and Eugenio Donato. Baltimore: Johns Hopkins University Press, 1972, 187–185.

Ibbet, John. "Gadamer, Application and the History of Ideas," *History of Political Thought* VIII, no. 3 (1987): 545–555.

Jäger, Hans. *Heidegger und die Sprache.* München: Francke, 1971.

Jaeger, Werner. *Aristotle: Fundamentals of the History of His Development,* 2nd ed. Trans. Richard Robinson. London: Oxford, 1948.

———. *Paideia: The Ideals of Greek Culture.* 3 vols. Trans. Gilbert Highet. New York: Oxford, 1944.

Jamme, Christoph. "Hegel and Hölderlin," *Clio* 15: 4 (1986): 359–377.

———. *"Ein ungelehrtes Buch": Die philosophische Gemeinschaft zwischen Hölderlin und Hegel in Frankfurt 1797–1800. Hegel-Studien.* Beiheft 23. Bonn: Bouvier Verlag, 1983.

Janicaud, Dominique. "The 'Overcoming' of Metaphysics in the Hölderlin Lectures." Sallis, ed. *Reading Heidegger,* 383–391.

Jung, Hwa Yol. "Martin Heidegger and the Homecoming of Oral Poetry," *Philosophy Today* (Summer 1982): 148–170.

Kahn, Charles. "The Greek Verb 'To Be' and the Concept of Being." *Foundations of Language* 2 (1966): 243–265.

———. *The Verb "Be" in Ancient Greek.* Foundations in Language Supplementary Series, vol. 16. Boston: Reidel, 1973.

Kerby, Anthony Paul. "Gadamer's Concrete Universal," *Man and World* 24 (1991): 49–61.

Kerferd, G. B. *The Sophistic Movement.* New York: Cambridge University Press, 1981.

Kettering, Emil. *NÄHE: Das Denken Martin Heidegger.* Pfüllingen: Neske, 1987.

Kisiel, Theodore. "The Genesis of *Being and Time,*" *Man and World* 25 (1992): 21–37.

———. *The Genesis of Heidegger's 'Being and Time.'* Berkeley: University of California Press, 1993.

———. "The Happening of Tradition." Hollinger 3–31.

———. "Hegel and Hermeneutics." Weise, 197–220.

———. "The Missing Link in the Early Heidegger." Kockelmans, ed., *Hermeneutic Phenomenology* 1–40.

———. "A Philosophical Postscript: On the Genesis of »Sein und Zeit,«" *Dilthey-Jahrbuch,* vol. 8 (1992–1993): 227–232.

———. "Repetition in Gadamer's Hermeneutics," *Analecta Husserliana,* vol. II (1972): 196–203.

———. "Towards the Topology of Dasein." Sheehan, ed., 95–106.

Kisiel, Theodor and John van Buren, eds. *Reading Heidegger from the Start: Essays in His Earliest Thought.* Albany: State University of New York Press, 1994.

Kockelmans, Joseph J. *On the Truth of Being: Reflections on Heidegger's Later Philosophy.* Bloomington: Indiana, 1984.

———, ed. *On Heidegger and Language.* Evanston: Northwestern University Press, 1972.

———. *Hermeneutic Phenomenology.* Lanham: University Press of America, 1988.

Kojève, Alexandre. *Introduction to the Reading of Hegel: Lectures on the 'Phenomenology of Spirit.'* Trans. James H. Nichols, Jr., ed. Allan Bloom. Ithaca: Cornell University Press, 1980.

Kolb, David. *The Critique of Pure Modernity: Hegel, Heidegger, and After.* Chicago: University of Chicago Press, 1986.

———. "Hegel and Heidegger as Critics," *Monist* 64 (Oct. 1981): 481–499.

Krell, David Farrell. *Intimations of Mortality: Time, Truth, and Finitude in Heidegger's Thinking of Being.* University Park: Penn State University Press, 1986.

———. *Of Memory, Reminiscence, and Writing: On the Verge.* Bloomington: Indiana University Press, 1990.

———. "The Oldest Program Towards a System in German Idealism," *The Owl of Minerva,* 17, 1 (Fall 1985): 5–19.

———. "Results," *Monist* 64 (Oct. 1981): 467–480.

Kusch, Martin. *Language as Calculus vs. Language as Universal Medium: A Study in Husserl, Heidegger, and Gadamer.* Dordrecht: Kluwer, 1989.

Lacoue-Labarthe, Philippe. "The Caesura of the Speculative." Fynsk, ed., 208–236.

———. *Heidegger, Art, and Politics: The Fiction of the Political.* Trans. Chris Turner. Oxford: Basil Blackwell, 1990.

———. "Hölderlin and the Greeks." Fynsk, ed., 236–247.

Lauer, Quentin. *Essays in Hegelian Dialectic.* New York: Fordham University Press, 1977.

Llewelyn, John. *Beyond Metaphysics? The Hermeneutic Circle in Contemporary Continental Thought.* Atlantic Highlands, NJ: Humanities Press, 1985.

Magliola, Robert. *Phenomenology and Literature.* West LaFayette: Purdue University Press, 1977.

Margolis, Joseph. "The Emergence of Philosophy." Robb, 228–242.

Marrou, Henri Irenee. *History of Education in Antiquity.* Trans. George Lamb. New York: Mentor, 1964.

Marshall, Donald G. "Deconstruction, Sophistic and Hermeneutics: Gadamer, Gorgias, Plato and Derrida." *Journal of Contemporary Literature and Aesthetics,* vol. 9, no. 1–2 (1986): 83–108.

Marshall, Donald G., ed. *Literature as Philosophy/Philosophy as Literature.* Iowa City: University of Iowa Press, 1987.

Marx, Werner. *Heidegger and the Tradition.* Trans. Theodore Kisiel and Murray Greene. Evanston: Northwestern University Press, 1971.

———. "The World in Another Beginning: Poetic Dwelling and the Role of the Poet." Kockelmans, ed., *Heidegger and Language,* 235–260.

McCumber, John. *The Company of Words: Hegel, Language, and Systematic Philosophy.* Evanston: Northwestern University Press, 1993.

McGaughey, Douglas R. "Husserl and Heidegger on Plato's Cave Allegory: A study of Philosophical Influence," *International Philosophical Quarterly* 16 (1976): 331–348.

McNeill, William. "The First Principle of Hermeneutics." Kisiel and van Buren, 393–408.

———. "Heimat: Heidegger on the Threshold." *Heidegger Toward the Turn: Essays on the Work of the 1930s.* Ed. James Risser. Albany: State University of New York Press (forthcoming).

———. "On the Concreteness of Heidegger's Thinking," *Philosophy Today* (Spring 1992): 83–94.

———. *The Glance of the Eye: Heidegger, Aristotle, and the Ends of Theory.* Albany: State University of New York Press. (forthcoming).

Meulen, Jan van der. *Heidegger und Hegel oder Widerstreit und Widerspruch,* 3rd ed. Meisenheim: Hain, 1959.

Mitscherling, Jeff. "Hegelian Elements in Gadamer's Notions of Application and Play," *Man and World* 25 (Jan. 1992): 61–67.

Mueller-Vollmer, Kurt, ed. *The Hermeneutics Reader: Texts from the German Tradition from the Enlightenment to the Present.* New York: Continuum, 1989.

Murray, Michael. "Husserl and Heidegger: Constructing and Deconstructing Greek Philosophy" *Review of Metaphysics* 41, no. 3 (March 1988): 501–518.

Nwodo, Christopher. "Friedländer Versus Heidegger: *A-letheia* Controversy," *JBSP,* vol. 10, no. 2 (May 1979): 84–93.

Olson, Alan M. "Renunciation and Metaphysics: An Examination of Dialectic in Hölderlin and Hegel During their Frankfurt Period," *Man and World* 15 (1982): 123–148.

Ormiston, Gayle, and Alan Schrift, eds. *The Hermeneutic Tradition: From Ast to Ricoeur.* New York, State University of New York Press, 1990.

———. *Transforming the Hermeneutic Context: From Nietzsche to Nancy.* New York: State University of New York Press, 1990.

Palmer, Richard E. *Hermeneutics: Interpretation Theory in Schleiermacher, Dilthey, Heidegger, and Gadamer.* Evanston: Northwestern University Press, 1969.

———. "The Postmodernity of Heidegger." Spanos, ed., 71–92.

Peacock, Ronald. *Hölderlin.* London: Metheun, 1973.

Peperzak, Adriaan T. "Einige Fragen zum Thema 'Hegel und Heidegger.' " Fresco, et al. 49–74.

———. "Heidegger and Plato's Idea of the Good." Sallis, ed., *Reading Heidegger,* 258–285.

Pfeiffer, Rudolf. *The History of Classical Scholarship.* Oxford: Clarendon, 1968.

Pöggeler, Otto. "Hegel und die Griechische Tragödie," *Hegel-studien* 1 (1964): 284–305.

———. *Heidegger und die hermeneutische Philosophie.* Freiburg: Alber Verlag, 1983.

———. *Martin Heidegger's Path of Thinking.* Trans. Daniel Magurshak and Sigmund Barber. Atlantic Highlands: Humanities Press, 1987.

———. "Metaphysics and the Topology of Being in Heidegger." Trans. Parvis Emad. Sheehan, ed., *Heidegger: The Man and the Thinker,* 173–186.

———. "Philosophy in the Wake of Hölderlin," *Man and World* 7 (May 1974): 158–176.

Pöggeler, Otto, ed. *Heidegger: Perspektiven zur Deutung seines Werks.* Königstein: Athenäum Verlag, 1984.

Prauss, Gerold. "Heidegger und die Praktische Philosophie." Gethmann-Siefert and Pöggeler, eds., 177–190.

Protevi, John. *Time and Exteriority: Aristotle, Heidegger, Derrida.* Lewisburg: Bucknell University Press, 1994.

Reynolds, L. D. and N. G. Wilson. *Scribes and Scholars: A Guide to the Transmission of Greek and Latin Literature.* 2nd edition. Oxford: Clarendon, 1974.

Richardson, William J., S. J. "Heidegger and Aristotle," *The Heythrop Journal,* vol. 5 (1964): 58–64.

———. "Heidegger and Plato," *The Heythrop Journal* vol. 4 (1963): 273–279.

Riedel, Manfred, ed. *Hegel und die antike Dialektik.* Frankfurt am Main: Suhrkamp, 1990.

Risser, James. "Poetic Dwelling in Gadamer's Hermeneutics," *Philosophy Today* (Winter 1994): 369–379.

Rist, John M. *The Mind of Aristotle: A Study in Philosophical Growth.* Toronto: University of Toronto, 1989.

Robb, Kevin, ed. *Language and Thought in Early Greek Philosophy.* LaSalle: Hegeler Institute 1983.

Rosen, Michael. *Hegel's Dialectic and Its Criticisms.* New York: Cambridge University Press, 1982.

Rosen, Stanley. *Hermeneutics as Politics.* New York: Oxford, 1987.

———. *The Quarrel Between Philosophy and Poetry: Studies in Ancient Thought.* New York: Routeledge, 1988.

Rosenfeld, Alvin H. "'The Being of Language and the Language of Being': Heidegger and Modern Poetics." Spanos, ed. 195–214.

Sallis, John. *Being and Logos: The Way of Platonic Dialogue,* 2nd ed. Atlantic Highlands: Humanities, 1986.

———. *Delimitations: Phenomenology and the End of Metaphysics.* Bloomington: Indiana University Press, 1986.

———. "World, Finitude and Temporality in the Philosophy of Martin Heidegger," *Philosophy Today* 9 (Spring 1965): 40–51.

Sallis, John, ed. *Reading Heidegger: Commemorations.* Bloomington: Indiana University Press, 1992.

———. *Studies in Phenomenology and the Human Sciences.* Atlantic Highlands: Humanities, 1979.

Santner, Eric L. *Friedrich Hölderlin: Narrative Vigilance and the Poetic Imagination.* New Brunswick: Rutgers, 1986.

Schalow, Frank. "Why Hegel?: Heidegger and Speculative Philosophy," *Southwest Philosophy Review* 6 (Jan. 1990): 29–35.

Schmidt, Dennis. "Between Hegel and Heidegger," *Man and World* 15 (1982): 17–32.

———. "Economics of Production: Heidegger and Aristotle on Poiēsis," *Crises in Continental Philosophy*. Eds. Arleen Dallery and Charles Scott. Albany: State University of New York Press, 1990.

———. "On the Obscurity of Origins: Hegel and Heidegger as Interpreters of Heraclitus," *Philosophy Today* (Winter 1982): 322–331.

———. *The Ubiquity of the Finite: Hegel, Heidegger, and the Entitlements of Philosophy*. Cambridge: MIT, 1988.

Schmitt, Gerhard. *The Concept of Being in Hegel and Heidegger*. Bonn: Bouvier, 1977.

Schneider, Herbert W. "Hegel, Heidegger, and 'Experience'—A Study in Translation," *Journal of the History of Philosophy* 10 (July 1972): 347–350.

Schuchman, Paul. "Aristotle's *Phronēsis* and Gadamer's Hermeneutics." *Philosophy Today* (Spring 1979): 41–50.

Schürmann, Reiner. "A Brutal Awakening to the Tragic Condition of Being: On Heidegger's *Beiträge zur Philosophie*." Harries and Jamme, 89–105.

———. *Heidegger on Being and Acting: From Principles to Anarchy*. Trans. Christine-Marie Gros. Bloomington: Indiana University Press, 1990.

———. "Questioning the Foundation of Practical Philosophy." Bruzina and Wilshire 11–22.

———. "Ultimate Double Binds." *Graduate Faculty Philosophy Journal*, vol. 14, no. 2 through vol. 15, no. 1 (1991): 213–236.

Scott, Charles. *The Language of Difference*. Atlantic Highlands: Humanities, 1987.

Segal, Charles. "Ancient Texts and Modern Literary Criticism," *Arethusa* 1 (1968): 1–25.

Serber, Jere Paul. "Heidegger's Critique of Hegel's Notion of Time," *Philosophy and Phenomenological Research* 39 (March 1979): 358–377.

Shahan, Robert W. and J. N. Mohanty, eds. *Thinking About Being: Aspects of Heidegger's Thought*. Norman: University of Oklahoma Press, 1984.

Shapiro, Gary and Alan Sica, eds. *Hermeneutics: Questions and Prospects*. Amherst: University of Massachusetts Press, 1984.

Sheehan, Thomas. "Heidegger, Aristotle and Phenomenology," *Philosophy Today* (Summer 1975): 87–94.

———. "Heidegger's Early Years: Fragments for a Philosophical Biography." Sheehan, *Heidegger: The Man and the Thinker* 3–20.

———. "Heidegger's Philosophy of Mind," *Contemporary Philosophy: A New Survey*, vol. 4, ed. G. Floistad. The Hague: Nijhoff, 1983. 287–318.

———. "On Movement and the Destruction of Ontology," *Monist* 64, 4 (1981): 534–542.

———. "The 'Original Form' of *Sein und Zeit*: Heidegger's *Begriff der Zeit* (1924)," *JBSP*, vol. 10, no. 2 (1979): 78–100.

———. "'Time and Being,' 1925–27." Shahan and Mohanty, 177–219.

Sheehan, Thomas, ed. *Heidegger: The Man and the Thinker.* Chicago: Precedent, 1981.

Silverman, Hugh. "Heidegger and Merleau-Ponty: Interpreting Hegel," *Research in Phenomenology* 7 (1977): 209–224.

Silverman, Hugh, ed. *Gadamer and Hermeneutics.* New York: Routledge, 1991.

Simon, Josef. *Das Problem der Sprache bei Hegel.* Stuttgart: Kohlhammer, 1966.

Sinaiko, Herman L. *Love, Knowledge, and Discourse in Plato: Dialogue and Dialectic in Phaedrus, Republic, Parmenides.* Chicago: University of Chicago Press, 1965.

Sinn, Dieter. *Die Kritik am Identitätsprinzip: von Heidegger zu Hegel.* Bonn: Bouvier, 1988.

Smith, P. Christopher. "Gadamer's Hermeneutics and Ordinary Language Philosophy," *Thomist* 43, 2 (April 1979): 286–321.

———. "Heidegger, Hegel, and the Problem of 'das Nichts,' " *International Philosophical Quarterly* 8 (1968): 397–405.

———. "Heidegger's Critique of Absolute Knowledge," *New Scholasticism* 45 (Winter 1971): 56–86.

———. *Hermeneutics and Human Finitude.* New York: Fordham University Press, 1991.

———. "H.-G. Gadamer's Heideggerian Interpretation of Plato." *JBSP*, vol. 12, no. 3 (Oct. 1981): 211–230.

———. "Gadamer on Language and Method in Hegel's Dialectic," *Graduate Faculty Journal* 5 (Fall 1975): 53–72.

———. "Plato as Impulse and Obstacle in Gadamer's Development of a Hermeneutical Theory." *Gadamer and Hermeneutics.* Ed. Hugh J. Silverman. New York: Routledge, 1991. 23–41.

Spanos, William V., ed. *Martin Heidegger and the Question of Literature: Toward a Postmodern Literary Hermeneutics*. Bloomington: Indiana University Press, 1979.

Sprague, R. K., ed. *The Older Sophists: A Complete Translation by Several Hands of the Fragments in 'Die Fragmente der Vorsokratiker'*. University of South Carolina Press, 1972.

Sprung, Mervyn, ed. and trans. *The Question of Being*. University Park: Pennsylvania University Press, 1978.

Stambaugh, Joan. *The Finitude of Being*. Albany: State University of New York Press, 1992.

———. "Time, Finitude, and Finality," *Philosophy East and West* 24 (April 1974): 129–135.

Starr, David E. *Entity and Existence: An Ontological Investigation of Aristotle and Heidegger*. New York: Burt Franklin & Co., 1975.

Stenzel, Julius. *Plato's Method of Dialectic*. Trans. and ed. D. J. Allan. New York: Arno Press, 1973.

Stratton, Jon D. "Identity and Difference as *Austrag*: Hegel and Heidegger," *Kinesis* 3 (Spring 1971): 81–92.

Sullivan, Robert R. *Political Hermeneutics: The Early Thinking of Hans-Georg Gadamer*. University Park: Pennsylvania State University Press, 1989.

Swearingen, C. Jan. "The Rhetor as Eiron: Plato's Defense of Dialogue," *Pre/Text*, vol. 3, no. 4 (1982): 289–336.

Sweeney, Leo, S.J. "Participation in Plato's Dialogues: *Phaedo, Parmenides, Sophist* and *Timaeus*." *New Scholasticism* 62 (1988): 125–149.

Szondi, Peter. "Hölderlin's Overcoming of Classicism," trans. Timothy Bahti, *Comparative Criticism*, 5 (1983): 251–270.

———. *On Textual Understanding and Other Essays*. Trans. Harvey Mendelsohn. Minneapolis: University of Minnesota Press, 1986.

Taminiaux, Jacques. "Finitude and Absolute: Remarks on Hegel and Heidegger." Sheehan, ed., *Heidegger: The Man and the Thinker*, 187–208.

———. *Heidegger and the Project of Fundamental Ontology*. Trans. & ed. Michael Gendre. Albany: State University of New York Press, 1991.

———. "The Interpretation of Greek Philosophy in Heidegger's Fundamental Ontology." *JBSP* 19 (1988): 3–14.

———. *Poetics, Speculation and Judgment: The Shadow of the Work of Art from Kant to Phenomenology*. Trans. Michael Gendre. Albany: State University of New York Press, 1993.

Taylor, Mark C., ed. *Deconstruction in Context: Literature and Philosophy*. Chicago: University of Chicago Press, 1986.

Teichert, Dieter. *Erfahrung, Erinnerung, Erkenntnis: Untersuchung zum Wahrheitsbegriff der Hermeneutik Gadamers*. Stuttgart: J. B. Metzler, 1991.

Torno, Timothy. *Finding Time: Reading for Temporality in Hölderlin and Heidegger*. New York: Peter Lang, 1995.

Unger, Richard. *Hölderlin's Major Poetry: The Dialectics of Unity*. Bloomington: Indiana University Press, 1975.

van Buren, John. *The Young Heidegger: Rumor of the Hidden King*. Bloomington: Indiana University Press, 1994.

———. "The Young Heidegger: Rumor of a Hidden King (1919–1926)," *Philosophy Today* (Summer 1989): 99–108.

Volpi, Franco. "*Being and Time*: A Translation of the *Nicomachean Ethics*?" Trans. John Protevi. Kisiel and van Buren, 195–212.

Vukïcevïc, Vladimir. *Logik und Zeit in der phänomenologischen Philosophie Martin Heideggers: 1925–1928*. Hildesheim: G. Olms, 1988.

Vycinas, Vincent. *Greatness and Philosophy: An Inquiry into Western Thought*. The Hague: Martinus Nijhoff, 1967.

Wachterhauser, Brice R. "Interpreting Texts: Objectivity or Participation?," *Man and World* 19 (1986): 439–457.

Wachterhauser, Brice R., ed. *Hermeneutics and Modern Philosophy*. Albany: State University of New York Press, 1986.

Walsh, Robert D. "When Love of Knowing Becomes Actual Knowing: Heidegger and Gadamer on Hegel's *die Sache Selbst*," *The Owl of Minerva* 17, 2 (Spring 1986): 153–164.

Warnke, Georgia. *Gadamer: Hermeneutics, Tradition and Reason*. Stanford: Stanford University, 1987.

Warminski, Andrzej. *Readings in Interpretation: Hölderlin, Hegel, Heidegger*. Minneapolis: University of Minnesota Press, 1987.

Watson, Stephen. "On the Errancy of Dasein," (Review of Christopher Fynsk's *Heidegger: Thought and Historicity*.) *Diacritics* 19.3–4 (Fall–Winter, 1989): 49–61.

Weise Frederick, ed. *Beyond Epistemology*. The Hague: Martinus Nijhoff, 1974.

Westphal, Merold. "Hegel and Gadamer." Wachterhauser, ed., 65–86.

———. *Hegel, Freedom, and Modernity*. Albany: State University of New York Press, 1992.

———, ed. *Method and Speculation in Hegel's Phenomenology.* Atlantic Highlands, NJ: Humanities Press, 1982.

White, Nicolas P. "*The Idea of the Good in Platonic-Aristotelian Philosophy,* by H.-G. Gadamer" (review article), *Noûs* XXIII, no. 2 (April 1989): 254–256.

White, Carol J. "Heidegger and the Beginning of Metaphysics," *JBSP,* vol. 19, no. 1 (January 1988): 34–50.

Williams, Robert R. "Hegel and Heidegger." Desmond, 135–162.

Wood, David. *Philosophy at the Limit: Problems of Modern European Thought.* London: Unwin Hyman, 1990.

Wood, Robert. *The Deconstruction of Time.* Atlantic Highlands: Humanities, 1989.

———. *A Path into Metaphysics: Phenomenological, Hermeneutical, and Dialogical Studies.* Albany: State University of New York Press, 1990.

Wright, Kathleen. "Gadamer: The Speculative Structure of Language." Wachterhauser, ed. 193–218.

———. "Heidegger and the Authorization of Hölderlin's Poetry." Harries and Jamme, 164–174.

———. "Heidegger's Hölderlin and the Mo(u)rning of History," *Philosophy Today* (Winter 1993): 423–435.

Wyschograd, Edith. *Spirit in Ashes: Hegel, Heidegger and Man-Made Mass Death.* New Haven: Yale, 1985.

Ziegler, Susanne. *Heidegger, Hölderlin und die Alētheia: Martin Heideggers Geschichtsdenken in seinen Vorlesungen 1934/35 bis 1944.* Berlin: Dunker & Humblot, 1991.

Zimmerman, Michael E. *Heidegger's Confrontation with Modernity: Technology, Politics, Art.* Bloomington: Indiana University Press, 1990.

Index

A

B

M

N

O

P

Q

R

S

T

U

V

W

Z